teach yourself®

beginner's hindi

rupert snell

For over 60 years, more than 50 million people have learnt over 750 subjects the **teach yourself** way, with impressive results.

be where you want to be
with **teach yourself**

For UK order enquiries: please contact Bookpoint Ltd, 130 Milton Park, Abingdon, Oxon, OX14 4SB. Telephone: +44 (0) 1235 827720. Fax: +44 (0) 1235 400454. Lines are open 09.00–17.00, Monday to Saturday, with a 24-hour message answering service. Details about our titles and how to order are available at www.teachyourself.co.uk

For USA order enquiries: please contact McGraw-Hill Customer Services, PO Box 545, Blacklick, OH 43004-0545, USA. Telephone: 1-800-722-4726. Fax: 1-614-755-5645.

For Canada order enquiries: please contact McGraw-Hill Ryerson Ltd, 300 Water St, Whitby, Ontario, L1N 9B6, Canada. Telephone: 905 430 5000. Fax: 905 430 5020.

British Library Cataloguing in Publication Data: a catalogue record for this title is available from the British Library.

Library of Congress Catalog Card Number: on file.

First published in UK 2003 by Hodder Arnold, 338 Euston Road, London, NW1 3BH.

First published in US 2003 by The McGraw-Hill Companies, Inc.

This edition published 2003.

Printed in Great Britain for Hodder Education, a division of Hodder Headline, 338 Euston Road, London, NW1 3BH, by Cox & Wyman Ltd, Reading, Berkshire.

Impression number 10 9 8 7
Year 2009 2008 2007 2006

contents

Welcome to *Beginner's Hindi* !

Is this the right course for you?

This course is designed for people who want a structured but user-friendly introduction to Hindi, whether studying alone or in a class. It aims to get you into the world of real Hindi as quickly as possible. Each of the twelve units prepares you for some new social or practical situations while also introducing the grammar gradually and simply. We begin with simple statements and questions using the verb 'to be'; then the various tenses and other structures are explained, steadily increasing the range of contexts that you can deal with. There are plentiful examples and exercises; all *numbered* questions are provided with answers, either immediately after the questions, or at the back of the book. The book often addresses you directly, asking questions about you and encouraging you to *use* the language as you learn it. The carefully graded vocabulary for each unit comes at the end, with full Hindi–English and English–Hindi glossaries bringing it all together at the back of the book.

The Sharma family

Most of the dialogues are based on the various members of the Sharma family, who live in Agra: Geeta (a doctor) and her husband Raju (a teacher), their children Manoj, Ram and Meena — and a dog, Moti. Because we're dealing with a set of known characters, it's easy to see the different levels of formality that are an important feature of Hindi: for example, we hear the children being addressed less formally than adults and strangers. One or two subsidiary characters, such as Pratap (a student visiting England), also appear in the book *Teach Yourself Hindi*, which gives a more detailed introduction to the language.

Script and pronunciation

The Hindi script, called 'Devanagari', is an extremely systematic writing system: each character represents a particular sound, making it the perfect guide to pronunciation. Although a 'roman' transliteration is given throughout the book, the small effort required to learn Devanagari is very well worthwhile!

Listen out for two important contrasts in pronunciation. The first is between 'retroflex' consonants (pronounced with the tongue touching the roof of the mouth, giving a 'hard' sound of the kind associated with Indian pronunciations of words like 'doctor') and 'dental' consonants (pronounced with the tongue touching the upper teeth, giving a 'soft' sound as in an Italian pronunciation of 'Italia'). The second contrast is between 'unaspirated' and 'aspirated' consonants, such as the pair क *ka* and ख *kha* — the first is much less 'breathy' than the second. Vowel sounds are very 'clean': the vowel ए *e* is more like the vowels in French 'été' than in English 'mayday'.

The recordings

This book is accompanied by recordings which will help bring the language alive for you. They introduce the sounds of Hindi, present the dialogues and other features from the book, and go beyond the book with several further listening and speaking exercises that will build your confidence in using Hindi in real conversations. Pause the recording whenever you need time to think, and practise imitating the Hindi voices as closely as possible, *speaking out loud.*

Where does this book lead?

After finishing this book, you may like to look at *Teach Yourself Hindi*, by Rupert Snell with Simon Weightman: this gives more detail on the grammar, and plenty of reading practice. The web-based course *A Door into Hindi* (**www.ncsu.edu/project/hindi_lessons**) has an interactive approach to the learning process; and Hindi films also offer a brilliant way of getting to know the language and the culture it expresses. Most importantly of all, you will find some 400 million Hindi-speakers waiting to talk to you: start speaking Hindi today!

Dictionaries: Rupert Snell's *Beginner's Hindi Dictionary* is designed for learners and gives a lot of help with sentence formation, while the *Oxford Hindi–English Dictionary* by R.S. McGregor is what you need if you want to start reading Hindi newspapers and magazines, many of which are available on the internet.

The Hindi script and sounds

Although a roman transliteration is provided for all the Hindi in this book, learning to read and write the Devanagari script is extremely worthwhile. Its phonetic basis makes it really easy to learn; and if you're in India, being able to read the Hindi all around you in signs and posters will bring its own reward, even before you start reading more ambitiously. As you begin to learn Devanagari, there's a very useful web-based 'Hindi script tutor' to help you learn the characters and their sounds: **http://www.avashy.com/hindiscripttutor.htm**; this website, devised by Richard Woodward, teaches and tests the script inter-actively, and demonstrates the sounds of Hindi. And for a detailed introduction to Devanagari, see Rupert Snell, *Beginner's Hindi Script* (Hodder & Stoughton, 2000).

The best way to learn the script is to copy out each character several times, pronouncing its sound as you do so. Start with the consonants. Each basic consonant is actually a complete syllable: for example the sign क stands for not just the consonant 'k' but the whole syllable 'ka'; it will sound similar to the first syllable of the word 'cup'. The 'a' vowel is always there unless replaced by some other vowel indicated by a special vowel sign. More on this later: for now, concentrate on copying and learning the consonants.

Write on lined paper, with the top line of the character falling on the printed line, and the rest of the character hanging below.

Aspiration

In the descriptions of the Hindi sounds you'll see many references to 'aspiration' — the amount of breath that escapes from the mouth when a sound is spoken. In English, the initial 'k' of 'kick' is strongly aspirated, the closing 'ck' much less so. In Hindi, such differences are represented by pairs of consonants such as क *ka* (unaspirated) and ख *kha* (aspirated). English consonants fall halfway between the two, so you'll have to make a special effort to cut back your aspiration for the one, and increase it for the other! All these things are best dealt with by listening to the recordings, and/or by asking a Hindi-speaker to demonstrate them for you.

On the facing page you'll find all the main characters of the script set out in a table; then each character is set out separately with its handwritten equivalent, and a note on pronunciation. The consonants are dealt with first (as is the tradition), though in dictionary order the vowels precede the consonants.

Devanagari: the basic characters

Independent vowel forms ('vowel characters')

अ *a*	आ *ā*	इ *i*	ई *ī*
उ *u*	ऊ *ū*	ऋ *ṛ*	
ए *e*	ऐ *ai*	ओ *o*	औ *au*

Consonants

क *ka*	ख *kha*	ग *ga*	घ *gha*	
च *ca*	छ *cha*	ज *ja*	झ *jha*	
ट *ṭa*	ठ *ṭha*	ड *ḍa*	ढ *ḍha*	ण *ṇa*
त *ta*	थ *tha*	द *da*	ध *dha*	न *na*
प *pa*	फ *pha*	ब *ba*	भ *bha*	म *ma*
य *ya*	र *ra*	ल *la*	व *va*	
श *śa*	ष *ṣa*	स *sa*	ह *ha*	

Dependent vowel forms ('vowel signs', based on क as an example)

क *ka*	का *kā*	कि *ki*	की *kī*
कु *ku*	कू *kū*	कृ *kṛ*	
के *ke*	कै *kai*	को *ko*	कौ *kau*

The consonants

क	*ka*	As in 'skin'; minimum aspiration.
क़	*qa*	Further back in the throat than undotted क (many speakers say 'ka' for both).
ख	*kha*	Aspirated version of क *ka.*
ख़	*kha*	Like the 'ch' in Scottish 'loch'.
ग	*ga*	As in 'gift'.
ग़	*ga*	A more guttural version of the above.
घ	*gha*	Aspirated version of ग; like the 'g h' in 'dog-house'. A *single* sound.
च	*ca*	As in 'cheap', but with the tongue positioned as for the 'ty' sound in 'tube'.
छ	*cha*	Aspirated form of the above.
ज	*ja*	As in 'jeep'.
ज़	*za*	As in 'zip'.
झ	*jha*	Aspirated form of ज *ja.*

The next seven consonants are 'retroflex': the tongue curls back to the palate (front part of the roof of the mouth), making a hard sound.

ट	*ṭa*	As in 'try', but harder.
ठ	*ṭha*	Aspirated version of the above.
ड	*ḍa*	As in 'dry', but harder.
ड़	*ṛa*	The tongue flicks past (rather than resting on) the retroflex position.
ढ	*ḍha*	Aspirated version of ड *ḍa.*

ढ़	*ṛha*	Aspirated version of ड़ *ṛa.*
ण	*ṇa*	An 'n' sound in the retroflex position.

The next five consonants are 'dental': the tongue touches the upper teeth, making a soft sound.

त	*ta*	As the first 't' in 'at the', very soft.
थ	*tha*	Aspirated version of the above.
द	*da*	As in 'breadth', very soft.
ध	*dha*	Aspirated version of the above.
न	*na*	As in 'anthology'.

'SONI DENTAL CHAMBER: [FALSE-] TEETH AND SPECTACLE-MAKER'

Ironically, the English word 'dental' is spelt with retroflex ड *ḍ* and ट *ṭ* in this signboard, whereas the Hindi word दाँत *dā̃t* 'tooth' has two dentals!

Now we come to 'labials', consonants produced with the lips.

प	*pa*	Much less aspiration than in 'pin'.
फ	*pha*	Aspirated version of the above.
ब	*ba*	As in 'bun'.
भ	*bha*	Aspirated version of the above.
म	*ma*	As in 'moon'.

Now for a sequence of four characters called 'semi-vowels':

य	*ya*	As in 'yes'.
र	*ra*	As in 'roll' — but lightly rolled!
ल	*la*	As in 'lullaby', but softer, more dental.
व	*va*	Neither a buzzy sound as in 'visa', nor as rounded as in 'we', but halfway between.

We're nearly done. Here are three 'sibilants':

श	*śa*	As 'sh' in 'ship'; pronounced 's' in some regional accents.
ष	*ṣa*	Strictly speaking a 'cerebral' (in which the tongue touches a high point in the roof of the mouth); but usually pronounced 'sh', the same as the previous character, श *śa*. It occurs in loanwords from Sanskrit only.
स	*sa*	As in 'sip'.

And finally an aspirate:

ह	*ha*	As in 'help'.

You'll have noticed that some characters have 'dotted' versions: these are for sounds which go beyond the range of Sanskrit, the classical language for which the script was first devised. They are क़ *qa*, ख़ *<u>kh</u>a*, ग़ *ġa*, ज़ *za*, and फ़ *fa* (typically for words borrowed from Arabic and Persian) and ड़ *ṛa*, ढ़ *ṛha* (late developers in the long history of Indian languages). These characters are not distinguished in dictionary order from their undotted equivalents. The showing of dots in print is often rather haphazard — but not in this book!

Remember that each consonant contains an inherent 'a' vowel as part of the deal. But it's important to notice that this 'inherent vowel' is *not* pronounced at the end of a word: thus the word for 'all', सब, reads *sab* (not '*saba*'), and the word for 'simple', सरल, reads *saral* (not '*sarala*'). Armed with this information you can now read and write these words:

कब	*kab*	when?	क़लम	*qalam*	pen
जब	*jab*	when	गरम	*garam*	warm
तब	*tab*	then	तरफ़	*taraf*	direction
पर	*par*	but; on	नमक	*namak*	salt
फल	*phal*	fruit	महल	*mahal*	palace
मन	*man*	mind	शहर	*śahar*	town
सब	*sab*	all	सड़क	*saṛak*	street
हम	*ham*	we, us	सरल	*saral*	simple

In the words महल *mahal* and शहर *śahar,* the ह *ha* has the effect of 'lightening' the adjacent vowels, making them sound more like the 'e' in 'mend' than the 'u' in 'mundane' (this will vary somewhat from speaker to speaker). Elsewhere, Hindi is remarkably free of such contextual changes: the Hindi script is a 'what you see is what you get' system.

The vowels

Now we move on to look at vowels. Each vowel has two different forms: one is the 'vowel *sign*', used after a consonant; the other is the 'vowel *character*', used in other positions. First, vowel signs.

A vowel sign is used when a vowel follows a consonant. It's a small mark that is added to the consonant, and it replaces the 'a' that is otherwise present as the inherent vowel. The examples below show the vowel *'e'* added to the consonants क *ka,* ख *kha,* ग *ga* and घ *gha.*

के *ke* खे *khe* गे *ge* घे *ghe*

Here now is the full range of such vowel signs, based on क —

का	*kā*	A long vowel, as in 'calm'.
कि	*ki*	A short vowel, as in 'kipper'.
की	*kī*	A long version of the above, as in 'keep'.
कु	*ku*	Short, as in 'put'.

कू	*kū*	A long version of the above, as in 'food'.
कृ	*kṛ*	A very short 'ri' sound, as in 'thrill'. It only occurs in Sanskrit loanwords.
के	*ke*	Like the French é in 'été'; *not* a rounded sound as in English 'payday'.
कै	*kai*	Similar to the vowel in 'cap', but flatter.
को	*ko*	A pure 'o', less rounded than in 'cold'.
कौ	*kau*	Similar to the vowel in 'hot'.

And here's some more reading and writing practice:

कान	*kān*	ear	पानी	*pānī*	water
कृपा	*kṛpā*	kindness	भारत	*bhārat*	India
खड़ा	*khaṛā*	standing	मकान	*makān*	house
चाय	*cāy*	tea	वाराणसी	*vārāṇasī*	Varanasi
तोता	*totā*	parrot	सितार	*sitār*	sitar
दुकान	*dukān*	shop	सौ	*sau*	hundred
दूर	*dūr*	far	है	*hai*	is

At this point you should practise writing out these vowel signs attached to *all* the consonants until they become really familiar.

These vowel signs can only be used when they have a consonant sign to cling to. In other positions, such as at the beginning of a word, the vowel is written with a vowel *character*. The first in the list is the 'inherent' vowel:

अ	*a*	अब *ab* now
आ	*ā*	आज *āj* today
इ	*i*	इधर *idhar* over here
ई	*ī*	ईरान *īrān* Iran

उ	*u*	उधर *udhar* over there
ऊ	*ū*	ऊपर *ūpar* up
ऋ	*ṛ*	ऋण *ṛṇ* debt
ए	*e*	एक *ek* one
ऐ	*ai*	ऐसा *aisā* such
ओ	*o*	ओर *or* direction
औ	*au*	और *aur* and

And here are three words in which vowel characters appear as the second of two sequential vowels (i.e. neither at the beginning of a word nor after a consonant):

कई *kaī* 'several' — ई *ī* follows the syllable क *ka*;

उबाऊ *ubāū* 'boring' — ऊ *ū* follows the syllable बा *bā*;

बनाओ *banāo* 'make' — ओ *o* follows the syllable ना *nā*.

Conjunct characters

When two consonant sounds come together without an intervening vowel, we have to cancel or 'kill off' the inherent vowel of the first consonant. For example, in the word 'Hindi' there is no 'a' between the 'n' and the 'd', so a shortened form of the first consonant, न, is physically joined to the second consonant, द, giving हिन्दी *hindī*.

क	+	य	=	क्य	क्या *kyā*	what?
च	+	च	=	च्च	बच्चा *baccā*	child
च	+	छ	=	च्छ	अच्छा *acchā*	good
ल	+	ल	=	ल्ल	बिल्ली *billī*	cat
स	+	त	=	स्त	हिन्दुस्तानी *hindustānī*	Indian

Conjuncts beginning with द *da* can be hard to recognize:

द	+	द	=	द्द	रद्द *radd*	cancelled
द	+	म	=	द्म	पद्म *padma*	lotus

द	+	य	=	द्य	विद्या	*vidyā* knowledge
द	+	व	=	द्व	द्वार	*dvār* gateway

When र is the first character of a compound it turns into a little curl (called रेफ *reph*) above the second character:

र	+	क़	=	र्क़	फ़र्क़	*farq* difference
र	+	थ	=	र्थ	अर्थ	*arth* meaning
र	+	द	=	र्द	दर्द	*dard* pain
र	+	मा	=	र्मा	शर्मा	*śarmā* Sharma
र	+	थी	=	र्थी	विद्यार्थी	*vidyārthī* student

The *reph* comes at the very *end* of the syllable in words like शर्मा *śarmā* (where it's above the vowel sign ा) and like विद्यार्थी *vidyārthī* (where it's above the vowel sign ी).

When र is the *second* character of a compound it turns into a little slanting line, tucked into a convenient nook of the first character:

ग	+	र	=	ग्र	सिग्रेट	*sigreṭ* cigarette
द	+	र	=	द्र	द्रोही	*drohī* hostile
प	+	र	=	प्र	प्रदेश	*pradeś* state, region

See what happens when no nook is available:

ट	+	र	=	ट्र	ट्रेन	*ṭren* train
ड	+	र	=	ड्र	ड्रामा	*ḍrāmā* drama

Some conjuncts stack vertically:

ट	+	ट	=	ट्ट	छुट्टी	*chuṭṭī* holiday
ट	+	ठ	=	ट्ठ	चिट्ठी	*ciṭṭhī* letter

Most conjuncts are easy to read, but there are some in which the conjunct has limited resemblance to its component parts, and these have to be learnt as new characters in their own right:

क	+	त	=	क्त	भक्ति	*bhakti* devotion
क	+	ष	=	क्ष	रक्षा	*rakṣā* protection

त	+	त	=	त्त	कुत्ता *kuttā* dog
त	+	र	=	त्र	मित्र *mitr* friend
द	+	भ	=	द्भ	अद्भुत *adbhut* wondrous
श	+	र	=	श्र	श्री *śrī* Mr
ह	+	म	=	ह्म	ब्रह्मा *Brahmā* Brahma (a deity)

The rare character ज्ञ *jña* is a conjunct of ज with ञ् *ña*, a nasal consonant (like the first 'n' in 'onion') that is not shown in our table because it never occurs alone; ज्ञ *jña* is usually pronounced 'gy'.

When pronouncing doubled consonants, just 'hold' the sound momentarily, as in distinguishing 'night train' from 'night rain'. Practise with कुत्ता *kuttā* 'dog', बिल्ली *billī* 'cat', बच्चा *baccā* 'child'.

Nasals

A nasalized vowel is produced by diverting part of the breath through the nose: speak while pinching your nose to hear what it sounds like! Nasalization is marked with a sign called *candrabindu*, 'moon-dot':

हाँ *hā̃* yes

कहाँ *kahā̃* where?

यहाँ *yahā̃* here

If there's a vowel sign above the top line, there won't be room for the moon (*candra*) , so the dot (*bindu*) is used alone:

नहीं *nahī̃* no

कहीं *kahī̃* somewhere

यहीं *yahī̃* right here

Nasalizing a vowel can change the meaning, as with है *hai* 'is' and हैं *haĩ* 'are'. Similarly, while यहीं *yahī̃* means 'right here', यही *yahī* *means* 'this one, this very one' — a completely different word!

Our little dot has a second function also (here with a new name — 'anusvār'); it can be used to indicate an 'n' or 'm' when such a letter is the first element of a conjunct:

अंडा	=	अण्डा	*aṇḍā* egg
हिंदी	=	हिन्दी	*hindī* Hindi
लंबा	=	लम्बा	*lambā* long, tall

Other signs

The word दुःख *duḥkh* 'sorrow' includes the colon-like sign called '*visarga*'; this rare sign indicates a lightly pronounced 'h' sound.

In situations where it's not possible or convenient to write or print a conjunct, an inherent vowel can be cancelled by hanging a little line called '*virām*' below it: चड्डी *caḍḍī* 'underpants'.

The 'full stop' is a standing line, as seen from Unit 1 onwards. Most other punctuation follows English usage.

Here are the numerals from 0 to 9:

० १ २ ३ ४ ५ ६ ७ ८ ९

Loanwords from English

When writing non-Indian words, transcribe the sounds, *not* the spelling; thus 'cycle' (bicycle) is written साइकिल *sāikil.* English 't' and 'd' usually become retroflex: 'doctor' is डाक्टर *ḍākṭar.*

Sometimes a little 'moon' sign is used to designate the Hindi pronunciation of an English 'o' like the first vowel in 'chocolate' — चॉकलेट. It doesn't have a standard transliteration in the roman script, and the sound isn't really affected: most people say चाकलेट *cāklet*, with the standard long 'ā' vowel.

Silent 'inherent vowels'

The inherent vowel 'a' is silent at the end of a word in Hindi — though not in Sanskrit, Hindi's classical ancestor. Thus the name राम is pronounced 'Rām' in Hindi, 'Rāma' in Sanskrit.

At the end of a word whose last syllable is a conjunct character, the inherent vowel is pronounced lightly in order to make the conjunct easier to say: अवश्य *avaśya* 'certainly', जन्म *janma* 'birth'.

Sometimes an inherent vowel is silent in the middle of a word, even though the spelling involves no conjunct. Here is a general (if imperfect) pair of rules:

In a word of three or more syllables that ends with a vowel other than the inherent vowel, the penultimate inherent vowel is not pronounced. Thus समझ *samajh*, but समझा *samjhā* (because it ends in long *ā*); रहन *rahan*, but रहना *rahnā* (likewise).

In a word that has three syllables in which the third is a long vowel and the second is the inherent vowel, the inherent vowel is not pronounced. Thus सोमवार *somvār* 'Monday', लिखता *likhtā* 'write, writing'.

01

नमस्ते
namaste
greetings

In this unit you will learn

- **how to say who you are, greet people and say goodbye**
- **how to ask questions about things and people**

Language points

- **the verb 'to be'**
- **basic sentence construction**
- **question formation**

1 Saying hello

The universal greeting in Hindi is the word नमस्ते *namaste*, which means both 'hello, good morning' etc. and also 'goodbye'. It comes from India's classical language of Sanskrit, where it means 'Salutation to you'. Though this literal meaning is now remote (like the 'God be with you' that underlies the English 'goodbye'), it is part of the elaborate code of respect that runs through the Hindi language.

To communicate well in Hindi, good clear pronunciation is as important as grammar, and the word नमस्ते *namaste* gives an ideal chance to practise right from the start. Your tongue should touch your upper teeth as you say the n and the t; and in the last syllable, aim for the é of French 'été' — the vowel is not the rounded 'ay' sound heard in English 'stay'.

In formal contexts the word नमस्ते *namaste* is accompanied by a gesture in which the palms are put together (though many people are more likely to offer a handshake these days). It's considered polite to say नमस्ते *namaste* to an older or senior person first, before he or she says it to you. Sometimes you will hear नमस्कार *namaskār* (in which the 's' may be pronounced 'sh'); this means the same thing.

नमस्ते *namaste* — you're speaking Hindi already!

▶ 2 Who and how people are

Here we meet Raju and Geeta, a married couple from Agra; later we'll meet their children Manoj (boy, 16), Meena (girl, 10), and Ram (boy, 8), and their dog Moti (male, age unknown).

'I am' is मैं हूँ *maĩ hū̃*, and 'I am not' is मैं नहीं हूँ *maĩ nahī̃ hū̃*. Notice how the verb हूँ *hū̃* 'am' comes at the end of the sentence.

मैं राजू हूँ ।
maĩ Rājū hū̃. I am Raju.

मैं ठीक हूँ ।
maĩ ṭhīk hū̃. I am OK.

मैं बीमार नहीं हूँ ।
maĩ bīmār nahī̃ hū̃. I am not ill.

मैं गीता हूँ ।

maĩ Gītā hū̃. I am Geeta.

मैं हिन्दुस्तानी हूँ ।

maĩ hindustānī hū̃. I am Indian.

मैं अँग्रेज़ नहीं हूँ ।

maĩ ãgrez nahī̃ hū̃. I am not English.

My and mine

The word मेरा *merā* means both 'my' and 'mine'; है *hai* means 'is'.

मेरा नाम राजू है ।

merā nām Rājū hai. My name is Raju.

मैं अध्यापक हूँ ।

maĩ adhyāpak hū̃. I'm a teacher.

गीता डाक्टर है ।

Gītā ḍākṭar hai. Geeta is a doctor.

सीता नर्स है ।

Sītā nars hai. Sita is a nurse.

Yes/no questions

A statement is turned into a question by simply adding the question-word क्या *kyā* at the beginning of the sentence; क्या *kyā* isn't translatable here: it just turns what follows into a question. There's no change in the word order: just add क्या *kyā* to make a question.

क्या मैं अध्यापक हूँ ?

kyā maĩ adhyāpak hū̃? Am I a teacher?

क्या गीता डाक्टर है ?

kyā Gītā ḍākṭar hai? Is Geeta a doctor?

क्या सीता नर्स है ?

kyā Sītā nars hai? Is Sita a nurse?

Because these questions can all be answered either जी हाँ *jī hā̃* 'yes' or जी नहीं *jī nahī̃* 'no', we'll call them 'yes/no' questions. Here are two more, with their answers:

क्या राजू ठीक है ?

kyā Rājū ṭhīk hai? Is Raju OK?

जी हाँ, राजू ठीक है ।

jī hã̄, Rājū ṭhīk hai. Yes, Raju is OK.

क्या गीता बीमार है ?

kyā Gītā bīmār hai? Is Geeta ill?

जी नहीं, गीता बीमार नहीं है ।

jī nahī̃, Gītā bīmār nahī̃ hai. No, Geeta isn't ill.

You

In order to begin real conversations, we need to add the word आप *āp* 'you' and the verb हैं *haĩ* 'are' — आप हैं *āp haĩ* 'you are'. Notice the difference between है *hai* 'is' and हैं *haĩ* 'are': the second is nasalized (a nasal sound is produced when some of the breath comes through the nose rather than through the mouth).

Now we're really talking:

क्या आप गीता हैं ?

kyā āp Gītā haĩ? Are you Geeta?

जी हाँ, मैं गीता हूँ ।

jī hã̄, maĩ Gītā hū̃. Yes, I am Geeta.

क्या आप डाक्टर हैं ?

kyā āp ḍākṭar haĩ? Are you a doctor?

जी हाँ, मैं डाक्टर हूँ ।

jī hã̄, maĩ ḍākṭar hū̃. Yes, I'm a doctor.

क्या मैं बीमार हूँ ?

kyā maĩ bīmār hū̃? Am I ill?

जी नहीं, आप बीमार नहीं हैं ।

jī nahī̃, āp bīmār nahī̃ haĩ. No, you're not ill.

क्या मैं ठीक हूँ ?

kyā maĩ ṭhīk hū̃? Am I all right?

जी हाँ, आप बिलकुल ठीक हैं !

jī hã̄, āp bilkul ṭhīk haĩ! Yes, you're quite all right!

Did you know?

In the tally of world languages, only English, Chinese and Spanish have more speakers than Hindi.

Practise what you've learnt

Practise these questions by speaking them out loud (and answering them) until you're completely at home with the format. Stay with this pattern until new words and phrases have been introduced.

क्या आप अँग्रेज़ हैं ?
kyā āp ãgrez haĩ? Are you English?

क्या आप डाक्टर हैं ?
kyā āp ḍākṭar haĩ? Are you a doctor?

क्या आप अध्यापक हैं ?
kyā āp adhyāpak haĩ? Are you a teacher?

क्या आप विद्यार्थी हैं ?
kyā āp vidyārthī haĩ? Are you a student?

क्या आप ठीक हैं ?
kyā āp ṭhīk haĩ? Are you OK?

क्या आप बीमार हैं ?
kyā āp bīmār haĩ? Are you ill?

क्या आप ख़ुश हैं ?
kyā āp khuś haĩ? Are you happy?

क्या आप नाराज़ हैं ?
kyā āp nārāz haĩ? Are you angry?

You may have noticed that Hindi doesn't have a word for 'a' (though sometimes the word एक *ek* — the number 'one' — serves this purpose). There isn't a word for 'the' either.

3 This and that; he, she, and it

So far we've seen the pronouns मैं *maĩ* 'I', and आप *āp* 'you'. Now we move on to the two words that mean, 'this, that, he, she, it'.

यह *yah* (often pronounced '*ye*') means 'this', and वह *vah* (often pronounced '*vo*') means 'that'.

यह लड़का राम है ।
yah laṛkā Rām hai. This boy is Ram.

यह लड़की मीना है ।
yah laṛkī Mīnā hai. This girl is Meena.

वह लड़का नाराज़ है, लेकिन ...
vah laṛkā nārāz hai, lekin... That boy is angry, but...

वह लड़की ख़ुश है ।
vah laṛkī khuś hai. that girl is happy.

यह *yah* and वह *vah* also mean 'he, she, it'. If the person referred to is near at hand ('this person here'), use यह *yah*; otherwise, use वह *vah*. Only use यह *yah* when indicating quite specifically 'this person/thing *here*': when referring to 'he, she, it' generally, वह *vah* is better.

राम ठीक नहीं है । वह बीमार है ।
Rām ṭhīk nahī̃ hai. vah bīmār hai. Ram isn't well. He's ill.

यह मोती है । *yah Motī hai.*
यह कुत्ता है । *yah kuttā hai.*
यह ख़ुश है । *yah khuś hai.*
यह मेरा है । *yah merā hai.*

There's no 'he/she' gender distinction in the Hindi pronoun. Later on you'll see that gender is distinguished by some verb endings.

In the plural, यह *yah* becomes ये *ye* ('these, they'), and वह *vah* becomes वे *ve* ('those, they'). And remember है *hai* 'is' and हैं *haĩ* 'are'.

यह आदमी अँग्रेज़ है ।
yah ādmī ãgrez hai. This man's English.

ये लोग अँग्रेज़ हैं ।
ye log ãgrez haĩ. These people are English.

वह आदमी अँग्रेज़ है ।
vah ādmī ãgrez hai. That man's English.

वे लोग अँग्रेज़ हैं ।
ve log ãgrez haĩ. Those people are English.

4 More questions

We saw just now that क्या *kyā* turns a statement into a question, without changing the word order: आप ठीक हैं *āp ṭhīk haĩ* 'You are OK' becomes क्या आप ठीक हैं? *kyā āp ṭhīk haĩ ?* 'Are you OK?'.

But in a second meaning, क्या *kyā* has the sense 'what?' Similarly कौन *kaun* means 'who?'

क्या
kyā what?

यह क्या है ?
yah kyā hai? What is this?

वह क्या है ?
vah kyā hai? What is that?

कौन
kaun who?

यह कौन है ?
yah kaun hai? Who is this?

वह कौन है ?
vah kaun hai? Who is that?

Notice how a reply copies the word-order of the question, the answer-word simply replacing the question-word. In the following pair of sentences, कौन *kaun* 'who?' is replaced by the answer मेरा दोस्त *merā dost* 'my friend'.

वह कौन है ?
vah kaun hai? Who is he?

वह मेरा दोस्त है ।
vah merā dost hai. He is my friend.

Our conversation possibilities are growing rapidly:

आप कौन हैं ?
āp kaun haĩ? Who are you?

मैं राजू हूँ ।
maĩ Rājū hū̃. I am Raju.

यह कौन है ?
yah kaun hai? Who is this?

यह मीना है ।
yah Mīnā hai. This is Meena.

वह क्या है ?
vah kyā hai? What is that?

वह सितार है ।
vah sitār hai. That is a sitar.

वह कौन है ?
vah kaun hai? Who is that?

वह मनोज है ।
vah Manoj hai. That is Manoj.

मनोज कौन है ?
Manoj kaun hai? Who is Manoj?

मनोज मेरा भाई है ।
Manoj merā bhāī hai. Manoj is my brother.

What's this?

Here's a chance for you to practise a very useful question-and-answer pattern — 'What's this?' 'It's a...'

यह क्या है ? *yah kyā hai?*
यह किताब है । *yah kitāb hai.*

यह क्या है ? *yah kyā hai?*
यह क़लम है । *yah qalam hai.*

यह क्या है ? *yah kyā hai?*
यह रेडियो है । *yah reḍiyo hai.*

यह क्या है ? *yah kyā hai?*
यह कुरसी है । *yah kursī hai.*

यह क्या है ? *yah kyā hai?*
यह मेज़ है । *yah mez hai.*

यह क्या है ? *yah kyā hai?*
यह मकान है । *yah makān hai.*

यह क्या है ? *yah kyā hai?*
यह कुत्ता है । *yah kuttā hai.*

यह क्या है ? *yah kyā hai?*
यह बिल्ली है । *yah billī hai.*

Remember that when क्या *kyā* comes at the beginning of the sentence, it turns a following statement into a question. When you've answered the following questions, make up more questions and answers of your own, using any everyday words from the glossary. (NB: you'll find answers to all *numbered* questions either after the questions or at the back of the book.)

१ क्या मोती बिल्ली है ?
kyā Motī billī hai?

२ क्या गीता डाक्टर है ?
kyā Gītā ḍākṭar hai?

३ क्या आप डाक्टर हैं ?
kyā āp ḍākṭar haĩ?

४ क्या राजू और गीता हिन्दुस्तानी हैं ?
kyā Rājū aur Gītā hindustānī haĩ?

५ क्या हिंदी आसान है ?
kyā hindī āsān hai?

Raju meets his new neighbour, Javed

You'll see a new pronoun here: उसका *uskā* 'his, her/hers, its'.

राजू	नमस्ते । मैं राजू हूँ । आप कौन हैं ?
जावेद	नमस्ते । मेरा नाम जावेद है ।
राजू	क्या आप ठीक हैं ?
जावेद	जी हाँ, शुक्रिया, मैं ठीक हूँ ।
राजू	वह लड़की कौन है ?
जावेद	उसका नाम बानो है ।
राजू	आपका पूरा नाम क्या है ?
जावेद	मेरा पूरा नाम जावेद ख़ाँ है ।

Rājū	*namaste. maĩ Rājū hū̃. āp kaun haĩ?*
Jāved	*namaste. merā nām Jāved hai.*
Rājū	*kyā āp ṭhīk haĩ?*
Jāved	*jī hā̃, śukriyā, maĩ ṭhīk hū̃.*
Rājū	*vah laṛkī kaun hai?*
Jāved	*uskā nām Bāno hai.*
Rājū	*āpkā pūrā nām kyā hai?*
Jāved	*merā pūrā nām Jāved Khā̃ hai.*

Raju	Hello. I am Raju. Who are you?
Javed	Hello. My name is Javed.
Raju	Are you OK?
Javed	Yes, thank you, I am OK.
Raju	Who is that girl?
Javed	Her name is Bano.
Raju	What is your full name?
Javed	My full name is Javed Khan.

Exercise 1a Translate:

Javed	What is this?
Manoj	This is my radio.
Javed	Who is that boy?
Manoj	He is my brother.
Javed	What's his name?

Manoj His name is Ram.
Javed Who is that girl?
Manoj Her name is Meena.
Javed Is she ill?
Manoj No, she isn't ill. She's OK.

Exercise 1b Answer the questions about the people described below. (New words: शादी-शुदा *śādī-śudā* 'married', दोनों *donõ* 'both'.)

सुरेश खन्ना Suresh Khanna	उमा देवी Uma Devi	विनोद कुमार Vinod Kumar
student	teacher	doctor
Indian	Indian	American
not married	not married	married
not happy	happy	happy

१ क्या सुरेश शादी-शुदा है ? *kyā Sureś śādī-śudā hai?*
२ क्या वह हिन्दुस्तानी है ? *kyā vah hindustānī hai?*
३ क्या वह अध्यापक है ? *kyā vah adhyāpak hai?*
४ उसका पूरा नाम क्या है ? *uskā pūrā nām kyā hai?*
५ क्या उमा हिन्दुस्तानी हैं ? *kyā Umā hindustānī hai?*
६ क्या वह डाक्टर है ? *kyā vah ḍākṭar hai?*
७ क्या वह शादी-शुदा है ? *kyā vah śādī-śudā hai?*
८ क्या वह सुखी है ? *kyā vah sukhī hai?*
९ क्या विनोद अँग्रेज़ है ? *kyā Vinod ãgrez hai?*

१० क्या वह अध्यापक है ? *kyā vah adhyāpak hai?*

११ उसका पूरा नाम क्या है ? *uskā pūrā nām kyā hai?*

१२ क्या वह शादी-शुदा है ? *kyā vah śādī-śudā hai?*

१३ क्या विनोद और सुरेश दोनों हिन्दुस्तानी हैं ?
kyā Vinod aur Sureś donõ hindustānī haĩ?

१४ क्या उमा और विनोद दोनों शादी-शुदा हैं ?
kyā Umā aur Vinod donõ śādī-śudā haĩ?

१५ क्या सुरेश और उमा दोनों अध्यापक हैं ?
kyā Sureś aur Umā donõ adhyāpak haĩ?

Glossary

The words in this glossary are on the recording at the end of the Introduction (track 1).

अँग्रेज़ *ãgrez* m., f. English person
अध्यापक *adhyāpak* m. teacher
अमरीकन *amrīkan* American
आदमी *ādmī* m. man
आप *āp* you
आपका *āpkā* your, yours
आसान *āsān* easy
इसका *iskā* his, her/hers, its
उसका *uskā* his, her/hers, its
एक *ek* a; one
और *aur* and
औरत *aurat* f. woman
क़लम *qalam* m./f. pen
किताब *kitāb* f. book
कुत्ता *kuttā* m. dog
कुरसी *kursī* f. chair
कौन *kaun* who?
क्या *kyā* what?; and question-marker
ख़ुश *khuś* pleased, happy
जी नहीं *jī nahī̃* no
जी हाँ *jī hā̃* yes
ठीक *ṭhīk* OK, all right
डाक्टर *ḍākṭar* m. doctor
दोनों *donõ* both
दोस्त *dost* m., f. friend
नमस्कार *namaskār* hello, goodbye
नमस्ते *namaste* hello, goodbye
नर्स *nars* m., f. nurse
नहीं *nahī̃* not, no
नाम *nām* m. name
नाराज़ *nārāz* angry, displeased
पूरा *pūrā* full, complete
बिलकुल *bilkul* quite, completely
बिल्ली *billī* f. cat
बीमार *bīmār* ill, sick
बेटा *beṭā* m. son
भाई *bhāī* m. brother
मकान *makān* m. house
मेज़ *mez* f. table
मेरा *merā* my, mine
मैं *maĩ* I
यह *yah* he, she, it, this
ये *ye* they, these
रेडियो *reḍiyo* m. radio

लड़का *laṛkā* m. boy
लड़की *laṛkī* f. girl
लेकिन *lekin* but
लोग *log* m. pl. people
वह *vah* he, she, it, that
विद्यार्थी *vidyārthī* m. student
वे *ve* they, those
शादी-शुदा *śādī-śudā* married
शुक्रिया *śukriyā* thank you
सुखी *sukhī* happy
सितार *sitār* m. sitar
हाँ *hā̃* yes
हिन्दी *hindī* f. Hindi
हिन्दुस्तानी *hindustānī* Indian
हूँ *hū̃* am
हैं *haĩ* are
है *hai* is

02

हमारा परिवार

hamārā

our family

In this unit you will learn

- about masculines and feminines
- about formal and informal ways of speaking to people

Language points

- agreement of number and gender
- cardinal and ordinal numbers

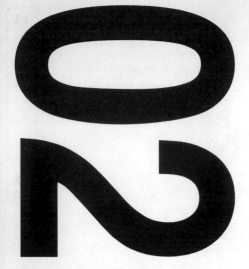

1 Gender matters

We saw earlier that लड़का *laṛkā* means 'boy' and लड़की *laṛkī* means 'girl'. This contrast between *-ā* in the masculine and *-ī* in the feminine appears in many nouns, adjectives, etc. — in fact it's a characteristic feature of Hindi. See how both adjective and noun change in the following:

मनोज बड़ा लड़का है ।
Manoj baṛā laṛkā hai. Manoj is a big boy.

मीना बड़ी लड़की है ।
Mīnā baṛī laṛkī hai. Meena is a big girl.

Masculine बड़ा *baṛā* becomes feminine बड़ी *baṛī*. Watch again:

मनोज लंबा और पतला है ।
Manoj lambā aur patlā hai. Manoj is tall and thin.

मीना लंबी और पतली है ।
Mīnā lambī aur patlī hai. Meena is tall and thin.

राम छोटा है ।
Rām choṭā hai. Ram is little.

क्या राम अच्छा लड़का है ?
kyā Rām acchā laṛka hai? Is Ram a good boy?

मोती मोटा नहीं है ।
Motī moṭā nahī̃ hai. Moti isn't fat.

क्या मनोज पतला है ?
kyā Manoj patlā hai? Is Manoj thin?

क्या मीना लंबी है ?
kyā Mīnā lambī hai? Is Meena tall?

Similarly, मेरा *merā* 'my, mine' becomes मेरी *merī* when describing a feminine noun:

यह लड़का मेरा छोटा भाई है ।
yah laṛkā merā choṭā bhāī hai. This boy is my little brother.

यह लड़की मेरी छोटी बहिन है ।
yah laṛkī merī choṭī bahin hai. This girl is my little sister.

मेरा बेटा ठीक है लेकिन मेरी बेटी बीमार है ।
merā beṭā ṭhīk hai lekin merī beṭī bīmār hai. My son is well but my daughter is sick.

The speaker of the three sentences above could be either male or female: the gender of मेरा/मेरी *merā/merī* depends on the thing or person possessed, *not* the possessor. It behaves just like any other adjective. Similarly आपका *āpkā* becomes आपकी *āpkī* in the feminine:

आपका बेटा काफ़ी लंबा है ।
āpkā beṭā kāfī lambā hai. Your son is quite tall.

आपकी बेटी बहुत सुंदर है ।
āpkī beṭī bahut sundar hai. Your daughter is very beautiful.

Practise what you've learnt

Think of a neighbour and answer these questions about him or her:

A male neighbour	A female neighbour
क्या आपका पड़ोसी लंबा है ? *kyā āpkā paṛosī lambā hai?*	क्या आपकी पड़ोसिन लंबी है ? *kyā āpkī paṛosin lambī hai?*
क्या आपका पड़ोसी पतला है ? *kyā āpkā paṛosī patlā hai?*	क्या आपकी पड़ोसिन पतली है ? *kyā āpkī paṛosin patlī hai?*
क्या आपका पड़ोसी अँग्रेज़ है ? *kyā āpkā paṛosī ãgrez hai?*	क्या आपकी पड़ोसिन अँग्रेज़ है ? *kyā āpkī paṛosin ãgrez hai?*
क्या वह नाराज़ है ? *kyā vah nārāz hai?*	क्या वह नाराज़ है ? *kyā vah nārāz hai?*
क्या वह बीमार है ? *kyā vah bīmār hai?*	क्या वह बीमार है ? *kyā vah bīmār hai?*
क्या वह सुंदर है ? *kyā vah sundar hai?*	क्या वह सुंदर है ? *kyā vah sundar hai?*

All nouns have a gender

You must learn the gender of every new noun you meet — it's not only animate beings that have gender. The words आशा *āśā* 'hope', अलमारी *almārī* 'cupboard' and तस्वीर *tasvīr* 'picture' are all feminine, while कमरा *kamrā* 'room', मकान *makān* 'house' and आदमी *ādmī* 'man' are all masculine. Try learning nouns with an appropriate adjective:

बड़ा कमरा, बड़ा आदमी

baṛā kamrā, baṛā ādmī   big room, big man

बड़ी तस्वीर, बड़ी किताब

baṛī tasvīr, baṛī kitāb   big picture, big book

बड़ा कुत्ता, छोटी बिल्ली

baṛā kuttā, choṭī billī   big dog, small cat

Some adjectives never change

Only those adjectives that end *-ā* in the masculine change to *-ī* in the feminine. Other adjectives never change, and so are called 'invariable'; ठीक *ṭhīk* 'OK' is a good example.

यह किताब ठीक है ।

yah kitāb ṭhīk hai.   This book is OK.

यह कमरा ठीक है ।

yah kamrā ṭhīk hai.   This room is OK.

मनोज ठीक है ।

Manoj ṭhīk hai.   Manoj is OK.

A few adjectives ending in *-ā* are invariable despite this ending. Examples are ज़िन्दा *zindā* 'alive' and शादी-शुदा *śādī-śudā* 'married'. A few adjectives ending in *-ī*, such as ख़ाली *khālī* 'vacant, empty, free', are also invariable.

क्या बिल्ली ज़िन्दा है ?

kyā billī zindā hai?   Is the cat alive?

गीता शादी-शुदा है ।

Gītā śādī-śudā hai.   Geeta is married.

यह कमरा ख़ाली है ।

yah kamrā khālī hai.   This room is free.

Did you know?

Though India's linguistic diversity has made it difficult for Hindi (or any other language) to gain the status of a true 'national language', Hindi is spoken by some 350 million people in the subcontinent — the 1991 census gives the figure of 337,272,114 (source: **www.censusindia.net**).

Role play

In this role play, your name is Geeta Sharma and you are married to Raju Sharma; you have a brother, Rakesh, and a sister, Sita — she's unwell, but everyone else is OK. Answer these questions:

१ क्या आप गीता हैं ? *kyā āp Gītā haĩ?*

२ आपका पूरा नाम क्या है ? *āpkā pūrā nām kyā hai?*

३ क्या आप शादी-शुदा हैं ? *kyā āp śādī-śudā haĩ?*

४ राकेश कौन है ? *Rākeś kaun hai?*

५ सीता कौन है ? *Sītā kaun hai?*

६ क्या आपकी बहिन ठीक है ? *kyā āpkī bahin ṭhīk hai?*

७ क्या आपका भाई बीमार है ? *kyā āpkā bhāī bīmār hai?*

८ क्या आप बीमार हैं ? *kyā āp bīmār haĩ?*

2 Number

English usually makes nouns singular plural by adding an 's', as in 'one book, two books'. In Hindi it's a bit more complicated, because masculine and feminine nouns behave differently. We'll look at masculine nouns first.

Two types of masculine noun

Most masculine nouns ending *-ā* in the singular change to *-e* in the plural. The same happens with most adjectives ending *-ā*.

बड़ा कमरा	बड़े कमरे
baṛā kamrā big room	*baṛe kamre* big rooms

Other masculine nouns don't change at all in the plural — they behave like the English word 'sheep'. In the following, though the noun आदमी *ādmī* doesn't change, its status as singular or plural is revealed by the adjective changing from singular *-ā* to plural *-e*:

बड़ा आदमी	बड़े आदमी
baṛā ādmī big man	*baṛe ādmī* big men

You'll sometimes find that neither the adjective *nor* the noun is of the changing type. As with the numerically ambiguous English phrase 'fat sheep', you can only tell the number from the context:

आसान काम

āsān kām easy work / easy jobs

साफ़ मकान

sāf makān clean house / clean houses

A handful of nouns ending in *-ā* belong to this 'non-changing' group: पिता *pitā* 'father', चाचा *cācā* 'uncle', राजा *rājā* 'king', नेता *netā* 'leader, politician.

मेरे पिता और चाचा दोनों नेता हैं ।

mere pitā aur cācā donõ netā haĩ. My father and uncle are both politicians.

Two types of feminine noun

Feminine nouns ending *-ī* (like लड़की *laṛkī* 'girl') or *-i* (शक्ति *śakti* 'power') change this ending to *-iyā̃* in the plural, but feminine adjectives stay the same in the plural:

छोटी लड़की *choṭī laṛkī* little girl	छोटी लड़कियाँ *choṭī laṛkiyā̃* little girls

Other feminine nouns are made plural be adding -एँ *-ẽ*.

एक मेज़ *ek mez* one table	दो मेज़ें *do mezẽ* two tables
एक औरत *ek aurat* one woman	तीन औरतें *tīn auratẽ* three women
एक मोटी महिला *ek moṭī mahilā* one fat lady	चार मोटी महिलाएँ *cār moṭī mahilāẽ* four fat ladies
मेरी बड़ी बहिन *merī baṛī bahin* my big sister	मेरी बड़ी बहिनें *merī baṛī bahinẽ* my big sisters

An adjective that refers to mixed genders is masculine, as in लंबे *lambe* below:

मनोज और मीना दोनों लंबे हैं ।

Manoj aur Mīnā donõ lambe haĩ. Manoj and Meena are both tall.

(Manoj is male, Meena female: the adjective लंबे *lambe* is masculine plural.)

Fill the gap!

Fill the gap with the appropriate word(s). Answers below.

१ ये औरतें बहुत .... हैं ।
ye auratẽ bahut .... haĩ. These women are very tall.

२ .... बहुत मोटे हैं ।
.... *bahut moṭe haĩ.* Those boys are very fat.

३ आपका दोस्त .... ।
āpkā dost .... Your friend is very thin.

४ सीता .... है ?
Sītā .... hai? Who is Sita?

५ .... मोती ठीक है ?
.... *Motī ṭhīk hai?* Is Moti OK?

Answers: 1 लंबी *lambī*; 2 वे लड़के *ve laṛke*; 3 बहुत पतला है *bahut patlā hai*; 4 कौन *kaun;* 5 क्या *kyā.*

Practising some plurals

Making nouns plural is an essential skill: practise singular/plural contrasts out loud, pronouncing every word as clearly as you can, and you'll feel the music of the language as you learn it.

एक आदमी *ek ādmī* one man	दो आदमी *do ādmī* two men
एक लड़का *ek laṛkā* one boy	दो लड़के *do laṛke* two boys
एक लड़की *ek laṛkī* one girl	दो लड़कियाँ *do laṛkiyā̃* two girls
एक मेज़ *ek mez* one table	दो मेज़ें *do mezẽ* two tables

Do this with a variety of different nouns and you'll soon get the hang of it — a certain amount of parrot-like repetition is essential when learning a new language! Throw in an adjective too —

एक बड़ा आदमी	दस बड़े आदमी	
ek baṛā ādmī	*das baṛe ādmī*	
one big man	ten big men	etc.

Some numbers

Talking of numbers — you should learn to count! Learn the numbers from 1 to 20 in groups of five as they're set out below. (You'll find a full list of numbers in Unit 12.6.) Hindi uses both the Arabic set of numerals (1 2 3 etc.) and the Devanagari set (१ २ ३ etc.).

१	1	एक	*ek*		११	11	ग्यारह	*gyārah*
२	2	दो	*do*		१२	12	बारह	*bārah*
३	3	तीन	*tīn*		१३	13	तेरह	*terah*
४	4	चार	*cār*		१४	14	चौदह	*caudah*
५	5	पाँच	*pā̃c*		१५	15	पंद्रह	*pandrah*
६	6	छह	*chah*		१६	16	सोलह	*solah*
७	7	सात	*sāt*		१७	17	सत्रह	*satrah*
८	8	आठ	*āṭh*		१८	18	अठारह	*aṭhārah*
९	9	नौ	*nau*		१९	19	उन्नीस	*unnīs*
१०	10	दस	*das*		२०	20	बीस	*bīs*

Bingo

If you have people you can practise with, have a game of bingo: everyone selects ten numbers of their choice (between 1 and 20) as shown below, then the caller calls out random numbers in Hindi between 1 and 20 until the winner declares a victory. No cheating!

Ordinal numbers: first, second, third

Ordinal numbers are made by adding *-vā̃* to the cardinal number, as in पाँचवाँ *pā̃cvā̃* fifth; but 'first', 'second', 'third', 'fourth', sixth' and 'ninth' are irregular:

पहला	*pahlā*	first	छठा	*chaṭhā*	sixth
दूसरा	*dūsrā*	second, other	सातवाँ	*sātvā̃*	seventh
तीसरा	*tīsrā*	third	आठवाँ	*āṭhvā̃*	eighth
चौथा	*cauthā*	fourth	नवाँ	*navā̃*	ninth
पाँचवाँ	*pā̃cvā̃*	fifth	दसवाँ	*dasvā̃*	tenth

The ordinal numbers agree as adjectives: दसवाँ कमरा *dasvā̃ kamrā* 'tenth room', दसवीं तस्वीर *dasvī̃ tasvīr* 'tenth picture'.

Ordinal numbers quiz

Answer the questions about these five fine fellows:

गणेश Ganesh

सुरेश Suresh

महेश Mahesh

दिनेश Dinesh

राजेश Rajesh

१ क्या पहला लड़का मोटा है ? *kyā pahlā laṛkā moṭā hai?*

२ पहला लड़का कौन है ? *pahlā laṛkā kaun hai?*

३ क्या तीसरा लड़का ख़ुश है ? *kyā tīsrā laṛkā <u>kh</u>uś hai?*

४ पाँचवाँ लड़का कौन है ? *pā̃cvā laṛkā kaun hai?*

५ क्या चौथा लड़का पतला है ? *kyā cauthā laṛkā patlā hai?*

६ चौथा लड़का कौन है ? *cauthā laṛkā kaun hai?*

७ क्या दूसरा लड़का महेश है ? *kyā dūsrā laṛkā Maheś hai?*

3 Getting familiar

We've already seen that आप *āp* means 'you' and आप हैं *āp haĩ* means 'you are'. But in an informal context (talking to a friend, or with someone perceived by the speaker to be in some way close or socially 'junior') the pronoun तुम *tum* 'you' is used instead. तुम *tum* has its own verb form: तुम हो *tum ho* 'you are'.

तुम कौन हो ?
tum kaun ho? Who are you?

क्या तुम राम हो ?
kyā tum Rām ho? Are you Ram?

When addressing someone as तुम *tum,* the word for 'your' is तुम्हारा *tumhārā.* Remember that such words must agree with the person or thing 'possessed'.

तुम्हारा भाई
tumhārā bhāī your brother

तुम्हारी बहिन
tumhārī bahin your sister

The important point here is that तुम *tum* is much more familiar and informal than आप *āp.* Used in the wrong context, तुम *tum* and तुम्हारा *tumhārā* could sound presumptuous or offensive, so you have to tread carefully here.

Even greater familiarity is shown by yet another pronoun, तू *tū* 'you', whose verb is है *hai* (the same as for यह *yah* and वह *vah*): तू है *tū hai* 'you are'. This is very intimate and is restricted to the closest of relationships, such as with partners, small children — and God!

राजू, तू मेरी जान है !
Rājū, tū merī jān hai! Raju, you are my darling!

गीता, तू मेरी जान है !
Gītā, tū merī jān hai! Geeta, you are my darling!

We won't be seeing much of तू *tū* in this book. Its intimacy restricts its usage; and if you know a Hindi-speaker well enough to use it, he or she will happily teach you all you need to know! Used in the wrong context, it can be insultingly blunt. All its verb forms (except the commands — see 4.1) are the same as for यह *yah* and वह *vah*.

Here then is the full range of 'you' words, with their verbs:

आप हैं
āp haĩ you are (formal and polite)

तुम हो
tum ho you are (familiar and casual)

तू है
tū hai you are (intimate or blunt)

Grammatically, तू *tū* is singular, and both आप *āp* and तुम *tum* are plural — whether addressing one person or more than one.

Did you know?

English used to have a similar singular/plural distinction, but the singular pronouns 'thou (thou art), thee, thy, thine' have been dropped — which is why even a single person is now addressed by the plural 'you are', rather than 'you is'.

How are you?

This is a good moment to introduce another new word, the very important कैसा *kaisā*, 'how?', as in 'how are you?'. (Later we'll see that it can also mean 'what kind of ?')

राजू, आप कैसे हैं ?
Rājū, āp kaise haĩ? Raju, how are you?

गीता, आप कैसी हैं ?
Gītā, āp kaisī haĩ? Geeta, how are you?

आपका भाई कैसा है ?
āpkā bhāī kaisā hai? How is your brother?

आपकी बहिन कैसी है ?
āpkī bahin kaisī hai? How is your sister?

आपके माता-पिता कैसे हैं ?
āpke mātā-pitā kaise haĩ? How are your parents?

राम, तुम कैसे हो ?

Rām, tum kaise ho? Ram, how are you?

मीना, तुम कैसी हो ?

Mīnā, tum kaisī ho? Meena, how are you?

4 Getting formal

As we have seen in the आप–तुम–तू *āp–tum–tū* distinction, Hindi has a hierarchy of formality: calling someone आप *āp* shows respect, and sets them 'above' people referred to as तुम *tum*, who in turn have higher status than those addressed as तू *tū*.

You may be familiar with similar systems in languages like French, with its distinction between 'vous' and 'tu' in the second person ('you'). But in Hindi, the system extends to the third person: 'he/she' can be expressed with the plural pronouns ये *ye* and वे *ve* instead of यह *yah* and वह *vah*. In effect, it's like referring to an individual person as 'they' rather than as 'he' or 'she'. The bad news is that verbs and adjectives must be plural to match!

As there's no difference between this 'honorific' plural and a numerical plural, some statements could be ambiguous:

वे अच्छे आदमी हैं ।

ve acche ādmī haĩ. He is a good man. / They are good men.

मेरे भाई लंबे हैं ।

mere bhāī lambe haĩ. My brother is tall. / My brothers are tall.

But this ambiguity only occurs in the masculine. In the feminine, only *numerically* plural nouns show plural forms. Compare the following:

ये लंबी महिला कौन हैं ?

ye lambī mahilā kaun haĩ? Who is this tall lady?

(Here the pronoun ये *ye* and verb हैं *haĩ* are honorific plural, but the noun महिला *mahilā* stays singular.)

ये लंबी महिलाएँ कौन हैं ?

ye lambī mahilāẽ kaun haĩ? Who are these tall ladies?

(Here ये *ye*, महिलाएँ *mahilāẽ* and हैं *haĩ* are all plural.)

Raju ji, Geeta ji

Respect can also be shown by adding जी *jī* to a name — written as one word or two (गीताजी *Gītājī*, or गीता जी *Gītā jī*). It's used with first names of both genders, or with surnames for males; also with titles and relationship terms (e.g. पिता जी *pitā jī* 'father'). It's sometimes a bit like 'Mr' or 'Mrs', but manages to combine respect and warmth more successfully than these rather stuffy English equivalents.

ये सीता जी हैं ।

ye Sītā jī haĩ. This is Sita ji.

शर्मा जी अच्छे अध्यापक हैं ।

Śarmā jī acche adhyāpak haĩ. Sharma ji is a good teacher.

Used alone, जी *jī* can be used as a polite way of addressing someone: नमस्ते जी ! *namaste jī!* English has no single equivalent.

We and our

Finally: 'we' and 'us' is हम *ham*, and 'our, ours' is हमारा *hamārā*.

हम आपके पड़ोसी हैं ।

ham āpke paṛosī haĩ. We're your neighbours.

मोती हमारा कुत्ता है ।

Motī hamārā kuttā hai. Moti is our dog.

मोती हमारा है ।

Motī hamārā hai. Moti is ours.

Javed asks Raju about his family

जावेद राजू जी, मनोज कौन है ?

राजू मनोज हमारा बड़ा बेटा है ।

जावेद अच्छा । मीना और राम कौन हैं ?

राजू मीना हमारी बेटी है और राम हमारा दूसरा बेटा है ।

जावेद और गीता जी आपकी पत्नी हैं ?

राजू जी हाँ, गीता मेरी पत्नी है ।

जावेद क्या आपके भाई डाक्टर हैं ?

राजू जी नहीं । वे अध्यापक हैं ।

जावेद वे कैसे अध्यापक हैं ?
राजू वे बहुत अच्छे अध्यापक हैं ।

Jāved *Rājū jī, Manoj kaun hai?*
Rājū *Manoj hamārā baṛā beṭā hai.*
Jāved *acchā. Mīnā aur Rām kaun haĩ?*
Rājū *Mīnā hamārī beṭī hai aur Rām hamārā dūsrā beṭā hai.*
Jāved *aur Gītā jī āpkī patnī haĩ?*
Rājū *jī hā̃, Gītā merī patnī hai.*
Jāved *kyā āpke bhāī ḍākṭar haĩ?*
Rājū *jī nahī̃. ve adhyāpak haĩ.*
Jāved *ve kaise adhyāpak haĩ?*
Rājū *ve bahut acche adhyāpak haĩ.*

Javed Raju ji, who is Manoj?
Raju Manoj is our elder ('big') son.
Javed Right. Who are Meena and Ram?
Raju Meena is our daughter and Ram is our second son.
Javed And Geeta ji is your wife?
Raju Yes, Geeta is my wife.
Javed Is your brother a doctor?
Raju No, he's a teacher.
Javed What kind of teacher is he? [i.e. 'is he good?']
Raju He's a very good teacher.

Exercise 2a Translate these sentences into Hindi.

(NB: 'There are' is हैं *haĩ*; 'only' is सिर्फ़ *sirf.)*

1 My name is Manoj. Raju and Geeta Sharma are my parents.
2 Meena is my little sister and Ram is my little brother.
3 Moti is our dog. He's very cute.
4 This is Meena. She is OK. She is little.
5 Our house isn't very big. There are only five rooms.
6 That boy is my friend; his name is Pratap [प्रताप *Pratāp*].
7 Javed sahab is our neighbour. [Use honorific plural.]

Exercise 2b Here are some sentences with singular subjects. Make them all numerically plural. (Make sure that all verbs, pronouns and adjectives agree!)

८ यह लड़का बहुत प्यारा है । *yah laṛkā bahut pyārā hai.*

९ यह कुत्ता हमारा नहीं है । *yah kuttā hamārā nahī̃ hai.*

१० वह लड़का कौन है ? *vah laṛkā kaun hai?*

११ यह आदमी कौन है ? *yah ādmī kaun hai?*

१२ मेरा दोस्त पंजाबी है । *merā dost panjābī hai.*

१३ क्या यह कुत्ता आपका है ? *kyā yah kuttā āpkā hai?*

१४ वह औरत कौन है ? *vah aurat kaun hai?*

१५ हमारा बेटा अच्छा लड़का है । *hamārā beṭā acchā laṛkā hai.*

१६ मेरी बेटी बीमार है । *merī beṭī bīmār hai.*

१७ क्या यह किताब महँगी है ? *kyā yah kitāb mahãgī hai?*

१८ यह मेज़ गंदी है । *yah mez gandī hai.*

Exercise 2c Change the sentences from आप *āp* to तुम *tum*, or vice versa, making sure that all the verb agreements (तुम हो *tum ho,* आप हैं *āp haĩ* etc.) work properly.

१९ तुम कौन हो ? *tum kaun ho?*

२० तुम्हारा नाम क्या है ? *tumhārā nām kyā hai ?*

२१ तुम्हारे माता-पिता बहुत अच्छे लोग हैं । *tumhāre mātā-pitā bahut acche log haĩ.*

२२ तुम्हारा भाई सुंदर नहीं है । *tumhārā bhāī sundar nahī̃ hai.*

२३ तुम दोनों लड़के लंबे हो । *tum donõ laṛke lambe ho.*

२४ तुम कैसे हो ? *tum kaise ho?*

२५ आपका नाम क्या है ? *āpkā nām kyā hai?*

२६ क्या आप ठीक हैं ? *kyā āp ṭhīk haĩ?*

२७ आप नाराज़ नहीं हैं ? *āp nārāz nahī̃ haĩ?*

२८ आप कैसी हैं ? *āp kaisī haĩ?*

Finally, go through all the sentences in sentences 1–28, underlining the subject of the verb; and make sure you can understand why each verb is singular or plural.

Glossary

(NB: Cardinal numbers up to 10 (and ordinals up to 'sixth') are included here. Higher cardinal numbers are given in Unit 12.6.)

अच्छा *acchā* good, nice
अलमारी *almārī* f. cupboard
आठ *āṭh* eight
आशा *āśā* f. hope
औरत *aurat* f. woman
कमरा *kamrā* m. room
काफ़ी *kāfī* quite, very; enough
काम *kām* m. work; job, task
कैसा *kaisā* how?
ख़ाली *khālī* empty, free, vacant
गंदा *gandā* dirty
चाचा *cācā* m. uncle (father's younger brother)
चार *cār* four
चौथा *cauthā* fourth
छठा *chaṭhā* sixth
छह *chah* six
छोटा *choṭā* small
ज़रूर *zarūr* of course
जान *jān* f. life, soul
ज़िंदा *zindā* (invariable *-ā* ending) alive
जी *jī* word of respect used after names etc. and as a short form of जी हाँ *jī hā̃* 'yes'
तस्वीर *tasvīr* f. picture
तीन *tīn* three
तीसरा *tīsrā* third
तुम *tum* you (familiar)
तुम्हारा *tumhārā* your, yours
तू *tū* you (intimate)
दस *das* ten
दूसरा *dūsrā* second; other
दो *do* two
नेता *netā* m. leader, politician
नौ *nau* nine
पड़ोसी *paṛosī* m., पड़ोसिन *paṛosin* f. neighbour
पतला *patlā* thin
पत्नी *patnī* f. wife
पहला *pahlā* first
पाँच *pā̃c* five; पाँचवाँ *pā̃cvā̃* fifth
पिता *pitā* m. father
प्यारा *pyārā* dear, sweet, cute
बड़ा *baṛā* big
बहिन *bahin* f. sister
बहुत *bahut* very
बेटी *beṭī* f. daughter
महँगा *mahā̃gā* expensive
महिला *mahilā* f. lady
माता *mātā* f. mother
माता-पिता *mātā-pitā* m. pl. parents
मोटा *moṭā* fat
राजा *rājā* m. king, raja
लंबा *lambā* tall
शक्ति *śakti* f. power
सात *sāt* seven
साफ़ *sāf* clean, clear
साहब *sāhab* sahib
सिर्फ़ *sirf* only
सुंदर *sundar* beautiful, handsome
हम *ham* we, us
हमारा *hamārā* our, ours
हो *ho* are (with तुम *tum*)

03

कमरे में
kamre
in the room

In this unit you will learn

- to say where people and things are
- to describe things
- to talk about ownership

Language points

- postpositions and case
- word order

1 Some more questions

You'll have noticed that question-words in Hindi begin with a 'k' — क्या *kyā*, कौन *kaun* etc. A further selection of such words will give us much more to talk about. We've already met कैसा *kaisā*, used in asking 'how' someone is; but it also means 'what kind of ?' And कितना *kitnā* means 'how much?'

कैसा मकान ?
kaisā makān? what kind of house?

यह कैसा मकान है ?
yah kaisā makān hai? What kind of house is this?

कितना पानी ?
kitnā pānī? how much water?

कितना पानी है ?
kitnā pānī hai? How much water is there?

Both कैसा *kaisā* and कितना *kitnā* inflect (OK, change their endings!) like adjectives: कैसा–कैसे–कैसी *kaisā–kaise–kaisī*, कितना–कितने–कितनी *kitna–kitne–kitnī.*

यह कैसा कमरा है ?
yah kaisā kamrā hai? What kind of room is this?

यह कैसी किताब है ?
ye kaisī kitāb hai? What kind of book is this?

ये कैसे कमरे हैं ?
ye kaise kamre haĩ? What kind of rooms are these?

कितने कमरे हैं ?
kitne kamre haĩ? How many rooms are there?

कितनी दुकानें हैं ?
kitnī dukānẽ haĩ? How many shops are there?

कितना पैसा है ?
kitnā paisā hai? How much money is there?

कितने लोग हैं ?
kitne log haĩ? How many people are there?

कितना समय है ?
kitnā samay hai? How much time is there?

What's this like?

When कैसा *kaisā* comes *after* the noun, it means 'what is something like?' Remember that it's also the usual way of asking about someone's health — such a commonly used expression that we'll look at some more examples:

यह कमरा कैसा है ?
yah kamrā kaisā hai? What's this room like?

मनोज कैसा है ?
Manoj kaisā hai? How is Manoj?

माता जी कैसी हैं ?
mātā jī kaisī haĩ? How is Mother?

राम, तुम कैसे हो ?
Rām, tum kaise ho? Ram, how are you?

शर्मा जी, आप कैसे हैं ?
Śarmā jī, āp kaise haĩ? Sharma ji, how are you?

गीता जी, आप कैसी हैं ?
Gītā jī, āp kaisī haĩ? Geeta ji, how are you?

Some questions for you

Answer the questions about the picture, using words from the list:

बूढ़ा *būṛhā*
elderly

पुराना *purānā*
old (of things)

कुल मिलाकर
kul milākar
in total

चूहा *cūhā* m.
mouse, rat

तोता *totā* m.
parrot

१ कितने आदमी हैं ? *kitne ādmī haĩ?*

२ यह कैसा आदमी है ? *yah kaisā ādmī hai?*

३ मेज़ कैसी है ? *mez kaisī hai?*

४ कितनी लड़कियाँ हैं ? *kitnī laṛkiyā̃ haĩ?*

५ कुल मिलाकर कितने लोग हैं ? *kul milākar kitne log haĩ?*

६ क्या दोनों लड़कियाँ लंबी हैं ? *kyā donõ laṛkiyā̃ lambī haĩ?*

७ कितने चूहे हैं ? *kitne cūhe haĩ?*

८ कितनी कुरसियाँ हैं ? *kitnī kursiyā̃ haĩ?*

९ क्या चूहे बहुत बड़े हैं ? *kyā cūhe bahut baṛe haĩ?*

१० कितने तोते हैं ? *kitne tote haĩ?*

2 Where? On the table

The word कहाँ *kahā̃* means 'where?' In order to say *where* something is, we need the words for 'on, in' and so on. Here's a little list:

पर	*par*	on, at
में	*mẽ*	in
से	*se*	from, with, by
तक	*tak*	up to, until
को	*ko*	to (and other meanings)

And here are some phrases:

मेज़ पर	*mez par*	on the table
कुरसी पर	*kursī par*	on the chair
घर पर	*ghar par*	at home
घर में	*ghar mẽ*	in the house
दिल्ली में	*dillī mẽ*	in Delhi
भारत में	*bhārat mẽ*	in India
आज तक	*āj tak*	until today

As you can see, the words पर *par,* में *mẽ* etc. come *after* the noun. Because of this they're called *post*positions rather than *pre*positions.

Practise what you've learnt

Answer these questions, using the postposition में *mẽ* 'in'.

दिल्ली कहाँ है ? *dillī kahā̃ hai?*

काठमांडु कहाँ है ? *kāṭhmāṇḍu kahā̃ hai?*

कराची कहाँ है ? *karācī kahā̃ hai?*

मुम्बई कहाँ है ? *mumbaī kahā̃ hai?*

लंदन कहाँ है ? *landan kahā̃ hai?*

आप कहाँ हैं ? *āp kahā̃ haĩ?*

Your answers should be दिल्ली भारत में है *dillī bhārat mẽ hai* etc.; and my answer to the last one is मैं लंदन में हूँ *maĩ landan mẽ hū̃.*

At home, at school, at work

पर *par* usually means 'on', but it means 'at' in phrases like घर पर *ghar par* 'at home'.

आज मनोज घर पर नहीं है ।
āj Manoj ghar par nahī̃ hai. Manoj isn't at home today.

राम स्कूल पर नहीं है ।
Rām skūl par nahī̃ hai. Ram isn't at school.

मेरे दोस्त काम पर हैं ।
mere dost kām par haĩ. My friends are at work.

शर्मा जी काम पर हैं ।
Śarmā jī kām par haĩ. Sharma ji is at work.

Word order

Look very closely at the difference between these two sentences:

मेज़ पर पंखा है ।
mez par pankhā hai. There's a fan on the table.

पंखा मेज़ पर है ।
pankhā mez par hai. The fan is on the table.

You'll see that the main piece of new information comes *just before the verb.* Another way of looking at these sentences is to see them as the answers to particular questions, with the new information simply slotting into the space that had been occupied by the question word:

मेज़ पर क्या है ?
mez par kyā hai? What is on the table?
मेज़ पर पंखा है ।
mez par pankhā hai. There's a fan on the table.

पंखा कहाँ है ?
pankhā kahā̃ hai? Where is the fan?
पंखा मेज़ पर है ।
pankhā mez par hai. The fan is on the table.

Where's the cat?

Answer the questions about the picture:

१ बिल्ली कहाँ है ? *billī kahā̃ hai?*
२ कुत्ता कहाँ है ? *kuttā kahā̃ hai?*
३ तस्वीर में कितनी कुरसियाँ हैं ? *tasvīr mẽ kitnī kursiyā̃ haĩ?*
४ तस्वीर में कितनी बिल्लियाँ हैं ? *tasvīr mẽ kitnī billiyā̃ haĩ?*
५ छोटी कुरसी पर क्या है ? *choṭī kursī par kyā hai?*
६ बड़ी कुरसी पर क्या है ? *baṛī kursī par kyā hai?*
७ मेज़ पर क्या है ? *mez par kyā hai?*
८ क्या कुत्ता और बिल्ली प्यारे हैं? *kyā kuttā aur billī pyāre haĩ?*

Do you have...

One postposition that you'll often need is के पास *ke pās*. We'll meet it more fully later, but we need it *now*. Its first meaning is 'near':

हमारी दुकान स्टेशन के पास है ।
hamārī dukān sṭeśan ke pās hai. Our shop is near the station.

But के पास *ke pās* can also indicate *ownership* of goods and chattels (or even time) — it's used in the meaning of 'to have':

मनोज के पास नया रेडियो है ।
Manoj ke pās nayā reḍiyo hai. Manoj has a new radio.

राम के पास कई नई किताबें हैं ।
Rām ke pās kaī naī kitābẽ haĩ. Ram has several new books.

मीना के पास कुछ नए कपड़े हैं ।
Mīnā ke pās kuch nae kapṛe haĩ. Meena has some new clothes.

राजू के पास कम्प्यूटर नहीं है ।
Rājū ke pās kampyūṭar nahī̃ hai. Raju doesn't have a computer.

पिताजी के पास समय नहीं है ।
pitājī ke pās samay nahī̃ hai. Father doesn't have time.

आपके पास कितना पैसा है ?
āpke pās kitnā paisā hai? How much money do you have?

When के पास *ke pās* is used with मेरे *mere*, तुम्हारे *tumhāre* or हमारे *hamāre*, the के *ke* is dropped:

मेरे पास समय नहीं है ।
mere pās samay nahī̃ hai. I don't have time.

तुम्हारे पास क्या है ?
tumhāre pās kyā hai? What have you got?

हमारे पास कुछ नहीं है ।
hamāre pās kuch nahī̃ hai. We have nothing.

Although के पास *ke pās* is used widely for a variety of possessions, it's not usually used with relatives ('I have a son' etc.); we'll come to a way of saying this in Unit 6.1. Meanwhile, a spirit of idle curiosity makes me ask *you* some questions:

क्या आप के पास ... *kyā āp ke pās...*

... साइकिल है ? *sāikil hai?*

... बहुत पैसे हैं ? *bahut paise haĩ?*

... नया रेडियो है ? *nayā reḍiyo hai?*

... नए हिन्दुस्तानी कपड़े हैं ? *nae hindustānī kapṛe haĩ?*

... नई गाड़ी है ? *naī gāṛī hai?*

3 Case

In the English phrase 'he speaks to him', the two pronouns can't be exchanged: 'him speaks to he' isn't impressive English! This is an example of a difference of 'case' — a system that shows how words relate to each other in a sentence. Stand by for a really important piece of grammar here.

Hindi has two main cases — the 'oblique', always used before postpositions, and the 'direct', used elsewhere.

In the following sentences, the underlined words are postpositions, and the **bold** words are oblique, because they're followed by those postpositions.

हम लोग **घर** में हैं ।
ham log ***ghar*** *mẽ haĩ.* We ['we people'] are in the house.

दिल्ली **भारत** में हैं ।
dillī ***bhārat*** *mẽ haĩ.* Delhi is in India.

क्या आप **लंदन** से हैं ?
kyā āp ***landan*** *se haĩ?* Are you from London?

शर्माजी **दुकान** पर हैं ।
Śarmājī ***dukān*** *par haĩ.* Sharma ji is at the shop.

In the first example, में *mẽ* 'in' affects only घर *ghar* 'house', giving the sense 'in the house' — it doesn't affect हम लोग *ham log* 'we' because this is the subject, and not part of the location. The same principle applies with the other examples.

Why say that these words are oblique, when they haven't changed their form at all? Because in the singular, only *some* nouns change in the oblique. Masculine *-ā* endings are the culprits here: they change to *-e*, as shown in the following list.

कमरा	*kamrā*	room
कमरे में	*kamre mẽ*	in the room
लड़का	*laṛkā*	boy
लड़के से	*laṛke se*	by the boy
आगरा	*āgrā*	Agra
आगरे तक	*āgre tak*	as far as Agra

Masculine *-ā* adjectives describing oblique nouns change similarly:

छोटा कमरा	*choṭā kamrā*	small room
छोटे कमरे में	*choṭe kamre mẽ*	in a/the small room
मोटा लड़का	*moṭā laṛkā*	fat boy
मोटे लड़के से	*moṭe laṛke se*	by the fat boy
मेरा बग़ीचा	*merā bagīcā*	my garden
मेरे बग़ीचे में	*mere bagīce mẽ*	in my garden

An *-ā* adjective changes like this with *all* types of masculine noun. So although घर *ghar* 'house' does not end in *-ā* and therefore cannot change visibly in the oblique, *-ā* adjectives qualifying it must change all the same:

बड़े घर में	*baṛe ghar mẽ*	in the big house
छोटे मकान में	*choṭe makān mẽ*	in the little house

Feminine nouns and adjectives are easier to deal with — they don't change at all in the oblique singular:

छोटी मेज़ पर	*choṭī mez par*	on the little table
मेरी बहिन को	*merī bahin ko*	to my sister

Plural nouns in the oblique case

In the oblique plural, all nouns take the ending *-õ* as shown:

मेज़	*mez*	table
मेज़ों पर	*mezõ par*	on tables
कमरा	*kamrā*	room
कमरों में	*kamrõ mẽ*	in rooms

लड़का	*laṛkā*	boy
लड़कों को	*laṛkõ ko*	to boys
कुत्ता	*kuttā*	dog
कुत्तों को	*kuttõ ko*	to dogs

... and masculine *-ā* adjectives keep their *usual* oblique *-e* ending:

कमरा	*kamrā*	room
छोटे कमरों में	*choṭe kamrõ mẽ*	in small rooms
लड़का	*laṛkā*	boy
बड़े लड़कों को	*baṛe laṛkõ ko*	to big boys
हमारा कुत्ता	*hamārā kuttā*	our dog
हमारे कुत्तों को	*hamāre kuttõ ko*	to our dogs

Nouns of either gender that end in *-i* change this to *iy* before adding the *-õ* ending. So they end *-iyõ.*

आदमी	*ādmī*	man
आदमियों से	*ādmiyõ se*	from men
लड़की	*laṛkī*	girl
लड़कियों से	*laṛkiyõ*	from girls

Well, after all that grammar you probably feel the need to sit or even lie down for a bit, so...

Sitting and lying

'Sitting' is बैठा *baiṭhā* and 'standing' is खड़ा *khaṛā*; 'lying' is पड़ा *paṛā* for an inanimate object (e.g. a book lying on the table), but लेटा *leṭā* for a person who is 'lying down'. These words need to agree with their nouns, like adjectives:

मनोज कमरे में बैठा है ।

Manoj kamre mẽ baiṭhā hai. Manoj is sitting in the room.

गीता बग़ीचे में खड़ी है ।

Gītā bagīce mẽ khaṛī hai. Geeta is standing in the garden.

आपके कपड़े कुरसी पर पड़े हैं ।

āpke kapṛe kursī par paṛe haĩ. Your clothes are lying on the chair.

दोनों लड़कियाँ फ़र्श पर लेटी हैं ।
donõ laṛkiyā̃ farś par leṭī haĩ. The two girls are lying on the floor.

House for rent

A Hindi-speaking friend has seen an advertisement in an English newspaper and needs your help in understanding it. Read the advertisement and then answer her questions.

New house for rent in Agra. 2 large & 2 small rooms, all well ventilated (windows in all rooms, ceiling fans in large rooms). Small garden with trees. Rent Rs. 5000.

१ घर कहाँ है ?
ghar kahā̃ hai?

२ क्या वह बहुत पुराना है ?
kyā vah bahut purānā hai?

३ कितने कमरे हैं ?
kitne kamre haĩ?

४ क्या सब कमरों में खिड़कियाँ हैं ?
kyā sab kamrõ mẽ khiṛkiyā̃ haĩ?

५ क्या पंखे भी हैं ?
kyā pankhe bhī haĩ?

६ बाहर क्या है ?
bāhar kyā hai?

७ क्या दुकानें दूर हैं ?
kyā dukānẽ dūr haĩ?

८ किराया कितना है ?
kirāyā kitnā hai?

Geeta's story

Geeta is telling us about her husband and her home.

मेरा नाम गीता है – श्रीमती गीता शर्मा । मैं वाराणसी से हूँ । मेरे पति श्री राजकुमार शर्मा हैं । वे दिल्ली से हैं । राजू अध्यापक हैं । यह हमारा घर है । हमारा घर आगरे में है । घर में एक बड़ा कमरा और चार छोटे कमरे हैं । यह हमारा बड़ा कमरा है । कमरे में एक बड़ी मेज़ है । मेज़ पर मेरा कम्प्यूटर है । एक पंखा भी है । फ़र्श पर कुछ किताबें पड़ी हैं । बग़ीचे में दो-तीन लंबे पेड़ हैं ।

merā nām Gītā hai – śrīmatī Gītā Śarmā. maĩ vārāṇasī se hū̃. mere pati śrī Rājkumār Śarmā haĩ. ve dillī se haĩ. Rājū adhyāpak haĩ. yah hamārā ghar hai. hamārā ghar āgre mẽ hai. ghar mẽ ek baṛā kamrā aur cār choṭe kamre haĩ. yah hamārā baṛā kamrā hai. kamre mẽ ek baṛī mez hai. mez par merā kampyūṭar hai. ek pankhā bhī hai. farś par kuch kitābẽ paṛī haĩ. bagīce mẽ do-tīn lambe peṛ haĩ.

My name is Geeta — Mrs Geeta Sharma. I'm from Varanasi. My husband is Mr Rajkumar Sharma. He's from Delhi. Raju is a teacher. This is our house. Our house is in Agra. In the house there's one big room and four small rooms. This is our big room. In the room there's one big table. On the table is my computer. There's a fan too. Some books are lying on the floor. In the garden there are two or three tall trees.

Two tasks for you

Underline all the words in the oblique case in Geeta's statement, then answer these questions:

१ गीता कहाँ से है ? *Gītā kahā̃ se hai?*

२ क्या गीता शादी-शुदा है ? *kyā Gītā śādī-śudā hai?*

३ क्या राजू दिल्ली से है ? *kyā Rājū dillī se hai?*

४ क्या राजू डाक्टर है ? *kyā Rājū ḍākṭar hai?*

५ क्या यह घर दिल्ली में है ? *kyā yah ghar dillī mẽ hai?*

६ घर में कितने कमरे हैं ? *ghar mẽ kitne kamre haĩ?*

७ बड़े कमरे में क्या है ? *baṛe kamre mẽ kyā hai?*

८ कम्प्यूटर कहाँ है ? *kampyūṭar kahā̃ hai?*

९ किताबें कहाँ हैं ? *kitābẽ kahā̃ haĩ?*

१० बग़ीचे में क्या है ? *bagīce mẽ kyā hai?*

A word that hates to be misplaced

The little word भी *bhī* 'also, too' is simple enough in itself, but it's incredibly fussy about where it goes in the sentence — it insists on following the word it emphasizes. Look closely at the difference between these two statements, both of which could be translated as 'this cloth is cheap too', leaving the emphasis ambiguous in English:

यह कपड़ा भी सस्ता है ।
yah kapṛā bhī sastā hai. This cloth too is cheap [i.e. as well as the other cloth we were just looking at].

यह कपड़ा सस्ता भी है ।
yah kapṛā sastā bhī hai. This cloth is cheap too [i.e. in addition to its other advantages — colour, texture, or whatever].

At school

अध्यापक	राम, तुम्हारी किताबें कहाँ हैं ?
राम	जी, मेरी किताबें यहाँ मेज़ पर पड़ी हैं ।
अध्यापक	तुम्हारी कुरसी पर क्या पड़ा है ?
राम	जी, मेरी कुरसी पर मेरे क़लम हैं ।
अध्यापक	तुम्हारे हाथों में क्या है ?
राम	मेरे हाथों में कुछ नहीं है ।
अध्यापक	आज तुम्हारी बहिन मीना कहाँ है ?
राम	जी, वह घर पर है । वह बीमार है ।

adhyāpak	*Rām, tumhārī kitābẽ kahā̃ haĩ?*
Rām	*jī, merī kitābẽ yahā̃ mez par paṛī haĩ.*
adhyāpak	*tumhārī kursī par kyā paṛā hai?*
Rām	*jī, merī kursī par mere qalam haĩ.*
adhyāpak	*tumhāre hāthõ mẽ kyā hai?*
Rām	*mere hāthõ mẽ kuch nahī̃ hai.*

adhyāpak	*āj tumhārī bahin Mīnā kahā̃ hai?*
Rām	*jī, vah ghar par hai. vah bīmār hai.*

Teacher	Ram, where are your books?
Ram	Sir, my books are lying here on the table.
Teacher	What's lying on your chair?
Ram	Sir, my pens are on my chair.
Teacher	What's in your hands?
Ram	There's nothing in my hands.
Teacher	Where is your sister Meena today?
Ram	Sir, she's at home. She's unwell.

At home

राजू	गीता, मनोज कहाँ है ?
गीता	वह स्कूल पर है ।
राजू	और राम कहाँ है ?
गीता	वह भी स्कूल पर है ।
राजू	अच्छा ! और मीना ?
गीता	मीना बग़ीचे में बैठी है ।
राजू	मेरा भाई कहाँ है ?
गीता	मालूम नहीं !

Rājū	*Gītā, Manoj kahā̃ hai?*
Gītā	*vah skūl par hai.*
Rājū	*aur Rām kahā̃ hai?*
Gītā	*vah bhī skūl par hai.*
Rājū	*acchā! aur Mīnā?*
Gītā	*Mīnā bagīce mẽ baiṭhī hai.*
Rājū	*merā bhāī kahā̃ hai?*
Gītā	*mālūm nahī̃!*

Raju	Geeta, where's Manoj?
Geeta	He's at school.
Raju	And where's Ram?
Geeta	He's at school too.
Raju	I see! And Meena?

Geeta	Meena's sitting in the garden.
Raju	Where's my brother?
Geeta	Don't know!

Exercise 3a Translate into Hindi:

1 My books are lying on the table.
2 Your brother is sitting in the garden.
3 I am standing in the big room.
4 Your books are in the little cupboard.
5 His house is not far from here.
6 How many people are there in your family?
7 How much money does your husband have?
8 How is your wife today? And how are you?
9 The children aren't at home, they're at school.
10 Is this little girl your sister?

▶ **Exercise 3b** Role play. You are Geeta Sharma (a doctor, remember), at home in Agra with your husband and children; they're in the garden and your husband's indoors. Answer these questions for a local government survey. (Say 'no' to 19, 'yes' to 23.)

११ आपका पूरा नाम क्या है ?
āpkā pūrā nām kyā hai?

१२ क्या आप डाक्टर हैं ?
kyā āp ḍākṭar haĩ?

१३ क्या आपके पति भी डाक्टर हैं ?
kyā āpke pati bhī ḍākṭar haĩ?

१४ क्या आपके पति घर पर हैं ?
kyā āpke pati ghar par haĩ?

१५ क्या आप लोग दिल्ली से हैं ?
kyā āp log dillī se haĩ?

१६ आपके मकान में कितने कमरे हैं ?
āpke makān mẽ kitne kamre haĩ?

१७ आपके परिवार में कितने बच्चे हैं ?
āpke parivār mẽ kitne bacce haĩ?

१८ क्या आपका छोटा लड़का आज स्कूल पर है ?
kyā āpkā choṭā laṛkā āj skūl par hai?

१९ क्या उसका स्कूल यहाँ से दूर है ?
kyā uskā skūl yahā̃ se dūr hai?

२० आपके दूसरे बच्चे कहाँ हैं ?
āpke dūsre bacce kahā̃ haĩ?

२१ क्या वह कुत्ता भी आपका है ?
kyā vah kuttā bhī āpkā hai?

२२ बहुत प्यारा है ! उसका नाम क्या है ?
bahut pyārā hai! uskā nām kyā hai?

२३ क्या आपके पास गाड़ी है ?
kyā āpke pās gāṛī hai?

२४ क्या आपके पास कम्प्यूटर है ?
kyā āpke pās kampyūṭar hai?

धन्यवाद ! बहुत धन्यवाद ! *dhanyavād! bahut dhanyavād!*

Glossary

अस्पताल *aspatāl* m. hospital
आज *āj* today; आजकल *ājkal* nowadays, these days
कई *kaī* several
कपड़ा *kapṛā* m. cloth, garment
कम्प्यूटर *kampyūṭar* m. computer
कराची *karācī* f. Karachi
काठमांडु *kāṭhmāṇḍu* m. Kathmandu
कहाँ *kahā̃* where?
कितना *kitnā* how much/many?
किराया *kirāyā* m. rent; fare
कुछ *kuch* some; something; कुछ और *kuch aur* some more; कुछ नहीं *kuch nahī̃* nothing
कुल मिलाकर *kul milākar* in total, all together
के पास *ke pās* near; in the possession of
को *ko* to
खड़ा *khaṛā* standing
खिड़की *khiṛkī* f. window
गाड़ी *gāṛī* f. car; train, vehicle
घर *ghar* m. house, home
चूहा *cūhā* m. mouse, rat
छुट्टी *chuṭṭī* f. holiday; free time, time off
तक *tak* up to, until, as far as
तोता *totā* m. parrot
दफ़्तर *daftar* m. office
दिल्ली *dillī* f. Delhi
दुकान *dukān* f. shop
दूर *dūr* far, distant
धन्यवाद *dhanyavād* thank you

नया *nayā* (f. नई *naī*; m. pl. नए *nae*) new
नेपाल *nepāl* m. Nepal
पंखा *pankhā* m. fan
पड़ा *paṛā* lying
पति *pati* m. husband
पर *par* on (and 'at' in 'at home' etc.)
परिवार *parivār* m. family
पाकिस्तान *pākistān* m. Pakistan
पानी *pānī* m. water
पास *pās*, पास में *pās mẽ* nearby
पुराना *purānā* old (only for inanimates)
पेड़ *peṛ* m. tree
पैसा *paisā* m. money
फ़र्श *farś* m. floor
फूल *phūl* m. flower
बग़ीचा *bagīcā* m. garden
बाहर *bāhar* outside
बूढ़ा *būṛhā* elderly, old (only for animates)
बैठा *baiṭhā* seated, sitting
भारत *bhārat* m. India
भी *bhī* also; even
मालूम नहीं *mālūm nahī̃* [I] don't know
मुंबई *mumbaī* f. Mumbai, Bombay
में *mẽ* in
यहाँ *yahā̃* here
या *yā* or
लन्दन *landan* m. London
लेटा *leṭā* lying, lying down
रास्ता *rāstā* m. road
वहाँ *vahā̃* there
वाराणसी *vārāṇasī* f. Varanasi, Banaras
श्री *śrī* Mr; श्रीमती *śrīmatī* Mrs
सब *sab* all
समय *samay* m. time
सस्ता *sastā* cheap
साइकिल *sāikil* f. bicycle
से *se* from
सोमवार *somvār* m. Monday
स्कूल *skūl* m. school
हज़ार *hazār* m. thousand
हाथ *hāth* m. hand

04

चाय पीजिए
cāy pījie
have some tea

In this unit you will learn
- how to make requests and give commands
- how to describe everyday events and habits

Language points
- imperative verbs
- imperfective present tense

1 Giving orders and making requests

Giving orders and making requests is easy in Hindi: but what you say depends on whom you're speaking to, because the imperative (command-giving) verb has different forms for तू *tū*, तुम *tum* and आप *āp* people. We're going to concentrate on the तुम *tum* and आप *āp* forms here. First, we have to define a couple of terms.

Dictionaries list verbs in their 'infinitive' form: बैठना *baiṭhnā* 'to sit'. Take away the -ना *-nā* ending and you are left with बैठ *baiṭh*, which is the basic building-block of the verb; it's called the 'verb stem'. Remember these terms, because we'll be using them quite often.

For commands to someone you call तुम *tum*, just add *-o* to the stem: बैठो *baiṭho* 'sit', etc.

For commands to someone you call आप *āp*, add *-ie* to the stem: बैठिए *baiṭhie* 'speak', etc. Because this is inherently polite, it more or less implies the sense 'please'.

As in English, the pronoun is optional: you can say either तुम बैठो *tum baiṭho* 'you sit', or just बैठो *baiṭho 'sit'.*

Spend some time getting to know these very common commands:

INFINITIVE	तुम *tum*	आप *āp*
बैठना *baiṭhnā* to sit	बैठो *baiṭho* sit	बैठिए *baiṭhie* please sit
बोलना *bolnā* to speak	बोलो *bolo* speak	बोलिए *bolie* please speak
जाना *jānā* to go	जाओ *jāo* go	जाइए *jāie* please go
आना *ānā* to come	आओ *āo* come	आइए *āie* please come
कहना *kahnā* to say	कहो *kaho* say	कहिए *kahie* please say
खाना *khānā* to eat	खाओ *khāo* eat	खाइए *khāie* please eat

Four of the commonest verbs are irregular (wouldn't you just know it?):

करना	करो	कीजिए
karnā to do	*karo* do	*kījie* please do
देना	दो	दीजिए
denā to give	*do* give	*dījie* please give
लेना	लो	लीजिए
lenā to take	*lo* take	*lījie* please take
पीना	पियो	पीजिए
pīnā to drink	*piyo* drink	*pījie* please drink

Commands to someone you call तू *tū* just use the verb stem — बैठ *baiṭh*, बोल *bol*, जा *jā*, आ *ā*, कह *kah*, खा *khā*, कर *kar*, दे *de*, ले *le*, पी *pī*. As their shortness suggests, these तू *tū* commands are very blunt (or, if you prefer, sharp!) — 'Speak!' 'Sit!'; used out of context, they could easily give offence. Care needed here!

Commands are made negative by न *na* or मत *mat* 'don't'. The latter is blunter.

यहाँ न बैठिए ।
yahā̃ na baiṭhie. Please don't sit here.

कुछ मत बोलो !
kuch mat bolo! Don't say anything!

Practise what you've learnt

Here are some आप *āp* commands for you to change into तुम *tum* commands. You'll find the new verbs in the glossary.

१ मत जाइए ! आइए, बैठिए । *mat jāie! āie, baiṭhie.*

२ बताइए, आप कैसे हैं ? *batāie, āp kaise haĩ?*

३ समोसा खाइए, पानी पीजिए । *samosā khāie, pānī pījie.*

४ यह दूसरा समोसा भी लीजिए । *yah dūsrā samosā bhī lījie.*

५ मोती को समोसा न दीजिए । *Motī ko samosā na dījie.*

६ और खाइए ! *aur khāie!* ['Have some more!']

७ ख़ाली प्लेट मेज़ पर रखिए । *khālī pleṭ mez par rakhie.*

८ अरे ! सिग्रेट न पीजिए ! *are! sigreṭ na pījie!*

९ और चाय लीजिए । *aur cāy lījie.* ['Have some more tea.']

The infinitive as a command

The infinitive too can be used as a command: हिन्दी में बोलना ! *hindī mẽ bolnā!* 'Speak in Hindi!'. Such commands are often meant to be obeyed at some time in the future, or generally at all times, rather than immediately.

झूठ मत बोलना ।
jhūṭh mat bolnā. Don't tell lies.

घर में सिग्रेट न पीना ।
ghar mẽ sigreṭ na pīnā. Don't smoke in the house.

आगरे से ख़त भेजना ।
āgre se khat bhejnā. Send [me] a letter from Agra.

Some conversational gambits

When you're learning Hindi you may find that people speak quite fast — you'll need to ask them to repeat things or to speak slowly etc. This section gives you some useful phrases to help you out!

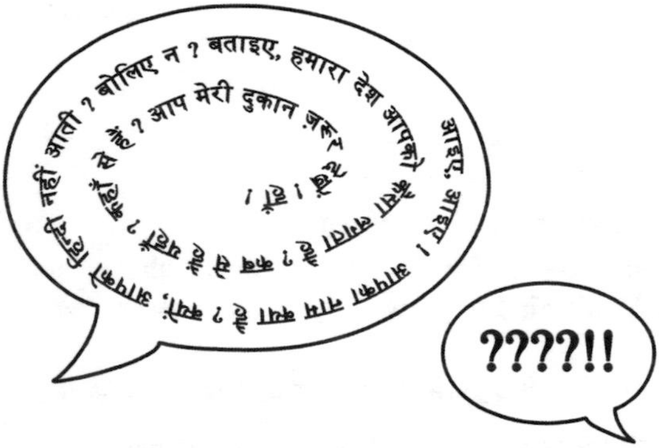

फिर से पूछिए ।
phir se pūchie. Please ask [me] again.

फिर से कहिए ।
phir se kahie. Please tell [me] again, say [it] again.

ज़ोर से बोलिए ।
zor se bolie. Please speak loudly.

धीरे धीरे बोलिए ।
dhīre dhīre bolie. Please speak slowly.

हिन्दी में बोलिए ।

hindī mẽ bolie. Please speak in Hindi.

हिन्दी में बोलिएगा ।

hindī mẽ boliegā. Be so kind as to speak in Hindi.

This sentence adds *-gā* to the command: बोलिए *bolie* becomes बोलिएगा *boliegā*. This gives a particularly polite command.

मैं नहीं समझा ।

maĩ nahī̃ samjhā. I don't/didn't understand. (male speaker)

मैं नहीं समझी ।

maĩ nahī̃ samjhī. I don't/didn't understand. (female speaker)

These sentences use the past tense, introduced in Unit 10.1.

2 Telling, saying, speaking, asking

When using verbs like 'to tell' and 'to ask', you may want to specify the person being spoken to. Most 'saying, asking' verbs make this link with से *se*, and here's a list of the common ones that do so:

कहना *kahnā* to say, tell

बोलना *bolnā* to speak

बात करना *bāt karnā* to converse

पूछना *pūchnā* to ask

माँगना *mā̃gnā* to ask for, demand

मिलना *milnā* to meet

राम से कहो ।

Rām se kaho. Tell Ram.

राम से बात करो, मनोज से नहीं ।

Rām se bāt karo, Manoj se nahī̃. Talk to Ram, not to Manoj.

मनोज से न पूछो, राम से पूछो ।

Manoj se na pūcho, Rām se pūcho. Don't ask Manoj, ask Ram.

राम से पैसा माँगो ।

Rām se paisā mā̃go. Ask Ram for money.

राम से मिलो ।

Rām se milo. Meet Ram.

But the verb बताना *batānā* 'to tell' uses को *ko* —

राम को बताओ । *Rām ko batāo.* Tell Ram.

Practise what you've learnt

Using both तुम *tum* and आप *āp* forms, make up some requests and commands from the following lists. Make some of your examples negative by using न *na* or मत *mat.* Here's an example:

यह किताब ध्यान से पढ़िए
yah kitāb dhyān se paṛhie. Read this book carefully.

OBJECTS

समोसा *samosā* m. samosa
किताब *kitāb* f. book
हिन्दी *hindī* f. Hindi
पानी *pānī* m. water
खाना *khānā* m. food
और चाय *aur cāy* f. more tea
घर *ghar* home
मेरी बात *merī bāt* f. what I say, my words
यह *yah* this
ये *ye* these

ADVERBS

अब *ab* now
अभी *abhī* right now
जल्दी से *jaldī se* quickly
ज़ोर से *zor se* loudly
धीरे धीरे *dhīre dhīre* slowly
यहाँ *yahā̃* here
यहीं *yahī̃* right here
ध्यान से *dhyān se* carefully
फिर से *phir* se again

VERBS

कहना *kahnā* to say
खाना *khānā* to eat
चलाना *calānā* to drive (vehicle)

जाना *jānā* to go
देखना *dekhnā* to see, look at
पढ़ना *paṛhnā* to read
पीना *pīnā* to drink
पूछना *pūchnā* to ask
बताना *batānā* to tell
बात करना *bāt karnā* to talk, converse
बैठना *baiṭhnā* to sit
बोलना *bolnā* to speak
रखना *rakhnā* to put, to keep
सीखना *sīkhnā* to learn
सुनना *sunnā* to listen

Did you know?

Like all the major languages of northern India, Hindi derives from Sanskrit, India's classical language. Sanskrit is a member of the Indo-European language family that includes Greek, Latin and the modern languages of Western Europe. So Hindi is a distant cousin of English, French, German etc.

3 Routine events

We now take a big step forward by learning how to to describe present-tense events and actions — starting with the verb बोलना *bolnā* 'to speak' and समझना *samajhnā* 'to understand':

मैं हिन्दी बोलता हूँ ।
maĩ hindī boltā hū̃. I speak Hindi. [male speaker]

मैं हिन्दी समझता हूँ ।
maĩ hindī samajhtā hū̃. I understand Hindi. [male speaker]

This is a present tense that describes actions that are done regularly or habitually. It is called the 'imperfective', and it consists of two parts. First, the word describing the action is बोलता *bolta*, which consists of the stem बोल *bol* plus the ending -ता *-tā*).

बोल + ता = बोलता *bol + tā = boltā*
समझ + ता = समझता *samajh + tā = samajhtā*

The second part is the verb 'to be' — here हूँ *hū̃* — already familiar to us from मैं हूँ *maĩ hū̃* 'I am'. Its purpose here is to show that the verb is in the present tense ('I speak', rather than 'I used to speak').

As you might expect, बोलता *boltā* changes to बोलते *bolte* in the masculine plural, and to बोलती *boltī* in the feminine; the part of the verb 'to be' also changes with the subject — वे बोलती हैं *ve boltī haĩ* etc.

मैं हिन्दी बोलती हूँ ।
maĩ hindī boltī hū̃. I speak Hindi. [female]

तुम हिन्दी बोलते हो ।
tum hindī bolte ho. You speak Hindi. [male]

तुम हिन्दी बोलती हो ।
tum hindī boltī ho. You speak Hindi. [female]

वह हिन्दी बोलता है ।
vah hindī boltā hai. He speaks Hindi.

वह हिन्दी बोलती है ।
vah hindī boltī hai. She speaks Hindi.

हम / आप / वे हिन्दी बोलते हैं ।
ham/āp/ve hindī bolte haĩ. We/you/they speak Hindi. [male]

हम / आप / वे हिन्दी बोलती हैं ।
ham/āp/ve hindī boltī haĩ. We/you/they speak Hindi. [female]

Where do you live? What do you do?

Let's look at examples of this tense using other verbs:

आप कहाँ रहती हैं ?
āp kahā̃ rahtī haĩ? Where do you live?

मैं दिल्ली में रहती हूँ ।
maĩ dillī maĩ rahtī hū̃. I live in Delhi.

आप क्या काम करती हैं ?
āp kyā kām kartī haĩ? What work do you do?

मैं संगीतकार हूँ; सितार बजाती हूँ ।
maĩ sangītkār hū̃; sitār bajātī hū̃. I'm a musician; I play the sitar.

क्या आपके पति भी सितार बजाते हैं ?
kyā āpke pati bhī sitār bajāte haĩ? Does your husband play the sitar too?

जी नहीं, वे अँग्रेज़ी पढ़ाते हैं ।
jī nahī̃, ve ãgrezī paṛhāte haĩ. No, he teaches English.

आपकी बेटी क्या करती है ?
āpkī beṭī kyā kartī hai? What does your daughter do?

वह अभी छोटी है । वह स्कूल जाती है ।
vah abhī choṭī hai. vah skūl jātī hai. She's still young; she goes to school.

What's this called?

The verb कहना *kahnā* 'to say' is useful in asking what something is called — a frequent event when learning a new language! Point to something and say:

इसको क्या कहते हैं ?
isko kyā kahte haĩ? What's this called?

You'll get answers like:

इसको किताब कहते हैं ।
isko kitāb kahte haĩ.
This is called a book.

इसको मेज़ कहते हैं ।
isko mez kahte haĩ.
This is called a table.

The question literally means 'What do [they] call this?', leaving the 'they' unexpressed because it's an impersonal kind of question. (The word इसको *isko* 'this' will be explained in Unit 5.)

Find the matching pairs of sentences

Each sentence numbered 1–7 matches up with one from the sequence A–G. Find the matching pairs. Answers below.

1 मनोज और राम सिनेमा जाते हैं ।
Manoj aur Rām sinemā jāte haĩ.

2 शर्मा जी अध्यापक हैं ।
Śarmā jī adhyāpak haĩ.

3 राम स्कूल जाता है ।
Rām skūl jātā hai.

4 कभी कभी मनोज और मीना चाय बनाते हैं ।
kabhī kabhī Manoj aur Mīnā cāy banāte haĩ.

5 गीता बहुत अच्छा खाना बनाती है ।
Gītā bahut acchā khānā banātī hai.

6 मीना बग़ीचे में बैठती है ।
Mīnā bagīce mẽ baiṭhtī hai.

7 तुम हमेशा हम से पैसा माँगते हो ।
tum hameśā ham se paisā mā̃gte ho.

A लेकिन वह बहुत ध्यान से नहीं पढ़ता ।
lekin vah bahut dhyān se nahī̃ paṛhtā.

B लेकिन हम को कुछ नहीं देते हो ।
lekin ham ko kuch nahī̃ dete ho.

C वे हिन्दी पढ़ाते हैं ।
ve hindī paṛhāte haĩ.

D वे हिन्दी फ़िल्में देखते हैं ।
ve hindī filmẽ dekhte haĩ.

E पर मनोज नहीं बनाता, सिर्फ़ खाता है !
par Manoj nahī̃ banātā, sirf khātā hai!

F वे काफ़ी भी बनाते हैं ।
ve kāfī bhī banāte haĩ.

G वह वहाँ बिल्ली से बात करती है ।
vah vahā̃ billī se bāt kartī hai.

Answers: 1D, 2C, 3A, 4F, 5E, 6G, 7B.

Language about language

Because the tense introduced in this chapter describes events that haven't been completed, it's called the 'imperfective' present. The form बोलता *boltā* is called the 'imperfective participle'.

The verb 'to be' (हूँ *hū̃*, है *hai* etc.) as used here is called the 'auxiliary', because it helps complete the meaning of the verb by specifying its timeframe. (English uses auxiliaries too: 'will' in the future tense 'I will go' is an example.)

Negative verbs

A final point here: the auxiliary can be dropped when the verb is in the negative — it's often optional, as shown by the brackets:

क्या तुम गोश्त खाते हो ?
kyā tum gośt khāte ho? Do you eat meat?

नहीं, मैं गोश्त नहीं खाता (हूँ) ।
nahī̃, maĩ gośt nahī̃ khātā (hū̃). No, I don't eat meat.

क्या वे शराब पीते हैं ?
kyā ve śarāb pīte haĩ? Do they drink alcohol?

नहीं, वे शराब नहीं पीते (हैं) ।
nahī̃, ve śarāb nahī̃ pīte (haĩ). No, they don't drink alcohol.

Javed and Raju get to know each other

जावेद राजू जी, आप एक कालेज में पढ़ाते हैं, न ?
राजू जी हाँ, मैं इतिहास पढ़ाता हूँ ।
जावेद और आपकी पत्नी ? क्या वे भी काम करती हैं ?
राजू हाँ ज़रूर, हम दोनों काम करते हैं ।
जावेद वे क्या काम करती हैं ?
राजू वे अस्पताल में काम करती हैं । डाक्टर हैं ।

Jāved *Rājū jī, āp ek kālej mẽ paṛhāte haĩ, na?*
Rājū *jī hā̃, maĩ itihās paṛhātā hū̃.*
Jāved *aur āpkī patnī? kyā ve bhī kām kartī haĩ?*
Rājū *hā̃ zarūr, ham donõ kām karte haĩ.*
Jāved *ve kyā kām kartī haĩ?*
Rājū *ve aspatāl mẽ kām kartī haĩ. ḍākṭar haĩ.*

Javed Raju ji, you teach in a college, don't you?
Raju Yes, I teach history.
Javed And your wife? Does she work too?
Raju Yes, of course, we both work.
Javed What work does she do?
Raju She works in a hospital. She's a doctor.

Notice that a pronoun can be dropped when its reference is clear from what's come before: डाक्टर हैं *ḍakṭar haĩ* [she] is a doctor. Look out for further examples of this in the second and third line below:

जावेद यह बताइए राजू जी, आप गोश्त खाते हैं ?
राजू जी हाँ, कभी कभी खाता हूँ । और आप ?
जावेद मैं भी खाता हूँ । लेकिन शराब नहीं पीता ।
राजू आप शराब नहीं पीते ? मैं पीता हूँ, लेकिन बहुत कम ।
जावेद क्या गीता जी भी पीती हैं ?
राजू जी नहीं, वे नहीं पीतीं ।

Jāved *yah batāie Rājū jī, āp gośt khāte haĩ?*
Rājū *jī hā̃, kabhī kabhī khātā hū̃. aur āp?*
Jāved *maĩ bhī khātā hū̃. lekin śarāb nahī̃ pītā.*
Rājū *āp śarāb nahī̃ pīte? maĩ pītā hū̃, lekin bahut kam.*
Jāved *kyā Gītā jī bhī pītī haĩ?*
Rājū *jī nahī̃, ve nahī̃ pītī̃.*

Javed Tell me this, Raju ji, do you eat meat?
Raju Yes, sometimes I do ['I eat']. And you?
Javed I do too. But I don't drink alcohol.
Raju You don't drink? I do, but very little.
Javed Does Geeta drink too?
Raju No, she doesn't drink.

वे नहीं पीतीं *ve nahī̃ pītī̃* — when पीती हैं *pītī haĩ* becomes negative it can drop the auxiliary हैं *haĩ*, leaving just वे नहीं पीतीं *ve nahī̃ pītī̃*. The nasal from the dropped हैं *haĩ* has been made homeless by this, so it jumps onto the participle पीती *pītī* ! This only happens with the feminine plural, and only in this tense.

Now look back at the list of verbs in section 4.1 and make up sentences from as many as you can, with yourself as subject (e.g.

मैं हिन्दी बोलता हूँ *maĩ hindī boltā hū̃*). Then do the same with other subjects such as 'she' or 'they'. Be sure to say your sentences *out loud*, with conviction; this will help you get used to this very important tense.

Exercise 4a Translate, using first तुम *tum* commands and then आप *āp* commands:

1 Don't drink alcohol in the house.
2 Listen carefully.
3 Send this letter to Manoj.
4 Go home.
5 Tell me his name.
6 Eat these two samosas.
7 Play the sitar.
8 Ask my neighbour.
9 Give this money to my wife.
10 Don't drive the car today.
11 Speak slowly.

Exercise 4b Fill the gap with the right postposition, then translate:

१२ राम......पूछिए । *Rām......pūchie.*
१३ बच्चों......मत बताना । *baccõ......mat batānā.*
१४ चाचा जी......हिन्दी बोलो । *cācā jī......hindī bolo.*
१५ मनोज......बात कीजिए । *Manoj......bāt kījie.*
१६ गीता......पैसा माँगना । *Gītā......paisā mā̃gnā.*

Exercise 4c Translate all the variations shown in these sentences:

17 My brother/sister lives in Delhi.
18 I/we understand Hindi.
19 The boy/girl drives the car very fast.
20 My husband/wife speaks Hindi.
21 Who [male/female] speaks English?

Glossary

अभी *abhī* right now; still
अरे *are* hey! oh!
आना *ānā* to come
और *aur* more
इतिहास *itihās* m. history
कभी *kabhī* ever; कभी कभी *kabhī kabhī* sometimes
कम *kam* little, less
करना *karnā* to do
कहना *kahnā* to say
काफ़ी *kāfī* f. coffee
काम *kām* work; काम करना *kām karnā* to work
कालेज *kālej* m. college
ख़त *khat* m. letter (correspondence)
खाना[1] *khānā* m. food
खाना[2] *khānā* to eat
गाना[1] *gānā* m. song, singing
गाना[2] *gānā* to sing
गोश्त *gośt* m. meat
चलाना *calānā* to drive
चाय *cāy* f. tea
जाना *jānā* to go
ज़ोर से *zor se* with force, loudly
झूठ *jhūṭh m.* a lie
तबला *tablā* m. tabla (drum)
देखना *dekhnā* to look, to see
देना *denā* to give
धीरे धीरे *dhīre dhīre* slowly
ध्यान *dhyān* m. attention; ध्यान से *dhyān se* attentively
न *na* don't; not
पढ़ना *paṛhnā* to read, to study
पढ़ाना *paṛhānā* to teach
पीना *pīnā* to drink; to smoke
पूछना *pūchnā* to ask
प्लेट *pleṭ* f. plate
फिर *phir;* फिर से *phir se* again
फ़िल्म *film* f. film
बजाना *bajānā* to play (music)
बताना *batānā* to tell
बनाना *banānā* to make
बात *bāt* f. thing said, idea; बात करना *bāt karnā* to talk, converse
बैठना *baiṭhnā* to sit
बोलना *bolnā* to speak
भेजना *bhejnā* to send
मत *mat* don't
माँगना *mā̃gnā* to ask for, demand
मिलना *milnā* to meet
यहीं *yahī̃* right here
रखना *rakhnā* to put, place, keep
लेना *lenā* to take
शराब *śarāb* f. alcoholic drink, liquor
संगीत *saṅgīt* m. music
संगीतकार *saṅgītkār* m. musician
समझना *samajhnā* to understand
समोसा *samosā* m. samosa
सिग्रेट *sigreṭ* m. cigarette
सिनेमा *sinemā* m. cinema
सीखना *sīkhnā* to learn
सुनना *sunnā* to hear, to listen
हमेशा *hameśā* always

05

आपको क्या चाहिए ?

āpko kyā

what do you want?

In this unit you will learn

- to talk about likes and needs
- expressions for 'to get' and 'to know'

Language points

- oblique-case expressions
- imperfective of 'to be'

1 Obliques again

Just when you thought you'd got things straight, we go oblique again! This time it's with the pronouns. To say 'to me', 'from her' etc., we need to use a postposition, which means that the pronoun must become oblique. (Look back to Unit 3 if you're uncertain about the use of obliques.)

The good news is that हम *ham*, आप *āp* and तुम *tum* don't change at all in the oblique:

हम को	*ham ko*	to us
आप को	*āp ko*	to you
तुम को	*tum ko*	to you

The bad news is that the others do change — like this:

DIRECT		OBLIQUE + को ko		
मैं	*maĩ*	मुझ को	*mujh ko*	to me
तू	*tū*	तुझ को	*tujh ko*	to you
यह	*yah*	इस को	*is ko*	to him, her, it, this
वह	*vah*	उस को	*us ko*	to him, her, it, that
ये	*ye*	इन को	*in ko*	to them, these
वे	*ve*	उन को	*un ko*	to them, those
कौन	*kaun*	किस को	*kis ko*	to whom (singular)
कौन	*kaun*	किन को	*kin ko*	to whom (plural)

उस को ये चीज़ें दीजिए ।
us ko ye cīzẽ dījie. Please give these things to him/her.

उन को मेरा पैसा दो ।
un ko merā paisā do. Give my money to them.

मुझ को बताइए ।
mujh ko batāie. Please tell me.

तुम मुझ को कुछ नहीं देती हो ।
tum mujh ko kuch nahī̃ detī ho. You give me nothing.

Pronoun + postposition are usually written together as one word (उसको *usko*), though on the page opposite they were written as two (उस को *us ko*), to show you more clearly what's going on.

Geeta talks to her children

Geeta is getting Manoj and Ram to help in the house. First, some new words:

कौनसा *kaunsā* which?
साफ़ करना *sāf karnā* to clean
जो *jo* which, who
अख़बार *a<u>kh</u>bār* m. newspaper

मनोज बेटा, ये किताबें तुम अलमारी में रखो । कौनसी किताबें ? हाँ ये, जो मेरी मेज़ पर पड़ी हैं । मीना कहाँ है ? उसको बुलाओ । अच्छा मीनू, तुम यहाँ हो ? तुम यह कमरा साफ़ करो । राम, तुम पिताजी से पूछो कि अख़बार कहाँ है । उनसे कहो कि चाचाजी बैठे हैं ।

Manoj beṭā, ye kitābẽ tum almārī mẽ rakho. kaunsī kitābẽ? hā̃ ye, jo merī mez par paṛī haĩ. Mīnā kahā̃ hai? usko bulāo. acchā Mīnū, tum yahā̃ ho? tum yah kamrā sāf karo. Rām, tum pitājī se pūcho ki a<u>kh</u>bār kahā̃ hai. unse kaho ki cācājī baiṭhe haĩ.

Manoj, son, put these books in the cupboard. Which books? Yes these, which are lying on my table. Where's Meena? Call her. Oh, Meena, you're here? You clean this room. Ram, ask father where the newspaper is. Tell him that Uncle is sitting [waiting].

Did you know?

At the level of everyday conversation, Hindi and Urdu are virtually identical — though Urdu is written in the Persian script (modified to represent Indian retroflex consonants). All the grammar taught in this book, and nearly all the vocabulary used here, is 'Urdu' as much as it is 'Hindi'.

2 What do you like, what do you want?

Liking things

In English, we can say 'I like London'; the subject of this is 'I'. But we could also say 'London appeals to me', which makes 'London' the subject. Hindi has many such constructions. They work like this:

मुझको दिल्ली पसंद है ।
mujhko dillī pasand hai. I like Delhi.

हमको दिल्ली पसंद है ।
hamko dillī pasand hai. We like Delhi.

These sentences translate literally as 'Delhi is pleasing to me/us'; the word दिल्ली *dillī* is the subject of the verb है *hai* 'is', with the 'me/us' expressed in the oblique. Here are some more examples.

क्या राम को यह जगह पसंद है ?
kyā Rām ko yah jagah pasand hai? Does Ram like this place?

हमको वह आदमी पसंद नहीं है ।
hamko vah ādmī pasand nahī̃ hai. We don't like that man.

मेरे दोस्त को ये तस्वीरें पसंद नहीं हैं ।
mere dost ko ye tasvīrẽ pasand nahī̃ haĩ. My friend doesn't like these pictures.

IMPORTANT!

GRAMMATICAL HEALTH WARNING

Constructions using को *ko* can damage your grammar

Take care: as you learn more Hindi you will see that this switch from English 'I' to Hindi मुझ को *mujh ko* 'to me' is very common. The focus of 'I' sentences is the person who experiences, but मुझको *mujhko* sentences have the *experience itself* as the focus. We can call these 'मुझको *mujhko*' constructions.

Needing and wanting things

Another मुझको *mujhko* construction expresses 'I need' or 'I want', using the word चाहिए *cāhie* — literally 'is wanted'. There's no है *hai* used with चाहिए *cāhie.*

तुमको क्या चाहिए ?
tumko kyā cāhie? What do you want/need?

मुझको काफ़ी चाहिए ।
mujhko kāfī cāhie. I want/need coffee.

हमको भी काफ़ी चाहिए ।
hamko bhī kāfī cāhie. We want/need coffee too.

किसको चाय चाहिए ?
kisko cāy cāhie? Who wants/needs tea?

राजू को चाय चाहिए ।
Rājū ko cāy cāhie. Raju wants/needs tea.

Remember that किस *kis* is the oblique of कौन *kaun* 'who?', as in किसको *kisko* 'to whom?'.

Knowing things

A similar construction means 'I know', using the word मालूम *mālūm* — literally 'known'. A difference from the चाहिए *cāhie* construction is that है *hai* is used here (though it can be dropped in the negative).

मुझको मालूम है ।
mujhko mālūm hai. I know.

मुझको नहीं मालूम / मुझको मालूम नहीं ।
mujhko nahī̃ mālūm / mujhko mālūm nahī̃. I don't know.

किसको मालूम है ?
kisko mālūm hai? Who knows?

उनको मालूम है कि मुझको चाबी चाहिए ।
unko mālūm hai ki mujhko cābī cāhie. They know that I want/need a key.

हमको मालूम है कि तुम यहाँ हो ।
hamko mālūm hai ki tum yahā̃ ho. We know that you're here.

मुझको मालूम है कि तुम कहाँ हो ।
mujhko mālūm hai ki tum kahā̃ ho. I know where you are.

उनको मालूम है कि मुझको क्या चाहिए ।
unko mālūm hai ki mujhko kyā cāhie. They know what I want.

Pratap goes shopping

Pratap, a visitor from England, is shopping in Delhi. He's forgotten the Hindi for some of the things he needs, but luckily for him, the shopkeeper knows some English and is able to help him out. We join them in the middle of their conversation.

प्रताप	मुझको टोर्च भी चाहिए ।
दुकानदार	"टोर्च" नहीं, "टार्च" ! यह लीजिए । और ?
प्रताप	मुझको ... क्या कहते हैं उस को ? ... एक छोटी किताब ... मैं कुछ लिखना चाहता हूँ ...
दुकानदार	अच्छा, आपको कापी चाहिए ।
प्रताप	हाँ, कापी ! एक क़लम भी दीजिए ।
दुकानदार	कैसा क़लम चाहिए ?
प्रताप	काला नहीं ... ब्लू ...
दुकानदार	यह लीजिए, नीला क़लम । और ?
प्रताप	मुझको वह चीज़ भी चाहिए ...
दुकानदार	कौनसी चीज़ ? यह डिब्बा ?
प्रताप	नहीं नहीं, वह लाल चीज़ जो डिब्बे पर पड़ी है ।
दुकानदार	अच्छा, चाक़ू ! आपको चाक़ू चाहिए । लीजिए ।

Pratāp	*mujhko ṭorc bhī cāhie.*
dukāndār	*'ṭorc' nahī̃, 'ṭārc'! yah lījie. aur?*
Pratāp	*mujhko... kyā kahte haĩ us ko?... ek choṭī kitāb... maĩ kuch likhnā cāhtā hū̃...*
dukāndār	*acchā, āp ko kāpī cāhie.*
Pratāp	*hā̃, kāpī! ek qalam bhī dījie.*
dukāndār	*kaisā qalam cāhie?*
Pratāp	*kālā nahī̃... blū...*
dukāndār	*yah lījie, nīlā qalam. aur?*
Pratāp	*mujhko vah cīz bhī cāhie...*
dukāndār	*kaunsī cīz? yah ḍibbā?*
Pratāp	*nahī̃ nahī̃, vah lāl cīz jo ḍibbe par paṛī hai.*
dukāndār	*acchā, cāqū! āp ko cāqū cāhie. lījie.*

Pratap	I need a torch too.
Shopkeeper	Not '*ṭorc*', '*ṭārc*'! What else?
Pratap	I... what's it called... a little book... I want to write something.
Shopkeeper	Oh, you need an exercise book.
Pratap	Yes, an exercise book! Give me a pen too.
Shopkeeper	What kind of pen do you want?
Pratap	Not black... 'blue'...
Shopkeeper	Here you are, a blue pen. What else?
Pratap	I need that thing too...
Shopkeeper	Which thing? This box?
Pratap	No no, that red thing that's lying on the box.
Shopkeeper	Oh, a penknife! You need a penknife. Here you are.

3 Availability — 'to get, to find'

Besides meaning 'to meet', मिलना *milna* also means 'to be available', and is the normal way to express the meaning 'to get, to find, to receive'. The subject here is not the person who gets or receives something, but the thing that's available or received.

इस दुकान में अच्छे जूते मिलते हैं ।
is dukān mẽ acche jūte milte haĩ. You can get good shoes in this shop. (Good shoes are available in this shop.)

दिल्ली में सब कुछ मिलता है ।
dillī mẽ sab kuch miltā hai.
You can get everything in Delhi.

हाथी भी मिलते हैं !
hāthī bhī milte haĩ!
You can even find elephants!

Notice that the sense of 'you' in 'you can get' is dropped, because the situation's an impersonal one, describing *general* availability.

सस्ते कपड़े कहाँ मिलते हैं ?
saste kapṛe kahā̃ milte haĩ? Where can you get cheap clothes?

अच्छी साड़ियाँ कहाँ मिलती हैं ?
acchī sāṛiyā̃ kahā̃ miltī haĩ? Where can you get good saris?

Practise what you've learnt

Match up items with locations, as in this example:

समोसे ढाबे में मिलते हैं ।

samose ḍhābe mẽ milte haĩ. Samosas are available in a café.

WHAT'S AVAILABLE

समोसे *samose* m. pl. samosas
सस्ता खाना *sastā khānā* m. cheap food
डाक टिकटें *ḍāk ṭikaṭẽ* f. pl. stamps
ताज़ा फल *tāzā phal* m. fresh fruit
अच्छा खाना *acchā khānā* m. good food
सिग्रेट *sigreṭ* m. pl. cigarette
सुंदर कपड़े *sundar kapṛe* m. pl. lovely clothes
अच्छे कमरे *acche kamre* m. pl. good rooms

WHERE TO FIND IT/THEM

डाक घर *ḍāk ghar* m. post office
मेरा कमरा *merā kamrā* m. my room
छोटी दुकान *choṭī dukān* f. small shop
यहाँ *yahā̃* here
ढाबा *ḍhābā* m. roadside cafe
भारत *bhārat* m. India
यह होटल *yah hoṭal* m. this hotel/restaurant
वह दुकान *vah dukān* f. that shop

The general and the particular

Look closely at these two sentences:

बनारसी साड़ियाँ बहुत अच्छी होती हैं ।

banārasī sāṛiyā̃ bahut acchī hotī haĩ. Banarasi saris are very good.

ये साड़ियाँ बहुत अच्छी हैं ।

ye sāṛiyā̃ bahut acchī haĩ. These saris are very good.

The participle होता *hotā* (from होना *honā* 'to be') is used in a statement that relates to a whole class of things: it's a *general* statement. Thus the first sentence above is about *all* saris from Banaras (a centre of fine sari making), while the second one is a *specific* one about a *particular* selection of saris.

4 Revision!

By now you should be reasonably confident in making basic sentences, using the verb 'to be' (है *hai* etc.) and the habitual tense of other verbs (मैं हिन्दी बोलता हूँ *maĩ hindī boltā hū̃*). The distinction between आप *āp* and तुम *tum* should be second nature, especially in making requests, and you should be able to make words agree with their subjects in number, gender and case. You can locate things using postpositions like में *mẽ* and पर *par*, and should always remember that nouns and pronouns that 'carry' postpositions must be in the oblique (कमरे में *kamre mẽ*, उस पर *us par*). You should be able to express 'need' using चाहिए *cāhie*, and मिलना *milnā* as 'to get' should be familiar too. You know that many constructions follow the format of 'X is pleasing to me' ('*mujhko* constructions') rather than 'I like X'. Look back now at anything you're unsure of.

Some hints on learning

- Listen to the recording until its dialogues and phrases are coming out of your ears! Try to catch the *music* of the language.
- Read *aloud*; and when reading longish sentences, break them up into smaller units, repeating each part until you're familiar with both its meaning and its construction.
- Read sentences *critically*: put yourself into the position of a teacher, explaining how each phrase is built up and why words are in the order and form in which you find them.
- If you have someone to practise with, act out the dialogues.
- You'll learn words and constructions much more thoroughly by using them yourself rather than just reading them passively. Write a Hindi diary, starting by noting 'habitual' things that you do every day, then gradually extending your range as new tenses are introduced; or write some dialogues of your own.

Raju visits a hotel

This section brings a revision dialogue in two parts. Visiting a small town for a teachers' conference, Raju tries his luck at the local hotel. There's no new grammar, but here are some useful new words:

कोई *koī* some, any, a
अच्छा-सा *acchā-sā* goodish, decent
दिखाना *dikhānā* to show
दिन *din* m. day
के लिए *ke lie* for

यानी *yānī* that is to say
शुक्रवार *śukravār* m. Friday
फ़ोन *fon* m. phone
शहर *śahar* m. town
ऐसा *aisā* such, of this kind
किराया *kirāyā* m. rent; fare
सौ *sau* m. hundred
रुपया *rupayā* m. rupee

शंकर	आइए साहब, आपको क्या चाहिए ?
राजू	मुझको कमरा चाहिए । कोई अच्छा-सा कमरा दिखाइए ।
शंकर	बहुत अच्छा । आपको कैसा कमरा चाहिए ?
राजू	मुझको बड़ा कमरा चाहिए ।
शंकर	बहुत अच्छा । कितने दिनों के लिए चाहिए ?
राजू	चार दिनों के लिए, यानी शुक्रवार तक ।
शंकर	बहुत अच्छा । आज से शुक्रवार तक हमारा एक बहुत अच्छा कमरा ख़ाली है ।
राजू	क्या कमरे में फ़ोन है ? फ़ोन चाहिए ।
शंकर	जी हाँ, है । बहुत अच्छा कमरा है । इस शहर में ऐसे कमरे मुश्किल से मिलते हैं ।
राजू	किराया कितना है ?
शंकर	सिर्फ़ सात सौ रुपये ।
राजू	कमरा दिखाइए ।
शंकर	बहुत अच्छा साहब । आइए, मैं कमरा दिखाता हूँ ।

Śankar	*āie sāhab, āpko kyā cāhie?*
Rājū	*mujhko kamrā cāhie. koī acchā-sā kamrā dikhāie.*
Śankar	*bahut acchā. āpko kaisā kamrā cāhie?*
Rājū	*mujhko baṛā kamrā cāhie.*
Śankar	*bahut acchā. kitne dinõ ke lie cāhie?*
Rājū	*cār dinõ ke lie, yānī śukravār tak.*
Śankar	*bahut acchā. āj se śukravār tak hamārā ek bahut acchā kamrā khālī hai.*
Rājū	*kyā kamre mẽ fon hai? fon cahie.*
Śankar	*jī hã, hai. bahut acchā kamrā hai. is śahar mẽ aise kamre muśkil se milte haĩ.*

Rājū *kirāyā kitnā hai?*
Śankar *sirf sāt sau rupaye.*
Rājū *kamrā dikhāie.*
Śankar *bahut acchā sāhab. āie, maĩ kamrā dikhātā hū̃.*

Shankar Please come [in], sir, what do you want?
Raju I need a room. Show me some decent room.
Shankar Very good. What kind of room do you want?
Raju I want a big room.
Shankar Very good. How many days do you want it for?
Raju For four days — that is, until Friday.
Shankar Very good. We have a very good room vacant from today until Friday.
Raju Is there a phone in the room? There needs to be a phone.
Shankar Yes, there is. It's a very good room. Such rooms are hard to find in this town.
Raju How much is the rent?
Shankar Only seven hundred rupees.
Raju Show me the room.
Shankar Very good, sir. Come, I'll show [you] the room.

(In this last line, Shankar's sentence मैं कमरा दिखाता हूँ *maĩ kamrā dikhātā hū̃* shows how the present tense can refer to something just about to be done.)

All seems to be going fine so far, and Shankar is obviously eager to please. But it's when he shows Raju the room that the problems start. Do you notice a change in tone in the way Raju addresses Shankar? (Look out for the pronouns.) But before we move on to the second part, some more new words:

ऊपर *ūpar* up, upstairs
दरवाज़ा *darvāzā* m. door
खोलना *kholnā* to open
करवाना *karvānā* to get done, caused to be done (by someone else)
काम करना *kām karnā* to work, to function
चालू करना *cālū karnā* to turn on, make work
घूमना *ghūmnā* to turn, revolve
लाइट *lāiṭ* f. electricity, electrical power
बिजली *bijlī* f. electricity
शुभ *śubh* good, auspicious (mainly used in the formula शुभ नाम *śubh nām* 'good name')
कोई दूसरा *koī dūsrā* another, some other one

The encounter continues:

(*दोनों आदमी ऊपर जाते हैं । शंकर एक दरवाज़ा खोलता है ।*)

शंकर	आइए जी ।
राजू	यह कमरा साफ़ नहीं है ।
शंकर	बहुत अच्छा साहब । मैं कमरा अभी साफ़ करवाता हूँ ।
राजू	क्या यह पुराना पंखा काम करता है ?
शंकर	जी हाँ, पंखा काम करता है । बहुत अच्छा पंखा है । आजकल ऐसे पंखे नहीं मिलते हैं ।
राजू	चालू करो ।
शंकर	बहुत अच्छा साहब ।

(*शंकर स्विच को "ऑन" करता है* [turns on the switch] *लेकिन पंखा घूमता नहीं ।)*

राजू	पंखा घूमता नहीं ।
शंकर	जी हाँ, क्योंकि लाइट नहीं है — बिजली नहीं है ।
राजू	तुम्हारा नाम क्या है ?
शंकर	जी, मुझको शंकर कहते हैं । और आपका शुभ नाम ?
राजू	मेरा नाम शर्मा है । श्री राजकुमार शर्मा ।
शंकर	बहुत अच्छा नाम है सर । मुझको आपका नाम बहुत पसंद है ।
राजू	शंकर, तुम "बहुत अच्छा" बहुत कहते हो । लेकिन यह कमरा बहुत अच्छा नहीं है । मुझ को पसंद नहीं है । कोई दूसरा कमरा दिखाओ ।
शंकर	बहुत अच्छा शर्मा जी । आइए ।

(*donõ ādmī ūpar jāte haĩ. Śankar ek darvāzā kholtā hai.*)

Śankar	*āie jī.*
Rājū	*yah kamrā sāf nahī̃ hai.*
Śankar	*bahut acchā sāhab. maĩ kamrā abhī sāf karvātā hū̃.*
Rājū	*kyā yah purānā pankhā kām kartā hai?*
Śankar	*jī hā̃, pankhā kām kartā hai. bahut acchā pankhā hai. ājkal aise pankhe nahī̃ milte haĩ.*

Rājū	*cālū karo.*
Śankar	*bahut acchā sāhab.*

(*Śankar svic ko 'ān' kartā hai* [turns on the switch] *lekin pankhā ghūmtā nahī̃.*)

Rājū	*pankhā ghūmtā nahī̃.*
Śankar	*jī hā̃, kyõki lāiṭ nahī̃ hai — bijlī nahī̃ hai.*
Rājū	*tumhārā nām kyā hai?*
Śankar	*jī, mujhko Śankar kahte haĩ. aur āpkā śubh nām?*
Rājū	*merā nām Śarmā hai. Śrī Rājkumār Śarmā.*
Śankar	*bahut acchā nām hai sar. mujhko āpkā nām bahut pasand hai.*
Rājū	*Śankar, tum 'bahut acchā' bahut kahte ho. lekin yah kamrā bahut acchā nahī̃ hai. mujhko pasand nahī̃ hai. koī dūsrā kamrā dikhāo.*
Śankar	*bahut acchā Śarmā jī. āie.*

(Both men go upstairs. Shankar opens a door.)

Shankar	Please come in, sir.
Raju	This room isn't clean.
Shankar	Very good, sir. I'll get the room cleaned at once.
Raju	Does this old fan work?
Shankar	Yes, the fan works. It's a very good fan. You can't get fans like this these days.
Raju	Turn it on.
	(Shankar switches on the fan, but the fan doesn't turn.)
Raju	The fan doesn't turn.
Shankar	Yes, sir [i.e. he agrees that it doesn't], because there's no 'light' — no electricity.
Raju	What's your name?
Shankar	Sir, I'm called Shankar. And what is your good name?
Raju	My name is Sharma. Mr Rajkumar Sharma.
Shankar	It's a very good name, sir. I like your name very much.
Raju	Shankar, you say 'very good' very much. But this room isn't very good. Show me some other room.
Shankar	Very good, Sharma ji. Please come.

In the first part of the dialogue, Raju had been calling Shankar आप *āp* (as is apparent from such commands as दिखाइए *dikhāie*; but in the second part, he calls Shankar तुम *tum* — the drop in honorific level indicating his declining patience!

Quantities

Expressing quantities or amounts in Hindi is simplicity itself:

एक किलो चावल
ek kilo cāval one kilo of rice

दो चम्मच चीनी
do cammac cīnī two spoons of sugar

तीन कप चाय
tīn kap cāy three cups of tea

There's no 'of' between the amount and the measured substance.

Exercise 5a You're doing some shopping in the market. Reply to the shopkeeper's questions:

१ आइए ! आज आपकी तबियत कैसी है ?
āie! āj āpkī tabiyat kaisī hai?

२ घर में सब लोग ठीक हैं ?
ghar mẽ sab log ṭhīk haĩ?

३ आपको क्या चाहिए ?
āpko kyā cāhie ?

४ कितना चाहिए ?
kitnā cāhie?

५ आपको और क्या चाहिए ?
āpko aur kyā cāhie?

६ साबुन वग़ैरह चाहिए?
sābun vagairah cāhie?

७ चाय, कॉफ़ी, बिस्कुट...?
cāy, kāfī, biskuṭ...?

८ आपका घर कहाँ है ?
āpkā ghar kahā̃ hai?

९ क्या ये चीज़ें भी आपकी हैं ?
kyā ye cīzẽ bhī āpkī haĩ?

१० आपकी गाड़ी बहुत दूर खड़ी है ?
āpkī gāṛī bahut dūr khaṛī hai?

Exercise 5b Translate into Hindi:

11 I need three samosas.

12 They don't like this house, they like the small house.

13 I don't like this room, show me another room.

14 Where do you live? We live in Old Delhi.

15 Your house isn't very far from my house. Come tomorrow.

16 I know that [कि *ki*] my teacher doesn't live here.

17 I know where your teacher lives.

18 Houses in Delhi are quite expensive.

19 Grandfather speaks very beautiful Hindi.

20 We don't want these black shoes.

Glossary

आधा *ādhā* m. half
ऊपर *ūpar* up, upstairs
ऐसा *aisā* such, of this kind
क़मीज़ *qamīz* f. shirt
किलो *kilo* m. kilo, kilogram
करवाना *karvānā* to get done (by someone else),to cause to be done
कल *kal* yesterday; tomorrow
काम करना *kām karnā* to work, to function
काला *kālā* black
कि *ki* that (conjunction)
किराया *kirāyā* m. rent; fare
कुरता *kurtā* m. kurta
के लिए *ke lie* for
कोई *koī* some, any, a; कोई दूसरा *koī dūsrā* some other, another
कौनसा *kaunsā* which?
क्यों *kyõ* why?
क्योंकि *kyõki* because
खोलना *kholnā* to open
घूमना *ghūmnā* to turn, revolve
चम्मच *cammac* m. spoon
चाक़ू *cāqū* m. knife, penknife
चाबी *cābī* f. key
चालू करना *cālū karnā* to turn on
चावल *cāval* m. rice
चाहना *cāhnā* to want, wish
चाहिए *cāhie* (is) wanted, needed
चीज़ *cīz* f. thing
चीनी *cīnī* f. sugar
जगह *jagah* f. place
ज़ुकाम *zukām* m. head cold
जूता *jūtā* m. shoe
जो *jo* who, which; the one who/which
टार्च *ṭārc* m. torch, flashlight

टिकिया *ṭikiyā* f. cake (of soap)
डाक *ḍāk* f. post; डाक घर *ḍāk ghar* m. post office; डाक की टिकट *ḍāk kī ṭikaṭ* f. stamp
डिब्बा *ḍibbā* m. box
ढाबा *ḍhābā* m. roadside cafe
तबियत *tabiyat* f. health, disposition
ताज़ा *tāzā* m. fresh
तो *to* so, then
दरवाज़ा *darvāzā* m. door
दिखाना *dikhānā* to show
दिन *din* m. day
नीला *nīlā* blue
पढ़ना *paṛhnā* to read; to study
पर *par* but
पसंद *pasand* pleasing (यह मुझको पसंद है *yah mujhko pasand hai* I like this)
फल *phal* m. fruit
फलवाला *phalvālā* m. fruitseller
फ़ोन *fon* m. phone; फ़ोन करना *fon karnā* to phone
बिजली *bijlī* f. electricity
बिस्कुट *biskuṭ* m. biscuit
बुख़ार *bu<u>kh</u>ār* m. fever
मालूम *mālūm* (is) known
मिलना *milnā* to meet, to be available
मुश्किल *muśkil* difficult; मुश्किल से *muśkil se* barely, hardly
यानी *yānī* in other words, that is to say
रहना *rahnā* to live, to stay
रुपया *rupayā* m. rupee
लाइट *lāiṭ* f. light, electric power
लाल *lāl* red
वग़ैरह *vagairah* etc., and so on
शहर *śahar* m. town, city
शायद *śāyad* maybe, perhaps
साबुन *sābun* m. soap
शुक्रवार *śukravār* m. Friday
शुभ *śubh* good, auspicious
सब कुछ *sab kuch* everything
-सा *-sā* '-ish' (suffix that qualifies an adjective, as in बड़ा-सा *baṛā-sā* 'biggish')
साड़ी *sāṛī* f. sari
साफ़ करना *sāf karnā* to clean
सौ *sau* m. hundred
हाथी *hāthī* m. elephant
होटल *hoṭal* m. hotel, restaurant, café

06

आप क्या काम करते हैं?

āp kyā

what work do you do?

In this unit you will learn

- how to talk about relationships
- how to ask about people's ages
- how to say 'I can' and 'let me'

Language points

- possessives
- verb stem and infinitive

1 Possession and 'to have'

You already know that मेरा *merā* means 'my, mine', आपका āpkā means 'your, yours', उसका *uskā* means 'his, her/hers, its', and हमारा *hamārā* means 'our, ours'. So much for showing possession with pronouns; now we need to see how possession works with names and nouns, as in 'Ram's friend' or 'my son's name'.

The phrase राम का कुत्ता *Rām kā kuttā* means 'Ram's dog'; मीना का कुत्ता *Mīnā kā kuttā* means 'Meena's dog'. So the little word का *kā* works like the apostrophe 's' in English. Some more examples:

मनोज का दोस्त	*Manoj kā dost*	Manoj's friend
गीता का पति	*Gītā kā pati*	Geeta's husband
राजू का बेटा	*Rājū kā beṭā*	Raju's son

This is a very important feature of the language and you should practise it thoroughly! Make some phrases of your own from the items provided:

डाक्टर *ḍākṭar*
पिता जी *pitā jī*
पड़ोसी *paṛosī*
विद्यार्थी *vidyārthī*
मेरी पत्नी *merī patnī*

कमरा *kamrā*
भाई *bhāī*
चाचा *cācā*
नाम *nām*
पैसा *paisā*

You'll have made phrases like मेरी पत्नी का पैसा *merī patnī kā paisā* 'my wife's money'. Great! Now look carefully at these phrases:

लड़के का दोस्त	*laṛke kā dost*	the boy's friend
लड़के की बहिन	*laṛke kī bahin*	the boy's sister
लड़के के माँ-बाप	*laṛke ke mā̃-bāp*	the boy's parents

Two things have happened: लड़का *laṛkā* has become oblique, and का *kā* has changed like an adjective to agree with the following word.

So का *kā* is a postposition that works like an adjective! This didn't show up earlier (in राम का कुत्ता *Rām kā kuttā* etc.) because non-inflecting masculine words had been cunningly chosen there. But from now on we'll have to keep an eye on this का *kā* business. For practice, make up phrases from the following lists, remembering to use oblique versions of words from the left-hand column, and to make का *kā* agree with the word chosen from the right-hand column:

वह् आदमी *vah ādmī*		चाबी *cabī*
मेरा दोस्त *merā dost*		बहिन *bhāī*
यह लड़का *yah laṛkā*	का / की / के	दो भाई *do bhāī*
फलवाला *phalvālā*	*kā kī ke*	माता *mātā*
उसका बेटा *uskā beṭā*		कपड़े *kapṛe*
ये लोग *ye log*		गाड़ी *gāṛī*

Do you have brothers and sisters?

Some time back we saw that Hindi doesn't have a verb 'to have', and that ownership of goods and chattels is indicated by के पास *ke pās*:

उसके पास दो चाबियाँ हैं ।
uske pās do cābiyā̃ haĩ. He/she has two keys.

But look at the following and notice the difference:

उसके दो भाई हैं ।
uske do bhāī haĩ. He/she has two brothers.

उसकी दो बहिनें हैं ।
uskī do bahinẽ haĩ. He/she has two sisters.

Yes, describing the 'ownership' or relatives involves का *kā* (or a pronoun like मेरा *merā*, or आपका *āpkā*) rather than के पास *ke pās.* The same applies for parts of the body:

रावण के दस सिर हैं ।
Rāvaṇ ke das sir haĩ.
Rāvaṇ has ten heads.

मेरा एक भाई है । उसके दो मकान हैं ।

merā ek bhāī hai. uske do makān haĩ. I have one brother. He has two houses.

मेरी कोई बहिन नहीं ।

merī koī bahin nahĩ. I don't have any sister(s).

2 The Sharma family

Now let's spend some quality time with the Sharmas. Here's their family tree, to remind you of the family relationships.

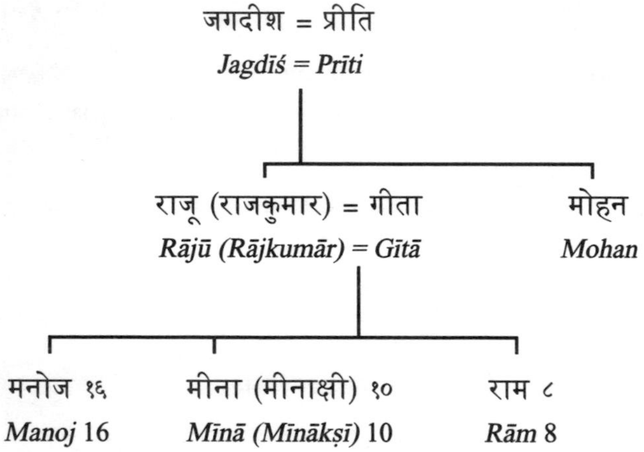

You have to sort out who's who. Test yourself by covering up the answers on the right of the page, then check your answers.

मनोज का छोटा भाई कौन है ?	राम
Manoj kā choṭā bhāī kaun hai?	*Rām*
राम और मनोज की बहिन कौन है ?	मीना
Rām aur Manoj kī bahin kaun hai?	*Mīnā*
बच्चों की माँ का नाम क्या है ?	गीता
baccõ kī mā̃ kā nām kyā hai?	*Gītā*
बच्चों के बाप का नाम क्या है ?	राजू
baccõ ke bāp kā nām kyā hai?	*Rājū*

राजू और गीता की बेटी का नाम क्या है ?	मीना
Rājū aur Gītā kī beṭī kā nām kyā hai?	*Mīnā*
बच्चों के दादा का नाम क्या है ?	जगदीश
baccõ ke dādā kā nām kyā hai?	*Jagdīś*
बच्चों की दादी का नाम क्या है ?	प्रीति
baccõ kī dādī kā nām kyā hai?	*Prīti*
मीना का पूरा नाम क्या है ?	मीनाक्षी शर्मा
Mīnā kā pūrā nām kyā hai?	*Mīnākṣī Śarmā*
बच्चों के चाचा का नाम क्या है ?	मोहन
baccõ ke cācā kā nām kyā hai?	*Mohan*
राजू के पिता का नाम क्या है ?	जगदीश
Rājū ke pitā kā nām kyā hai?	*Jagdīś*

And a final question:

राजू के बच्चों के कुत्ते का नाम क्या है ?	मोती
Rājū ke baccõ ke kutte kā nām kyā hai?	*Motī*

How old are you?

Another use of का–के–की *kā–ke–kī* is to give people's ages. It's used with the word साल *sāl* m. 'year':

मनोज सोलह साल का है ।

Manoj solah sāl kā hai. Manoj is sixteen ('is of 16 years').

मीना दस साल की है ।

Mīnā das sāl kī hai. Meena is ten.

गीता कितने साल की है ?

Gītā kitne sāl kī hai? How old is Geeta?

राम कितने साल का है ?

Rām kitne sāl kā hai? How old is Ram?

राम आठ साल का है ।

Rām āṭh sāl kā hai. Ram is eight.

The word for 'age' is उम्र *umra* (f.), often pronounced '*umar*'.

आपकी कितनी उम्र है ?

āpkī kitnī umra hai? How old are you?

Someone is here

The word कोई *koī* 'any' also means 'anyone' or 'someone' (and कोई नहीं *koī nahī̃* means 'no one'). कोई *koī* can also refer to inanimates, as in कोई दुकान *koī dukān* 'some shop (or other)'. Its oblique form is किसी *kisī*, as in किसी का बेटा *kisī kā beṭā* 'someone's son'.

Don't confuse किसी *kisī* with किस *kis*, which is the oblique of कौन *kaun* and of क्या *kyā*: किसको *kisko* 'to whom/what?', किसका भाई *kiskā bhāī* 'whose brother?'

कोई है ?

koī hai? Anyone there?

घर में कोई नहीं है ।

ghar mẽ koī nahī̃ hai. There's nobody in the house.

किसी के घर में कोई चूहा रहता था ।

kisī ke ghar mẽ koī cūhā rahtā thā. In somebody's house there lived a certain mouse.

Here's a very useful little phrase:

कोई बात नहीं ।

koī bāt nahī̃. Never mind, it doesn't matter, don't mention it.

Used with a number, कोई *koī* means 'about', just as 'some' does in English:

कोई बारह गाड़ियाँ

koī bārah gāṛiyā̃ some twelve cars

As we've already seen, कुछ *kuch* means 'some' (कुछ पैसा *kuch paisā* some money) or 'something'. It doesn't change in the oblique.

क्या मेज़ पर कुछ है ?

kyā mez par kuch hai? Is there something on the table?

हमको कुछ दूध चाहिए ।

hamko kuch dūdh cāhie. We need some milk.

घर में कुछ नहीं है ।

ghar mẽ kuch nahī̃ hai. There's nothing in the house.

कुछ लोगों के पास कुछ नहीं है ।

kuch logõ ke pās kuch nahī̃ hai. Some people have nothing.

Manoj introduces Pratap to his father

मनोज प्रताप, मेरे पिताजी से मिलो ।[1]
प्रताप नमस्ते जी ।
राजू हलो प्रताप, क्या हाल है ?[2]
प्रताप ठीक है, शुक्रिया ।
राजू तुम्हारी उम्र कितनी है प्रताप ?
प्रताप मैं इक्कीस साल का हूँ ।
राजू तुम्हारे कितने भाई और बहिनें हैं ?
प्रताप मेरा एक भाई है, मेरी कोई बहिन नहीं है ।

Manoj *Pratāp, mere pitājī se milo.*[1]
Pratāp *namaste jī.*
Rājū *halo Pratāp, kyā hāl hai?*[2]
Pratāp *ṭhīk hai, śukriyā.*
Rājū *tumhārī umr kitnī hai Pratāp?*
Pratāp *maĩ ikkīs sāl kā hū̃.*
Rājū *tumhāre kitne bhāī aur bahinẽ haĩ?*
Pratāp *merā ek bhāī hai, merī koī bahin nahī̃ hai.*

Manoj Pratap, meet my father.
Pratap Hello ji.
Raju Hello, Pratap, how's things?
Pratap Fine, thank you.
Raju How old are you, Pratap?
Pratap I'm twenty-one.
Raju How many brothers and sisters do you have?
Pratap I have one brother, I don't have any sister(s).

1 मिलना *milnā* 'to meet' uses the linking word से *se* 'with' — पिताजी से मिलो *pitājī se milo* 'Meet (with) Father'.

2 क्या हाल है? *kyā hāl hai?* 'How's things?' (lit. 'what's the condition?') This is a very common way of asking how someone is — a more colloquial equivalent to तुम कैसे हो? *tum kaise ho?* 'How are you?'

Some questions for you

आपके कितने भाई हैं ?
āpke kitne bhāī haĩ?

आपकी कितनी बहिनें हैं ?
āpkī kitnī bahinẽ haĩ?

क्या आपके घर में कोई कुत्ता है ?
kyā āpke ghar mẽ koī kuttā hai?

Practise what you've learnt

We're going to have another look at the present-tense verbs that we met earlier. Match the subject with the activity:

फलवाला *phalvālā* fruit-seller	किताबें लिखता है । *kitābẽ likhtā hai.*
अध्यापिका *adhyāpikā* teacher (female)	कालेज में पढ़ता है । *kālej mẽ paṛhtā hai.*
लेखक *lekhak* writer	फल बेचता है । *phal bectā hai.*
दर्ज़ी *darzī* tailor	मरीज़ों का इलाज करता है । *marīzõ kā ilāj kartā hai.*
विद्यार्थी *vidyārthī* student	कालेज में पढ़ाती है । *kālej mẽ paṛhātī hai.*
ट्रेन *ṭren* train	माल बेचता है । *māl bectā hai.*
डाक्टर *ḍākṭar* doctor	कपड़े बनाता है । *kapṛe banātā hai.*
दुकानदार *dukāndār* shopkeeper	तेज़ चलती है । *tez caltī hai.*

3 You can go

'You can go' is आप जा सकते हैं *āp jā sakte haĩ.* This features the special verb सकना *saknā* — special because it never stands alone, but always follows the stem of the main verb (here जा *jā* from जाना *jānā* 'to go').

आप मेरी हिन्दी समझ सकते हैं ?

āp merī hindī samajh sakte haĩ? You can understand my Hindi?

मैं यह काम नहीं कर सकता ।

maĩ yah kām nahī̃ kar saktā.   I can't do this work.

यह कैसे हो सकता है ?

yah kaise ho sakta hai? How can this be?

Now turn these 'I do' sentences into 'I can do' sentences, following this example:

मैं हिन्दी बोलता हूँ ।	मैं हिन्दी बोल सकता हूँ ।
maĩ hindī boltā hũ	*maĩ hindī bol saktā hũ.*
I speak Hindi.	I can speak Hindi.

१   हम सिनेमा जाते हैं ।   *ham sinemā jāte haĩ.*

२   चाचा जी घर पर रहते हैं ।   *cācā jī ghar par rahte haĩ.*

३   मैं अध्यापक से पूछता हूँ ।   *maĩ adhyāpak se pūchtā hũ.*

४   बच्चे बग़ीचे में खेलते हैं ।   *bacce bagīce mẽ khelte haĩ.*

५   मैं अख़बार पढ़ती हूँ ।   *maĩ akhbār paṛhtī hũ.*

६   हम बच्चों को सब कुछ बताते हैं ।   *ham baccõ ko sab kuch batāte haĩ.*

७   तुम शराब नहीं पीते हो ।   *tum śarāb nahī̃ pīte ho.*

८   वह कुछ नहीं कहता है ।   *vah kuch nahī̃ kahtā hai.*

▶ There's nobody in the house

Manoj is talking to Pratap. He thinks they're alone!

मनोज   एक सिग्रेट पियो प्रताप ! घर में कोई नहीं है ।

प्रताप   नहीं, मैं सिग्रेट नहीं पीता । तुम पी सकते हो ।

मनोज   हाँ मैं रोज़ दो-तीन सिग्रेट पीता हूँ ।

प्रताप   ये सिग्रेट तुम्हारे हैं ?

मनोज   नहीं, ये मेरे बाप के हैं ।

प्रताप   उनके सिग्रेट क्यों पीते हो ?

मनोज मेरे पास पैसे नहीं हैं । मैं सिग्रेट नहीं ख़रीद सकता ।
राजू (*दूसरे कमरे से*) मनोज ! ओ मनोज ! तुम कहाँ हो ?
प्रताप तुम्हारे पिताजी की आवाज़ !
(*राजू कमरे में आता है*)
राजू अरे, यह क्या ? वह तुम्हारे हाथ में क्या है मनोज ?
मनोज पिताजी ! देखिए, यह प्रताप का सिग्रेट है ...
राजू मनोज, बकवास मत कर । प्रताप, तुम जा सकते हो ।
मनोज लेकिन ... लेकिन ...

Manoj *ek sigreṭ piyo Pratāp! ghar mẽ koī nahī̃ hai.*
Pratāp *nahī̃, maĩ sigreṭ nahī̃ pītā. tum pī sakte ho.*
Manoj *hā̃ maĩ roz do-tīn sigreṭ pītā hū̃.*
Pratāp *ye sigreṭ tumhāre haĩ?*
Manoj *nahī̃, ye mere bāp ke haĩ.*
Pratāp *unke sigreṭ kyõ pīte ho?*
Manoj *mere pās paise nahī̃ haĩ. maĩ sigreṭ nahī̃ kharīd saktā.*
Rājū *(dūsre kamre se) Manoj! O Manoj! tum kahā̃ ho?*
Pratāp *tumhāre pitājī kī āvāz!*
(Rājū kamre mẽ ātā hai)
Rājū *are, yah kyā? vah tumhāre hāth mẽ kyā hai Manoj?*
Manoj *pitājī! dekhie, yah Pratāp kā sigreṭ hai.*
Rājū *Manoj, bakvās mat kar. Pratāp, tum jā sakte ho.*
Manoj *lekin... lekin...*

Manoj Have a cigarette, Pratap! there's no one in the house.
Pratap No, I don't smoke. You can.
Manoj Yes, I smoke two or three cigarettes every day.
Pratap These cigarettes are yours?
Manoj No, they're my dad's.
Pratap Why do you smoke his cigarettes?
Manoj I don't have any money. I can't buy cigarettes.
Raju [*from another room*] Manoj! Oh Manoj! Where are you?
Pratap Your father's voice!
[*Raju comes into the room.*]
Raju Hey, what's this? What's that in your hand, Manoj?

Manoj Father! Look, this is Pratap's cigarette...
Raju Manoj, don't talk nonsense. Pratap, you can go.
Manoj But... but...

True or false?

Are these statements right (सही *sahī* 'correct', सच *sac* 'true') or wrong (ग़लत *galat*)? Answers below.

		सही *sahī*	ग़लत *galat*
१	प्रताप सिग्रेट पीना चाहता है । *Pratāp sigreṭ pīnā cāhtā hai.*	☐	☐
२	मनोज सोचता है कि राजू घर पर नहीं है । *Manoj soctā hai ki Rājū ghar par nahī̃ hai.*	☐	☐
३	मनोज के पास उसके पिता के सिग्रेट हैं । *Manoj ke pās uske pitā ke sigreṭ haĩ.*	☐	☐
४	मनोज हमेशा सच बोलता है । *Manoj hameśā sac boltā hai.*	☐	☐
५	राजू के सिग्रेट प्रताप के हाथ में हैं । *Rājū ke sigreṭ Pratāp ke hāth mẽ haĩ.*	☐	☐
६	राजू कहता है कि दोनों लड़के जा सकते हैं । *Rājū kahtā hai ki donõ laṛke jā sakte haĩ.*	☐	☐

Answers: Only 2 and 3 are true.

4 Let me go!

'Let me go' is मुझको जाने दो *mujhko jāne do*. The sense 'to let, to allow' uses the verb देना *denā*, whose literal meaning is 'to give'; it's like saying 'give me [permission] to go'. As you can see in मुझको जाने दो *mujhko jāne do*, it's used with the infinitive of the main verb. The infinitive ends *-e* in this construction (here, the infinitive जाना *jānā* changes to oblique जाने *jāne*), and the person who is 'allowed to do' takes को *ko*.

हम बच्चों को खेलने देते हैं ।
ham baccõ ko khelne dete haĩ. We let the kids play.

पर हम उनको सड़क पर खेलने नहीं देते ।

par ham unko saṛak par khelne nahī̃ dete. But we don't let them play on the road.

हमको सोचने दीजिए ।

hamko socne dījie. Please let us think.

मनोज को बाहर जाने दो ।

Manoj ko bāhar jāne do. Let Manoj go out.

Manoj has a dream

Manoj is dreaming. In this dream, his mother is talking to his father, trying to persuade him to go easy on Manoj and to let him do all the things he wants to do:

मनोज का सपना ।

गीता —"मनोज के बाप, मनोज को सिग्रेट पीने दो, उसको शराब भी पीने दो । वह बहुत अच्छा लड़का है; वह स्कूल में बहुत ध्यान से पढ़ता है । उसको गाड़ी क्यों नहीं चलाने देते हो ? और हाँ, छुट्टियों में उसको अमरीका जाने दो !"

Manoj kā sapnā
Gītā — 'Manoj ke bāp, Manoj ko sigreṭ pīne do, usko śarāb bhī pīne do. vah bahut acchā laṛkā hai; vah skūl mẽ bahut dhyān se paṛhtā hai. usko gāṛī kyõ nahī̃ calāne dete ho? aur hā̃, chuṭṭiyõ mẽ usko amrīkā jāne do!'

Manoj's dream

Geeta — 'Manoj's father, let Manoj smoke, and let him drink too. He's a very good boy; he studies very hard at school. Why don't you let him drive the car? Oh and yes, let him go to America in the holidays!'

Turning 'I want to' into 'let me'

Here you have to convert the 'I want to' sentences into 'let me' sentences, following the example:

मैं घर जाना चाहता हूँ ।	मुझको घर जाने दीजिए / दो ।
maĩ ghar jānā cāhtā hū̃.	*mujhko ghar jāne dījie / do*
I want to go home.	Let me go home.

१ मैं अमरीका जाना चाहता हूँ ।
maĩ amrīkā jānā cāhtā hū̃.

२ मैं गाड़ी चलाना चाहती हूँ ।
maĩ gāṛī calānā cāhtā hū̃.

३ मैं खाना खाना चाहता हूँ ।
maĩ khānā khānā cāhtā hū̃.

४ मैं काम करना चाहती हूँ ।
maĩ kām karnā cāhtī hū̃.

५ मैं आपसे बात करना चाहता हूँ ।
maĩ āpse bāt karnā cāhtā hū̃.

Continue doing the same with sentences 6–10. These feature people other than 'I', as in this example:

वह सोना चाहता है ।	उसको सोने दीजिए / दो ।
vah sonā cāhtā hai.	*usko sone dījie / do*
He wants to sleep.	Let him sleep.

६ वह सिग्रेट पीना चाहता है ।
vah sigreṭ pīnā cāhtā hai.

७ हम अध्यापक से कुछ कहना चाहते हैं ।
ham adhyāpak se kuch kahnā cāhte haĩ.

८ वह हिन्दी सीखना चाहती है ।
vah hindī sīkhnā cāhtī hai.

९ बच्चे समोसे खाना चाहते हैं ।
bacce samose khānā cāhte haĩ.

१० हम यहाँ रहना चाहते हैं ।
ham yahā̃ rahnā cāhte haĩ.

Repeating formulas like this is a very efficient way of learning new expressions. Say them over and over again, out loud. And try making up new examples, choosing any new verbs from the glossary.

Exercise 6a Answer these questions about occupations:

१ फलवाला क्या बेचता है ? *phalvālā kyā bectā hai?*

२ अख़बारवाला क्या बेचता है ? *a<u>kh</u>bārvālā kyā bectā hai?*

३ दूधवाला क्या बेचता है ? *dūdhvālā kyā bectā hai?*

४ अध्यापक क्या करता है ? *adhyāpak kyā kartā hai?*

५ स्कूल में बच्चे क्या करते हैं ? *skūl mẽ bacce kyā karte haĩ?*

६ घर पर बच्चे क्या करते हैं ? *ghar par bacce kyā karte haĩ?*

७ ड्राइवर क्या करता है ? *ḍrāivar kyā kartā hai?*

८ दुकानदार क्या करता है ? *dukāndār kyā kartā hai?*

Exercise 6b Answer these questions addressed to you:

९ आप कहाँ रहते हैं / रहती हैं ?
āp kahā̃ rahte haĩ / rahtī haĩ?

१० आप क्या काम करते हैं / करती हैं ?
āp kyā kām karte haĩ / kartī haĩ?

११ क्या आप सितार बजाते हैं / बजाती हैं ?
kyā āp sitār bajāte haĩ / bajātī haĩ?

१२ आप कौनसा अख़बार पढ़ते / पढ़ती हैं ?
āp kaunsā a<u>kh</u>bār paṛhte haĩ / paṛhtī haĩ?

१३ आप कितनी भाषाएँ बोलते हैं / बोलती हैं ?
āp kitnī bhāṣāẽ bolte haĩ / boltī haĩ?

Exercise 6c Translate the following:

14 Jagdish reads Manoj's newspaper.
15 My two brothers work in a big office.
16 My sister drives my brother's car.
17 He only speaks Hindi, he doesn't speak English.
18 Our teachers teach three languages.
19 His children play cricket in the garden.

20 Our parents don't eat meat.
21 Where do you work? Where do you live?
22 What does your younger ('little') brother do?
23 How many languages does your mother speak?

Glossary

अख़बार *akhbār* m. newspaper
अख़बारवाला *akhbārvālā* m. newspaper seller
अध्यापिका *adhyāpikā* f. teacher
आवाज़ *āvāz* f. voice; sound
इलाज *ilāj* m. cure, treatment
उम्र *umra, umar* f. age
ओ *o* oh!
का–की–के *kā–kī–ke* (shows possession, like English 's)
कोई *koī* any, some; somebody; कोई नहीं *koī nahī̃* nobody
किसी *kisī* oblique of कोई *koī*
क्रिकेट *kriket* m. cricket
ख़रीदना *kharīdnā* to buy
खेलना *khelnā* to play (a game)
ट्रेन *tren* f. train
ड्राइवर *ḍrāivar* m. driver
दर्ज़ी *darzī* m. tailor
दादा *dādā* m. grandfather (father's father)
दादी *dādī f.* grandmother (father's mother)
दुकानदार *dukāndār* m. shopkeeper
दूध *dūdh* m. milk
दूधवाला *dūdhvālā* m. milkman
देना *denā* to give; to allow to, let (with oblique infinitive: हमको जाने दो *hamko jāne do* 'Let us go')
बकवास *bakvās* f. nonsense, idle chatter
बच्चा *baccā* m. child
बाप *bāp* m. dad
बेचना *becnā* to sell
भाषा *bhāṣā* f. language
मरीज़ *marīz* m. patient
माँ *mā̃* f. mother; माँ-बाप *mā̃-bāp* m. pl. parents
माल *māl* m. goods, stuff
रोज़ *roz* every day
लिखना *likhnā* to write
लेखक *lekhak* m. writer
सकना *saknā* to be able (with verb stem: तुम जा सकते हो *tum jā sakte ho* 'You can go')
सच *sac* m. truth; adj. true
सड़क *saṛak* f. road, street
सपना *sapnā* m. dream; सपना देखना *sapnā dekhnā* to dream, to have a dream
साल *sāl* m. year
सोचना *socnā* to think
सोना *sonā* to sleep
हाल *hāl* m. condition, state (in क्या हाल है ? *kyā hāl hai?* 'How's things? How are you?')

07

भूत-काल
bhūt-kāl
the past

In this unit you will learn
- how to talk about memories and routine events in the past
- how to add nuance to what you say

Language points
- past imperfective tenses
- direct objects
- use of emphatics

1 In the past

So far, we've been working in the present all the time. Moving into the past is very easy. It involves these words from the verb 'to be':

	was	were
MASCULINE	**था** *thā*	**थे** *the*
FEMININE	**थी** *thī*	**थीं** *thī̃*

We can use this tense in two ways. Firstly, here's 'was/were' alone:

कल सोमवार था ।
kal somvār thā. Yesterday was Monday.

कल आप घर पर थे ।
kal āp ghar par the. Yesterday you were at home.

कल वह बीमार थी ।
kal vah bīmār thī. Yesterday she was ill.

कल प्रीति जी कहाँ थीं ?
kal Prīti jī kahā̃ thī̃? Where was Priti ji yesterday?

Unlike है *hai* and हैं *haĩ*, था–थे–थी–थीं *thā–the–thī–thī̃* distinguish gender as well as number, so we know that the second sentence above refers to males (or one male, honorific plural), and the third to a female.

The second use is in the 'imperfective' tense used for routine actions, and introduced in section 4.3. Simply changing है *hai* to था *thā* converts present into past — 'I used to...'.

PRESENT	PAST
मैं यहाँ रहता हूँ ।	मैं यहाँ रहता था ।
maĩ yahā̃ rahtā hū̃.	*maĩ yahā̃ rahtā thā.*
I live here.	I used to live here.

दादा जी वाराणसी में रहते थे ।
dādā jī vārāṇasī mẽ rahte the. Grandpa used to live in Varanasi.

वे एक दुकान में काम करते थे ।
ve ek dukān mẽ kām karte the. He used to work in a shop.

उनकी बहिनें घर में खेलती थीं ।

unkī bahinẽ ghar mẽ kheltī thī̃. His sisters used to play at home.

उनके भाई स्कूल जाते थे ।

unke bhāī skūl jāte the. His brothers used to go to school.

वे बहुत ध्यान से पढ़ते थे ।

ve bahut dhyān se paṛhte the. They used to study very hard.

Memories of Varanasi

Jagdish Sharma is in nostalgic mood and has begun writing some memories of his childhood. There are notes to help you follow what he's written, and later there'll be some questions for you to answer.

किनारा *kinārā* m. bank, edge
ज़माना *zamānā* m. period, time
कमी *kamī* f. lack, shortage
आँगन *ā̃gan* m. courtyard
नदी *nadī* f. river
शाम *śām* f. evening
नाव *nāv* f. boat
सैर *sair* f. trip
याद *yād* f. memory
ठंडा *ṭhaṇḍā* cold; ठंडा-सा *ṭhaṇḍā-sā* coldish
हवा *havā* f. air, breeze
चलना *calnā* to move, blow, flow
छत *chat* f. roof

हम लोग[1] वाराणसी में रहते थे । हमारा घर गंगा[2] के किनारे पर था । बड़ा-सा[3] घर था । हम तीन भाई थे, और चार बहिनें । हम तीनों[4] लड़के स्कूल जाते थे; लड़कियाँ घर पर रहती थीं । उस ज़माने में बहुत कम लड़कियाँ स्कूल जाती थीं । पैसे की कमी थी, और लोग यह सोचते थे कि औरतों की जगह घर में है ।

पिताजी स्कूल में पढ़ाते थे — लेकिन हमारे स्कूल में नहीं । उनका स्कूल हमारे घर से काफ़ी दूर था । वे साइकिल से स्कूल जाते थे । सब लोग उनको "मास्टर जी"[5] कहते थे । हम उनको "पापा" कहते थे और माताजी को "माँ" कहते थे ।[6]

कितना सुंदर मकान था हमारा ! कोई बग़ीचा नहीं था, लेकिन हम बच्चे लोग आँगन में ख़ूब खेलते थे । कभी कभी हम सड़कों पर या नदी के किनारे पर भी खेलते थे । शाम को हम नदी पर नाव में सैर करते थे । ठंडी-सी हवा चलती थी । रात को हम छत पर सोते थे । मुझको उन दिनों की यादें बहुत आती हैं ।[7]

ham log[1] *vārāṇasī mẽ rahte the. hamārā ghar gaṅgā*[2] *ke kināre par thā. baṛā-sa*[3] *ghar thā. ham tīn bhāī the, aur cār bahinẽ. ham tīnõ*[4] *laṛke skūl jāte the; laṛkiyā̃ ghar par rahtī thī̃. us zamāne mẽ bahut kam laṛkiyā̃ skūl jātī thī̃. paise kī kamī thī, aur log yah socte the ki auratõ kī jagah ghar mẽ hai.*

pitājī skūl mẽ paṛhāte the — lekin hamāre skūl mẽ nahī̃. unkā skūl hamāre ghar se kāfī dūr thā. ve sāikil se skūl jāte the. sab log unko 'māsṭar jī'[5] *kahte the. ham unko 'pāpā' kahte the aur mātājī ko 'mā̃' kahte the.*[6]

kitnā sundar makān thā hamārā! koī bagīcā nahī̃ thā, lekin ham bacce log ā̃gan mẽ khūb khelte the. kabhī kabhī ham saṛakõ par yā nadī ke kināre par bhī khelte the. śām ko ham nadī par nāv mẽ sair karte the. ṭhaṇḍī sī havā caltī thī. rāt ko ham chat par sote the. mujhko un dinõ kī yādẽ bahut atī haĩ.[7]

We used to live in Varanasi. Our house was on the bank of the Ganges. It was a biggish house. We were three brothers and four sisters. All three of us boys used to go to school; the girls used to stay at home. In those days very few girls went to school. Money was short, and people used to think that women's place was in the home.

Father taught in a school — but not in our school. His school was quite far from our house. He used to go to school by bicycle. Everyone called him 'Master ji'. We called him 'Papa' and we called mother 'Ma'.

What a beautiful house we had! There wasn't a garden, but we children used to play to our hearts' content in the courtyard. Sometimes we would play on the roads or on the riverbank. In the evening we used to take a ride in a boat on the river. A cool breeze would blow. At night we used to sleep on the roof. I think of those days a lot.

Notes

1 हम लोग *ham log* 'we, we people, we guys' — the word लोग *log* can indicate a group; compare बच्चे लोग *bacce log* 'the children, the kids'.

2 गंगा *gangā* — like all rivers (and the word for 'river', नदी *nadī*), the Ganges is feminine.

3 The suffix -सा -सी -से *-sā -sī -se* is similar to '-ish' in English: बड़ा-सा घर *baṛā-sā ghar* 'a biggish house', अच्छी-सी गाड़ी *acchī-sī gāṛī* 'quite a good car', अच्छे-से लोग *acche-se log* 'quite decent people'.

4 तीनों *tīnõ* — 'all three'; this is a special 'inclusive' use of the oblique plural. Compare दोनों *donõ* 'both', चारों *cārõ* 'all four'.

5 'Master ji' is a title used for schoolmasters (and for tailors — masters of their craft).

6 When a plural subject comprises both males and females, as here, the verb is masculine.

7 Literally 'memories of those days come to me a lot' — a typical मुझको *mujhko* expression.

Some question about Jagdish's memories

१ जगदीश जी किस शहर में रहते थे ?
Jagdīś jī kis śahar mẽ rahte the?

२ उनके परिवार में कितने बच्चे थे ?
unke parivār mẽ kitne bacce the?

३ क्या उनकी बहिनें स्कूल जाना नहीं चाहती थीं ?
kyā unkī bahinẽ skūl jānā nahī̃ cahtī thī̃?

४ जगदीश के पिता का स्कूल कहाँ था ?
Jagdīś ke pitā kā skūl kahā̃ thā?

५ क्या जगदीश के पिता जी पैदल स्कूल जाते थे ?
kyā Jagdīś ke pitā jī paidal skūl jāte the?

Did you know?

Modern Hindi has developed within the last 200 years or so on the basis of a dialect called Khari Boli (खड़ी बोली), whose original home is the region around Delhi. Many other dialects are still spoken within the 'Hindi belt' of northern India; two of them, Braj Bhasha (ब्रजभाषा) and Awadhi (अवधी), were important literary languages between about AD 1500 and 1850, and poetry from this period is still well-loved today.

2 Getting specific

The word को *ko* means 'to':

यह ख़त गीता को दो ।

yah khat Gītā ko do. Give this letter to Geeta.

टिकट मुझको दीजिए ।

ṭikaṭ mujhko dījie. Please give the ticket to *me.*

हम बच्चों को पैसे देते हैं ।

ham baccõ ko paise dete haĩ. We give money to the children.

In these sentences the 'thing given' (e.g. the letter) is the direct object and the recipient (e.g. Geeta) is the indirect object. It's the recipient who is marked with को *ko*.

Usually, को *ko* isn't needed at all with a direct object. In the following, the direct objects are फल *phal* 'fruit' and पानी *pānī* 'water' respectively:

फल खाओ, पानी पियो ।

phal khāo, pānī piyo. Eat fruit, drink water.

The meaning here is a general one — 'any fruit, any water'. But if a more specific fruit/water is meant, को *ko* is added (and 'the' is used in English):

फल को खाओ, पानी को पियो ।

phal ko khāo, pānī ko piyo. Eat the fruit, drink the water.

The contrast between having को *ko* and not having it isn't always this clearcut: but in general को *ko* tends to be added to an object that's in some way specific or individualized. For this reason, references to people (and other specific creatures such as animals!) normally *do* take को *ko* —

बच्चों को घर में बुलाओ ।

baccõ ko ghar mẽ bulāo. Call the children inside the house.

मोती को मत मारो !

Motī ko mat māro! Don't hit Moti!

उन लोगों को देखो !

Un logõ ko dekho! Look at those people!

Marking an object with को *ko* doesn't necessarily change the meaning much at all. The two sentences यह ख़त पढ़ो *yah <u>kh</u>at paṛho* and इस ख़त को पढ़ो *is <u>kh</u>at ko paṛho* both translate as 'read this letter', even though the second version suggests a greater focus on the individual letter (and maybe a closer scrutiny of it also).

3 A shortcut

The word को *ko* is a multi-purpose tool; we saw some of its uses in Unit 5. Whereas English expressions about a person tend to have that person as the grammatical subject (as if individuals were the centre of the universe of experience), Hindi prefers to have the *experience itself* as the subject:

आपको बुख़ार है ।

āpko bu<u>kh</u>ār hai. You have a fever.

तुमको ज़ुकाम है ।

tumko zukām hai. You have a cold.

मुझको मालूम है कि आपको क्या चाहिए।

mujhko mālūm hai ki āpko kyā cāhie I know what you need.

किसको मालूम है कि यह क्या है ?

kisko mālūm hai ki yah kyā hai? Who knows what this is?

उनको नए जूते चाहिए ।

unko nae jūte cāhie. They need new shoes.

हमको यह तस्वीर पसंद है ।

hamko yah tasvīr pasand hai. We like this picture.

मुझको लिखने का शौक़ है ।

mujhko likhne kā śauq hai. I'm fond of writing

उनको संगीत का शौक़ है ।

unko sangīt kā śauq hai. They are keen on music.

This type of construction, with its heavy reliance on को *ko*, is so common that the 'pronoun + को *ko*' combination has an alternative short form: for example, मुझको *mujhko* has the alternative मुझे *mujhe*. Only आपको *āpko* refuses to be shortened. These pairs of forms are completely interchangeable: it makes no difference at all which member of a pair you choose to use.

मुझको *mujhko*	=	मुझे *mujhe*
हमको *hamko*	=	हमें *hamẽ*
तुझको *tujhko*	=	तुझे *tujhe*
तुमको *tumko*	=	तुम्हें *tumhẽ*
इसको *isko*	=	इसे *ise*
इनको *inko*	=	इन्हें *inhẽ*
उसको *usko*	=	उसे *use*
उनको *unko*	=	उन्हें *unhẽ*
किसको *kisko*	=	किसे *kise*
किनको *kinko*	=	किन्हें *kinhẽ*

Remember that किस *kis* (singular) and किन *kin* (plural) are the oblique forms of कौन *kaun* 'who' and क्या *kyā* 'what':

किसे मालूम है कि राम कहाँ है ?
kise mālūm hai ki Rām kahā̃ hai? Who knows where Ram is?

तुम पत्र किन्हें लिखते हो?
tum patr kinhẽ likhte ho? To whom [plural] do you write letters?

The main point to bear in mind here is that many expressions in Hindi are based on a मुझको *mujhko* pattern rather than a मैं *maĩ* pattern. You need to develop the skill of using both types of sentences, switching freely between one and the other. For example, these two sentences have the same meaning:

मुझे मालूम है कि वह कौन है ।
mujhe mālūm hai ki vah kaun hai. I know who he is.

मै जानता हूँ कि वह कौन है ।
maĩ jāntā hū̃ ki vah kaun hai. I know who he is.

When getting to grips with the मुझको *mujhko* pattern, think of the individual as being subjected to the effects of experiences from the world around him or her:

मुझे मालूम है कि तुम कौन हो ।
mujhe mālūm hai ki tum kaun ho.

मुझे हिन्दी आती है ।
mujhe hindī ātī hai.

मुझे तुम्हारा चेहरा बहुत पसंद है !
mujhe tumhārā cehrā bahut pasand hai!

मुझे गाने का बहुत शौक़ है ।
mujhe gāne kā bahut śauq hai.

▶ Raju recalls some childhood experiences

While reading this passage, look out for two things in particular: 'used to' verbs describing habitual things in the past, and the numerous constructions using को ko.

बचपन में मुझे पत्र लिखने का बहुत शौक़ था । कभी कभी मैं प्रधान मंत्री को भी पत्र लिखता था । मुझे मालूम नहीं था कि उन्हें मेरे पत्र पसंद थे कि नहीं, क्योंकि वे जवाब नहीं देते थे । एक समय मेरा छोटा भाई कई महीनों तक बीमार था । उसे बहुत बुख़ार था इसलिए हमें बहुत चिंता थी । मुझको मालूम था कि उसे दवा की ज़रूरत थी लेकिन हमारे पास पैसे कहाँ थे । लोग कहते थे कि प्रधान मंत्री बहुत दयालु आदमी हैं । इस लिए. . .

आदरणीय प्रधान मंत्री जी ।

सादर नमस्ते । मुझे मालूम है कि आपको बहुत काम है लेकिन हमें बहुत चिंता है क्योंकि मेरे छोटे भाई को बुख़ार है । हमारे पास पैसे नहीं हैं । क्या आप कुछ कर सकते हैं ? हमको आप पर पूरा भरोसा है ।

शुभकामनाओं सहित

आपका राजकुमार शर्मा

bacpan mẽ mujhe patr likhne kā bahut śauq thā. kabhī kabhī maĩ pradhān mantrī ko bhī patr likhtā thā. mujhe mālūm nahī̃ thā ki unhẽ mere patr pasand the ki nahī̃, kyõki ve javāb nahī̃ dete the. ek samay merā choṭā bhāī kaī mahīnõ tak bīmār thā. use bahut bukhār thā islie hamẽ bahut cintā thī. mujhko mālūm thā ki use davā kī zarūrat thī lekin hamāre pās paise kahā̃ the. log kahte the ki pradhān mantrī bahut dayālu admī haĩ. is lie…

ādaraṇīy pradhān mantrī jī,

sādar namaste. mujhe mālūm hai ki āpko bahut kām hai lekin hamẽ bahut cinta hai kyõki mere choṭe bhāī ko bukhār hai. hamāre pās paise nahī̃ haĩ. kyā āp kuch kar sakte haĩ? hamko āp par pūrā bharosā hai.

śubhkāmnāõ sahit

āpkā Rājkumār Śarmā.

In childhood I was very fond of writing letters. Sometimes I would even write letters to the Prime Minister. I didn't know if he liked my letters or not, because he used not to reply. One time my younger brother was ill for several months. He had a high fever and so we were very worried. I knew that he needed medicine but we didn't have the money [literally 'where was the money?']. People used to say that the Prime Minister was a very kindly man. So...

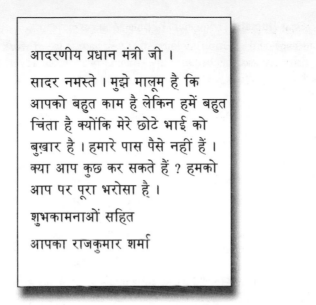

Dear [literally 'respected'] Prime Minister ji,

Respectful greetings. I know that you have a lot of work but we are very anxious because my younger brother has fever. We don't have any money. Can you do something? We have full trust in you.

With best wishes, yours, Rajkumar Sharma.

See Unit 8 for the Prime Minister's reply!

4 Adding emphasis

Three little words can add various kinds of subtle emphasis to a Hindi sentence. We have already met भी *bhī* 'also, even', and we saw how fussy it was about its position in the word order (see 3.2). We now add the other two — ही *hī* 'only' etc., and तो *to* 'as for...'. All three follow the words or phrases that they emphasize, but they are *not* postpositions (see 3.2), so they don't involve any change of case.

Firstly, भी *bhī* means 'also', 'even', etc.; it gives an *inclusive* emphasis. Look out for the effect of भी *bhī* in these sentences:

अजय पतला है; वह लंबा भी है ।

Ajay patlā hai; vah lambā bhī hai. Ajay is thin; he's *tall* too.

अजय पतला है; विजय भी पतला है ।

Ajay patlā hai; Vijay bhī patlā hai. Ajay is thin; *Vijay* is thin too.

In the first sentence, भी *bhī* emphasizes लंबा *lambā*; in the second it emphasizes the name विजय *Vijay*. Where does the emphasis fall in the following?

मुझे बुख़ार है । मुझे ज़ुकाम भी है ।

mujhe bukhār hai. mujhe zukām bhī hai. I've got a fever. I've got a cold too.

मुझे बुख़ार है । तुम्हें भी बुख़ार है ।

mujhe bukhār hai. tumhẽ bhī bukhār hai. I've got a fever. You've got a fever too.

Yes, it's on ज़ुकाम *zukām* and तुम्हें *tumhẽ* respectively. So you see again how sensitive the position of भी *bhī* is. The same applies with our second emphatic word, ही *hī*, which means 'only', or stresses what's just been said; it gives an *exclusive* emphasis.

मैं चाय ही पीता हूँ ।

maĩ cāy hī pītā hū̃. I only drink *tea* (nothing but tea).

मैं ही चाय पीता हूँ ।

maĩ hī cāy pītā hū̃. Only *I* drink tea (or *'I* drink tea').

यह चाय बहुत ही अच्छी है !

yah cāy bahut hī acchī hai! This tea is *really* good!

Thirdly: तो *to* emphasizes one thing by implying a contrast to another; this *contrastive* emphasis may be 'explicit', in the sense that it can name both parts of the contrast:

अजय तो ठीक है, पर विजय थोड़ा पागल है ।

Ajay to ṭhīk hai, par Vijay thoṛa pāgal hai. *Ajay's* OK, but Vijay's a bit crazy.

...or it may be merely implied, leaving a 'but...' hanging in the air:

अजय तो ठीक है ।

Ajay to ṭhīk hai. *Ajay's* OK (implication: 'but that other guy...').

क़मीज़ तो काफ़ी सुंदर है ।

qamīz to kāfī sundar hai. The *shirt's* quite nice (implication: 'but the jacket's a nightmare!').

क़मीज़ सुंदर तो है ।

qamīz sundar to hai. The shirt is quite *nice* (implication: 'but have you seen the price ticket?').

Finally, notice how ही *hī* merges with certain words:

यह *yah*	यही *yahī*	this very one, the same one
इस *is*	इसी *isī*	this very one, the same one
वह *vah*	वही *vahī*	that very one, the same one
उस *us*	उसी *usī*	that very one, the same one
यहाँ *yahā̃*	यहीं *yahī̃*	right here, in this very place
वहाँ *vahā̃*	वहीं *vahī̃*	right there, in that very place

For now, it's enough to get a general understanding of how these emphatic words operate: they'll gradually become more familiar.

Exercise 7a Convert the sentences in Exercise 6c into the past tense (e.g. 'Jagdish used to read Manoj's newspaper') and translate into Hindi.

Exercise 7b Translate the following, bringing out the emphasis given by तो *to* and ही *hī.*

११ जगदीश जी के परिवार में लड़के ही स्कूल जाते थे ।
Jagdīś jī ke parivār mẽ laṛke hī skūl jāte the.

१२ उनका स्कूल उनके घर से बहुत ही दूर था ।
unkā skūl unke ghar se bahut hī dūr thā.

१३ स्कूल में बच्चे ही नहीं, सब लोग उन्हें "मास्टर जी" कहते थे ।
skūl mẽ bacce hī nahī̃, sab log unhẽ 'māsṭar jī' kahte the.

१४ उनकी नौकरी में तनख़्वाह तो बहुत अच्छी नहीं थी ।
unkī naukarī mẽ tankhvāh to bahut acchī nahī̃ thī.

१५ जगदीश की माँ हिन्दी ही बोलती थीं ।
Jagdīś kī mā̃ hindī hī boltī thī̃.

१६ उस ज़माने में बच्चे तो बहुत ख़ुश थे ।
us zamāne mẽ bacce to bahut khuś the.

१७ बग़ीचा तो नहीं था, लेकिन खेलने की जगहें बहुत थीं ।
bagīcā to nahī̃ thā, lekin khelne kī jagahẽ bahut thī̃.

१८ बच्चे लोग तो छत पर ही सोते थे ।
bacce log to chat par hī sote the.

१९ बचपन में तो राजू को पत्र लिखने का शौक़ था ।
bacpan mẽ to Rājū ko patr likhne kā śauq thā.

२० प्रधान मंत्री दयालु तो थे लेकिन उन्हें बहुत काम होता था ।
pradhān mantrī dayālu to the lekin unhẽ bahut kām hotā thā.

Exercise 7c Write a passage of 100 words or so about childhood memories — yours or imagined ones. Try to use a wide range of vocabulary and constructions; remember that you can always supplement your vocabulary from the glossaries at the back of the book.

Glossary

अँग्रेज़ी *ãgrezī* f. English (language); and adj.
आँगन *ãgan* m. courtyard
आदरणीय *ādaraṇīy* 'respected' (used for 'Dear...' in formal corresponence)
इसलिए *islie* so, because of this
कमी *kamī* f. lack, shortage
किनारा *kinārā* m. bank, edge
ख़ूब *khūb* a lot, freely
गंगा *gangā* f. Ganges
गरमी *garmī* f. heat; गरमियाँ *garmiyā̃* f. pl. summer
चलना *calnā* to move, blow, flow
चिंता *cintā* f. anxiety
चेहरा *cehrā* m. face
छत *chat* f. roof
ज़माना *zamānā* m. period, time
ज़रूरत *zarūrat* f. need
जवाब *javāb* m. answer, reply; जवाब देना *javāb denā* to reply
जानना *jānnā* to know
ज़िंदगी *zindagī* f. life
टिकट *ṭikaṭ* f./m. ticket; stamp
ठंडा *ṭhaṇḍā* cold
तनख़्वाह *tankhvāh*, तनख़ाह *tankhāh* f. pay, wages
तो *to* as for...
थोड़ा *thoṛā* (a) little
दयालु *dayālu* compassionate, kind
दवा *davā* f. medicine
नदी *nadī* f. river
नाव *nāv* f. boat
नौकरी *naukarī* f. job, employment
पत्र *patr* m. letter (correspondence)
पसंद आना *pasand ānā* to appeal to, to be liked
पागल *pāgal* mad, crazy
पापा *pāpā* m. papa, father
पैदल *paidal* on foot
प्रधान मंत्री *pradhān mantrī* m prime minister
बचपन *bacpan* m. childhood
भरोसा *bharosā* m. trust, reliance
महीना *mahīnā* m. month
मारना *mārnā* to hit, beat, strike
मेहनत *mehnat* f. hard work
मेहनती *mehntī* hard-working
याद *yād* f. memory
शाम *śām* f. evening
शुभकामना *śubhkāmnā* f. good wish
शौक़ *śauq* m. liking, hobby, interest
सहित *sahit* with (formal)
सादर *sādar* respectful
सैर *sair* f. trip
हवा *havā* f. air, breeze
ही *hī* only (emphatic)

08

क्या हो रहा है ?

what's happening?

In this unit you will learn

- how to make comparisons
- a tense for describing what's going on right now
- how to say *how* things happen

Language points

- comparatives and superlatives
- continuous tenses
- adverbs and postpositions

1 Comparisons: bigger and smaller

English has two main ways of showing comparisons, firstly as in 'harder' (using an '-er' comparative word) and secondly as in 'more difficult' (using 'more' with the ordinary adjective). Hindi prefers this second type. The word for 'more' is ज़्यादा *zyādā* or और *aur*.

यह होटल ज़्यादा/और अच्छा है ।
yah hoṭal zyādā/aur acchā hai. This hotel is better.

वह होटल ज़्यादा/और महँगा है ।
vah hoṭal zyādā/aur mahãgā hai. That hotel is more expensive.

When comparing one thing directly to another, the word से *se* 'than' is used, and the ज़्यादा/और *zyādā/aur* can be dropped:

दिल्ली आगरे से बड़ी है ।
dillī āgre se baṛī hai. Delhi is bigger than Agra.

आगरा दिल्ली से छोटा है ।
āgrā dillī se choṭā hai. Agra is smaller than Delhi.

'Less' is कम *kam* —

यह कमरा कम अच्छा है ।
yah kamrā kam acchā hai. This room is less good.

यह किताब (उस किताब से) कम अच्छी है ।
yah kitāb (us kitāb se) kam acchī hai. This book is less good (than that book).

वह होटल (ताज से) कम महँगा है ।
vah hoṭal (tāj se) kam mahãgā hai. That hotel is less pricey (than the Taj).

Superlatives follow the model of सबसे अच्छा *sabse acchā* 'best of all':

यही दवा सबसे अच्छी है ।
yahī davā sabse acchī hai. *This* medicine is the best.

मनोज सबसे बड़ा लड़का है ।
Manoj sabse baṛā laṛkā hai. Manoj is the biggest/eldest boy.

राम सबसे छोटा लड़का है ।
Rām sabse choṭā laṛkā hai. Ram is the smallest/youngest boy.

Four children

Answer the questions about these four siblings, shown in age order (Shiv is the eldest).

शिव m.	रीता f.	ओम m.	शंकर m.
Śiv	*Rītā*	*Om*	*Śankar*

१ क्या ओम शंकर से बड़ा है ?
kyā Om Śankar se baṛā hai?

२ कितने बच्चे रीता से छोटे हैं ?
kitne bacce Rītā se choṭe haĩ?

३ सबसे बड़ा लड़का कौन है ?
sabse baṛā laṛkā kaun hai?

४ सबसे छोटा लड़का कौन है ?
sabse choṭā laṛkā kaun hai?

५ ओम कितने बच्चों से बड़ा है ?
Om kitne baccõ se baṛā hai?

६ क्या रीता शिव से बड़ी है ?
kyā Rītā Śiv se baṛī hai?

७ क्या रीता ओम से छोटी है ?
kyā Rītā Om se choṭī hai?

८ क्या रीता शंकर से छोटी है ?
kyā Rītā Śankar se choṭī hai?

९ आपको किस बच्चे की तस्वीर सबसे ज़्यादा पसंद है ?
āpko kis bacce kī tasvīr sabse zyādā pasand hai?

2 Continuous tense: '-ing' verbs

'I speak Hindi' (मैं हिन्दी बोलता हूँ *maĩ hindī boltā hũ̃*) describes something that's done regularly or habitually; but 'I am speaking Hindi' describes something that's going on *at the time*. In Hindi, the '-ing' sense is conveyed like this:

मैं हिन्दी बोल रहा हूँ ।
maĩ hindī bol rahā hũ̃. I am speaking Hindi.

मैं हिन्दी बोल रहा था ।
maĩ hindī bol rahā thā. I was speaking Hindi.

This is called the 'continuous' tense. It has three elcments:

A thc verb stem बोल *bol* (or सीख *sīkh*, कर *kar,* लिख *likh*, कह *kah* etc.) supplies the basic meaning;

B रहा रही रहे *rahā–rahī–rahe* delivers the '-ing' aspect;

C the auxiliary verb 'to be' (हूँ *hũ̃*, है *hai*, था *thā* etc.) confirms the timeframe, i.e. past or present.

Some more examples:

वह रो रही है ।
vah ro rahī hai. She is crying.

पिताजी क्यों मुस्करा रहे हैं ?
pitājī kyõ muskarā rahc haĩ? Why is Father smiling?

तुम क्यों हँस रहे हो ?
tum kyõ hãs rahe ho? Why are you laughing?

मेरी बहिन कोई हिन्दी फ़िल्म देख रही थी ।
merī bahin koī hindī film dekh rahī thī. My sister was watching some Hindi film.

क्या तुम तमिल सीख रहे हो ?
kyā tum tamil sīkh rahe ho? Are you learning Tamil?

दादी जी गुजराती में कुछ पत्र लिख रही थीं ।
dādī jī gujarātī mẽ kuch patr likh rahī thĩ. Grandma was writing some letters in Gujarati.

Geeta phones home

Listen in on a phone conversation between Geeta and Raju with *lots* of verbs in the continuous tense. Here's the new vocabulary:

सहेली *sahelī* f. girl's or woman's female friend
के साथ *ke sāth* with, in the company of
कब *kab* when?
देर *der* f. a while, period of time
रात का खाना *rāt kā khānā* m. dinner
मदद *madad* f . help
आज रात (को) *āj rāt (ko)* tonight
लाना *lānā* to bring
बाप रे बाप *bāp re bāp* Oh God!

गीता हलो राजू, मैं गीता बोल रही हूँ ।[1]
राजू कहाँ से बोल रही हो ?[2]
गीता ताज होटल से ।
राजू तुम क्या कर रही हो वहाँ ?
गीता मैं कुछ सहेलियों के साथ चाय पी रही हूँ !
राजू बच्चे क्या कर रहे हैं ?
गीता वे तो यहाँ बग़ीचे में खेल रहे हैं ।
राजू तो क्या मनोज भी खेल रहा है ?
गीता नहीं, वह किसी लड़की से बात कर रहा है ।
राजू ओहो ! तुम लोग घर कब आ रहे हो ?[3]
गीता हम अभी आ रहे हैं, थोड़ी देर में । क्यों ?
राजू क्योंकि मैं रात का खाना बना रहा हूँ । मुझे मदद चाहिए ।
गीता क्यों ? आज रात को कोई आ रहा है ?
राजू हाँ, जावेद आ रहा है । उसके कुछ दोस्त[4] भी आ रहे हैं ।
गीता बाप रे बाप ! अच्छा, मैं अभी आती हूँ ।
राजू वहाँ ताज में ज़्यादा पैसा मत ख़र्च करना !

Gītā *halo Rājū, maĩ Gītā bol rahī hū̃.*[1]
Rājū *kahā̃ se bol rahī ho?*[2]
Gītā *tāj hoṭal se.*
Rājū *tum kyā kar rahī ho vahā̃?*
Gītā *maĩ kuch saheliyõ ke sāth cāy pī rahī hū̃!*

Rājū	*bacce kyā kar rahe haĩ?*
Gītā	*ve to yahā̃ bagīce mẽ khel rahe haĩ.*
Rājū	*to kyā Manoj bhī khel rahā hai?*
Gītā	*nahī̃, vah kisī laṛkī se bāt kar rahā hai.*
Rājū	*oho! tum log ghar kab ā rahe ho?*[3]
Gītā	*ham abhī ā rahe haĩ, thoṛī der mẽ. kyõ?*
Rājū	*kyõki maĩ rāt kā khānā banā rahā hū̃. mujhe madad cāhie.*
Gītā	*kyõ? āj rāt ko koī ā rahā hai?*
Rājū	*hā̃, Jāved ā rahā hai. uske kuch dost*[4] *bhī ā rahe haĩ.*
Gītā	*bāp re bāp! acchā, maĩ abhī ātī hū̃.*
Rājū	*vahā̃ tāj mẽ zyādā paisā mat <u>kh</u>arc karnā!*

Geeta	Hello, Raju, this is Geeta speaking.
Raju	Where are you speaking from?
Geeta	From the Taj Hotel.
Raju	What are you doing there?
Geeta	I'm having tea with some friends!
Raju	What are the children doing?
Geeta	They're playing in the garden here.
Raju	So is Manoj playing too?
Geeta	No, he's talking to some girl.
Raju	Oho! When are you all coming home?
Geeta	We're just coming in a little while. Why?
Raju	Because I'm making dinner. I need help.
Geeta	Why? Is someone coming tonight?
Raju	Yes, Javed's coming. Some of his friends are coming too.
Geeta	Oh my God! OK, I'm just coming.
Raju	Don't spend too much money there in the Taj!

1 This is the usual way of announcing yourself on the phone — 'I Geeta am speaking', i.e. 'This is Geeta'.

2 Remember that a pronoun (here तुम *tum*) can be dropped when context makes it clear who is meant.

3 The continuous tense can be used for the immediate future (as in English) — 'when are you coming home?'.

4 उसके कुछ दोस्त *uske kuch dost* — 'some friends of his'. Note the word order.

Practise what you've learnt

Look at each picture below, then choose a verb from the list to describe who's doing what. Here's the first answer to show you the format: 1. जावेद पत्र लिख रहा है *Jāved patr likh rahā hai* 'Javed is writing a letter.' Keep an eye on gender and number!

खाना तैयार करना *khānā taiyār karnā* to prepare food

शराब पीना *śarāb pīnā* to drink (alcohol)

ताश खेलना *tāś khelnā* to play cards

पत्र लिखना *patr likhnā* to write a letter

दौड़ना *dauṛnā* to run

बरतन माँजना *bartan mā̃jnā* to wash dishes

सोना *sonā* to sleep

फ़ोन पर बात करना *fon par bāt karnā* to talk on the phone

1

जावेद
Jāved

2

दो लड़कियाँ
do laṛkiyā̃

3

कोई आदमी
koī ādmī

4

कुत्ता
kuttā

5

सीता
Sītā

6

गीता और राजू
Gītā aur Rājū

7

राम
Rām

8

उषा
Uṣā

The verbs we've met so far

Now that we're more than halfway through the book, here's a summary of all the verb forms we've seen so far, listed by unit and section. Our example verb here is बोलना *bolnā* 'to speak'.

	GRAMMAR	EXAMPLES
1.2	होना *honā* 'to be'	है *hai* , हैं *haĩ*
4.1	infinitive	बोलना *bolnā*
4.1	stem	बोल *bol*
4.1	command	बोल, बोलो, बोलिए *bol, bolo, bolie*
4.3	imperfective participle	बोलता *boltā*
4.3	imperfective present	वह बोलता है *vah boltā hai*
7.1	imperfective past	वह बोलता था *vah boltā thā*
8.2	continuous present	वह बोल रहा है *vah bol rahā hai*
8.2	continuous past	वह बोल रहा था *vah bol rahā thā*

Now is the time to look back if you need to revise any of these!

3 Raju is reading 'his own' newspaper

Consider this statement: 'Javed is sitting in Raju's house; Raju is reading his newspaper.' Hmm: 'his' is ambiguous here — is Raju reading his *own* newspaper or Javed's? Hindi has no such ambiguity, because the pronoun अपना *apnā* replaces उसका *uskā* whenever the sense 'his/her *own*' is meant:

राजू अपना अख़बार पढ़ रहा है ।

Rājū apnā akhbār paṛh rahā hai. Raju is reading his (own) paper.

राजू उसका अख़बार पढ़ रहा है ।

Rājū uskā akhbār paṛh rahā hai. Raju is reading his (someone else's) paper.

अपना *apnā* is not restricted to 'his/her', it can mean 'my', 'our', 'your' and so on.

मैं अपना काम कर रहा हूँ ।

maĩ apnā kām kar rahā hũ. I am doing my work.

हम अपना काम कर रहे हैं ।

ham apnā kām kar rahe haĩ. We are doing our work.

तुम अपना काम करो !

tum apnā kām karo. Do your work!

अपना पैसा लीजिए ।

apnā paisā lījie. Please take your money.

When to use अपना *apnā* is a vexing question for all learners of Hindi. As a rule of thumb, it has to be used whenever the 'possessor' is the subject of the main verb. The subjects in the next two sentences (using धोना *dhonā* 'to wash') are मैं *maĩ* 'I' and वे *ve* 'they' respectively:

मैं अपने कपड़े धो रहा हूँ ।

maĩ apne kapṛe dho rahā hū̃. I'm washing my clothes.

वे अपने कपड़े नहीं धोते ।

ve apne kapṛe nahī̃ dhote. They don't wash their (own) clothes.

Revising with Gopal and Jagdish

The difference between the continuous and imperfective tenses should be reasonably clear by now. Here's a dialogue to remind you of the imperfective. A young lad called Gopal comes timidly to Jagdish Sharma's shop looking for work.

नौकरी *naukarī* f. job
मेहनती *mehnatī* hard-working
ज़रूरत *zarūrat* f. need; मुझको X की ज़रूरत है *mujhko X kī zarūrat hai* 'I need X'
मेहनत *mehnat* f. hard work
पास में *pās mẽ* nearby
जानना *jānnā* to know
थोड़ा *thoṛā* a little
अँग्रेज़ी *ãgrezī* f. English (language)
तनख़ाह *tankhāh* f. pay, wages

गोपाल नमस्ते शर्माजी ।

जगदीश नमस्ते । क्या चाहिए बेटा ?

गोपाल जी, मुझको आपकी दुकान में नौकरी चाहिए ।

जगदीश हाँ, मुझको एक मेहनती लड़के की ज़रूरत तो है ।

गोपाल मैं बहुत मेहनत करता हूँ शर्मा जी !

जगदीश तुम्हारी उम्र कितनी है ?

गोपाल जी, मैं सोलह साल का हूँ ।

जगदीश कहाँ रहते हो ?

गोपाल पास में । हमारा घर यहाँ से दूर नहीं है ।

जगदीश क्या तुम पढ़ना-लिखना जानते हो ?

गोपाल जी हाँ, और मुझे थोड़ी अँग्रेज़ी भी आती है ।

जगदीश ठीक है, कल से आना ।

गोपाल बहुत शुक्रिया । शर्माजी, एक बात बताइए ।

जगदीश बोलो, क्या बात है ?

गोपाल तनख़्वाह् ... ?

जगदीश यह तुम अभी मत पूछो !

Gopāl *namaste Śarmājī.*
Jagdīś *namaste. kyā cāhie beṭā?*
Gopāl *jī, mujhko āpkī dukān mẽ naukarī cāhie.*
Jagdīś *hā̃, mujhko ek mahnatī laṛke kī zarūrat to hai.*
Gopāl *maĩ bahut mehnat kartā hū̃ Śarmā jī!*
Jagdīś *tumhārī umr kitnī hai?*
Gopāl *jī, maĩ solah sāl kā hū̃.*
Jagdīś *kahā̃ rahte ho?*
Gopāl *pās mẽ. hamārā ghar yahā̃ se dūr nahī̃ hai.*
Jagdīś *kyā tum paṛhnā-likhnā jānte ho?*
Gopāl *jī hā̃, aur mujhe thoṛī ā̃grezī bhī ātī hai.*
Jagdīś *ṭhīk hai, kal se ānā.*
Gopāl *bahut śukriyā. Śarmājī, ek bāt batāie.*
Jagdīś *bolo, kyā bāt hai?*
Gopāl *tan<u>kh</u>vāh...?*
Jagdīś *yah tum abhī mat pūcho!*

Gopal Hello Sharma ji.
Jagdish Hello. What do you want, son?
Gopal Sir, I need a job in your shop.
Jagdish Yes, I *do* need a hard-working lad.
Gopal I work very hard, Sharma ji!
Jagdish How old are you?
Gopal Sir, I'm sixteen.
Jagdish Where d'you live?

Gopal Nearby. Our house isn't far from here.
Jagdish Do you know how to read and write?
Gopal Yes, and I know a little English too.*
Jagdish All right, come from tomorrow.
Gopal Thank you very much. Sharma ji, please tell me one thing.
Jagdish Speak, what is it?
Gopal The wages...?
Jagdish Don't ask this just now!

*Literally 'a little English comes to me'. This is a common usage with languages: मुझे उर्दू आती है *mujhe urdū ātī hai* 'I know Urdu'; मेरे भाई को चार भाषाएँ आती हैं *mere bhāī ko cār bhāṣāẽ ātī haĩ* 'my brother knows four languages'. Used with an infinitive verb, this construction means 'knowing how to do something', 'having a skill': मुझे खाना बनाना आता है *mujhe khānā banānā ātā hai,* 'I know how to cook.'

True or false?

Are these statements right (सही *sahī*) or wrong (ग़लत *galat*)? Answers below.

		सही *sahī*	ग़लत *galat*
१	गोपाल दुकान में कुछ ख़रीदना चाहता है । *Gopāl dukān mẽ kuch kharīdnā cāhtā hai.*	☐	☐
२	गोपाल दुकान में काम करना चाहता है । *Gopāl dukān mẽ kām karnā cāhtā hai.*	☐	☐
३	गोपाल को मेहनत करना पसंद नहीं है । *Gopāl ko mehnat karnā pasand nahī̃ hai.*	☐	☐
४	जगदीश को एक लड़के की ज़रूरत है । *Jagdīś ko ek laṛke kī zarūrat hai.*	☐	☐
५	जगदीश गोपाल के बाप से मिलना चाहता है । *Jagdīś Gopāl ke bāp se milnā cāhtā hai.*	☐	☐
६	गोपाल तनख़ाह के बारे में जानना चाहता है । *Gopāl tankhāh ke bāre mẽ jānnā cāhtā hai.*	☐	☐

Answers: 2, 4, 5 and 6 are true.

The PM writes back

Ah, here's the Prime Minister's reply to the letter that Raju wrote when he was little. (For reasons of confidentiality we can't show the signature.)

प्रिय राजू,

तुम जानते हो कि प्रधान मंत्री का जीवन कैसा होता है ? वह अपने लिए तो कुछ नहीं कर सकता है लेकिन दूसरों के लिए कुछ कर सकता है ! तुम अपने भाई की चिंता न करो । मैं अपने ही डाक्टर से तुम्हारे भाई के लिए कुछ दवा भिजवा रहा हूँ । अपने अगले पत्र में उसका हाल लिखना । और अपनी तबियत का भी ध्यान रखना ।

तुम्हारा (...)

priy Rajū,

tum jānte ho ki pradhān mantrī kā jīvan kaisā hotā hai? vah apne lie to kuch nahī̃ kar saktā hai lekin dūsrõ ke lie kuch kar saktā hai! tum apne bhāī kī cintā na karo. maĩ apne hī ḍākṭar se tumhāre bhāī ke lie kuch davā bhijvā rahā hū̃. apne agle patr mẽ uskā hāl likhnā. aur apnī tabiyat kā bhī dhyān rakhnā.

tumhārā (...)

Dear Raju,

Do you know what a Prime Minister's life is like? He can't do anything for himself but he can do something for others! Don't worry about your brother. I'm getting some medicine sent by my very own doctor. In your next letter write how he is. And take care of your own health too!

Yours (...)

4 These days, in and out, up and down

Here are some sentences with adverbs (words or phrases like 'quickly' or 'these days', that describe the *manner* or *context* in which something happens). Look carefully at the words in bold:

इन दिनों तुम क्या कर रहे हो ?
in dinõ *tum kyā kar rahe ho?* What are you doing these days?

उस दिन हम काम कर रहे थे ।
us din *ham kām kar rahe the.* That day, we were working.

पिछले हफ़्ते मेरी तबियत ख़राब थी ।
pichle hafte *merī tabiyat <u>kh</u>arāb thī.* I was unwell last week.

वह **अगले महीने** घर जा रहा है ।
vah ***agle mahīne*** *ghar jā rahā hai.* He's going home next month.

Notice anything? The words in bold print are in the oblique case — as if followed by invisible postpositions. This is usual with adverbs of time; here you have to forget the hard-learned rule that the oblique case is only used when a postposition requires it! Think of the time-words as being haunted by the ghosts of dropped postpositions.

These next sentences involve destinations — 'Agra', 'your house':

हम आगरे जा रहे हैं ।
ham āgre jā rahe haĩ. We're going to Agra.

वे आपके घर आ रहे हैं ।
ve āpke ghar ā rahe haĩ. They're coming to your house.

Here the obliques (आगरे *āgre*, oblique of आगरा *āgrā*; and आपके घर *āpke ghar*, oblique of आपका घर *āpkā ghar*) are again haunted by the ghosts of postpositions. To put it another way, the oblique case alone is the equivalent for the English 'to' in these sentences. It's significant that both sentences involve verbs of motion.

Finally, we find something very similar happening in the following sentences, which use आना *ānā* or जाना *jānā* with a sense of purpose:

वे आपसे मिलने आ रहे हैं ।
ve āpse milne ā rahe haĩ. They're coming to meet you.

हम फ़िल्म देखने जा रहे हैं ।
ham film dekhne jā rahe haĩ. We're going to see a film.

These sentences have a sense of *purpose* or *intention* which is expressed by the मिलने *milne* and देखने *dekhne* (infinitives ending *-e*) — as if here too some postposition had been dropped.

About adverbs and postpositions

Now here are some more sentences using adverbs. These ones (again shown in bold text) describe place:

मनोज **बाहर** खड़ा है ।

Manoj ***bāhar*** *khaṛā hai.* Manoj is standing outside.

मीना **अंदर** बैठी है ।

Mīnā ***andar*** *baiṭhī hai.* Meena is sitting inside.

ऊपर देखो ।

ūpar *dekho.* Look up.

नीचे आओ ।

nīce *āo.* Come down.

The thing to notice here is that adverbs and postpositions work differently from each other. Let's take the pair बाहर *bāhar* and के बाहर *ke bāhar*, both meaning 'outside', as an example. बाहर *bāhar* on its own is an adverb that means 'outside' without reference to any other place: वह बाहर खड़ा है *vah bāhar khaṛā hai* 'he's standing outside'. But के बाहर *ke bāhar* is a postposition that means 'outside *in relation to* something': मकान के बाहर *makān ke bāhar* 'outside the house'. There are many such pairings: for example, the adverb ऊपर *ūpar* means 'up, upstairs' (ऊपर जाओ *ūpar jāo* 'go up' or 'go upstairs'), while the postposition के ऊपर *ke ūpar* means 'on top of, above' (मेज़ के ऊपर *mez ke ūpar* 'on top of the table').

हमारे मकान के बाहर

hamāre makān ke bāhar outside our house

इस कमरे के अंदर

is kamre ke andar inside this room

अलमारी के ऊपर

almārī ke ūpar on top of the cupboard

इस मेज़ के नीचे

is mez ke nīce under this table

There are many such postpositions consisting of two (or even three) words. Grammarians (who are always fond of long names for short things!) call them 'compound postpositions'.

के नज़दीक	*ke nazdīk*	near
के पास	*ke pās*	near; in the possession of
के अलावा	*ke alāvā*	as well as
के यहाँ	*ke yahā̃*	at the place of, at X's place
के लिए	*ke lie*	for
की तरफ़ / ओर	*kī taraf / or*	towards
की तरह	*kī tarah*	like

When using these with the pronouns मैं *maĩ* (मेरे *mere*), तू *tū* (तेरे *tere*), तुम *tum* (तुम्हारे *tumhāre*), हम *ham* (हमारे *hamāre*) and अपना *apnā* (अपने *apne*) the के/की *ke/kī* component is absent:

उनके यहाँ	*unke yahā̃*	at their place
मेरे यहाँ	*mere yahā̃*	at my place
मकान की ओर	*makān kī or*	towards the house
हमारी ओर	*hamārī or*	towards us

You'll find many more of these compound postpositions listed in the Hindi–English glossary under के *ke* and की *kī*.

Practise what you've learnt

Make up phrases (such as मेरे घर के पीछे *mere ghar ke pīche* 'behind my house') from the following, remembering to make the first column oblique:

कौन *kaun* [oblique किस *kis* 'whom']	के लिए *ke lie* for
मेरा दोस्त *merā dost*	के बाद *ke bād* after
वह बड़ा पेड़ *vah baṛā peṛ*	की तरह *kī tarah* like
सोमवार *somvār*	के पहले *ke pahle* before
हमारा स्कूल *hamārā skūl*	के पीछे *ke pīche* behind
यह होटल *yah hoṭal*	की तरफ़ *kī taraf* towards

पुराना स्टेशन *purānā sṭeśan*	के नज़दीक *ke nazdīk* near
मेरा घर *merā ghar*	के नीचे *ke nīce* under, below
ये लोग *ye log*	के यहाँ *ke yahā̃* at the place of
तुम्हारा घर *tumhārā ghar*	के चारों ओर *ke cārõ* all around

Exercise 8a Translate:

1 You are not cleverer than them. (clever: होशियार *hośiyār*)
2 I (f.) am older than my brother but younger than you.
3 My other sister is the cleverest.
4 Some people say that Hindi is easier than English.
5 Mother thinks that my sister is more beautiful than me.
6 Father knows more than Mother but he can't say anything.
7 Their house is bigger and more beautiful than ours.
8 I am cleverer than you.
9 Your language is more difficult than my language.

Exercise 8b Rewrite these sentences in the continuous tense, translating the rewritten version. (Raju is speaking throughout.)

मैं रेडियो सुनता हूँ ।	मैं रेडियो सुन रहा हूँ ।
maĩ reḍiyo suntā hū̃.	*maĩ reḍiyo sun rahā hū̃.*
I listen to the radio.	I am listening to the radio.

१० हम लोग अपने दोस्तों को खाना खाने बुलाते हैं ।
ham log apne dostõ ko khānā khāne bulāte haĩ.

११ मैं खाना तैयार करता हूँ ।
maĩ khānā taiyār kartā hū̃.

१२ वे लोग शाम को आते हैं ।
ve log śām ko āte haĩ.

१३ वे अपने बच्चों और दोस्तों को भी लाते हैं ।
ve apne baccõ aur dostõ ko bhī lāte haĩ.

१४ मेरी पत्नी कहती है कि उनके बच्चे मोती को मारते हैं ।
merī patnī kahtī hai ki unke bacce Motī ko mārte haĩ.

१५ दादी जी हमारी मदद नहीं करती हैं, सिर्फ़ रेडियो सुनती हैं ।
dādī jī hamārī madad nahī̃ kartī haĩ, sirf reḍiyo suntī haĩ.

१६ हमारा कुकर ['cooker'] ठीक से काम नहीं करता ।
hamārā kukar ['cooker'] *ṭhīk se kām nahī̃ kartā.*

१७ हमारे दोस्त कहते हैं कि बाथरूम में पानी नहीं आ रहा है ।
hamāre dost kahte haĩ ki bāthrūm mẽ pānī nahī̃ ā rahā hai.

Exercise 8c Answer the questions:

१८ अपने ख़ाली समय में आप क्या करते/करती हैं ?
apne <u>kh</u>ālī samay mẽ āp kyā karte/kartī haĩ?

१९ आपको घर पर रहना या बाहर जाना ज़्यादा पसंद है ?
āpko ghar par rahnā yā bāhar jānā zyādā pasand hai?

२० आप हिन्दी क्यों सीख रहे/रही हैं ?
āp hindī kyõ sīkh rahe/rahī haĩ?

२१ क्या हिन्दी अँग्रेज़ी से ज़्यादा आसान है ?
kyā hindī ãgrezī se zyādā āsān hai?

२२ क्या आपके कुछ दोस्त भी हिन्दी बोलते हैं ?
kyā āpke kuch dost bhī hindī bolte haĩ?

२३ आज आप क्या कर रहे/रही हैं ?
āj āp kyā kar rahe/rahī haĩ?

२४ आप अपनी छुट्टियों में कहाँ जाते/जाती हैं ?
āp apnī chuṭṭiyõ mẽ kahā̃ jāte/jātī haĩ?

२५ अभी आप क्या सोच रहे/रही हैं ?
abhī āp kyā soc rahe/rahī haĩ?

Glossary

अंदर *andar* inside
अगला *aglā* next
अपना *apnā* one's own (my, your, his etc.)
आज रात को *āj rāt ko* tonight; आज शाम को *āj śām ko* this evening
कब *kab* when?
की ओर *kī or* towards
की तरफ़ *kī taraf* towards
की तरह *kī tarah* like
के अंदर *ke andar* inside
के अलावा *ke alāvā* as well as
के ऊपर *ke ūpar* above, on top of
के नज़दीक *ke nazdīk* near
के नीचे *ke nīce* below, under
के बाहर *ke bāhar* outside
के यहाँ *ke yahā̃* at the place of
के साथ *ke sāth* with, in the company of
ख़र्च *kharc m.* expenditure; ख़र्च करना *kharc karnā* to spend
गुजराती f. Gujarati
ज़रूरत *zarūrat f.* need; मुझको X की ज़रूरत है *mujhko X kī* zarūrat *hai* I need X
जीवन *jīvan* m. life
ज़्यादा *zyādā* more, much
तमिल *tamil* f. Tamil
ताश m. playing cards
तैयार *taiyār* ready, prepared; तैयार करना *taiyār karnā* to prepare
थोड़ी देर *thoṛī der* f. a little while
दुखी *dukhī* sad
दौड़ना *dauṛnā* to run
धोना *dhonā* to wash
ध्यान रखना *dhyān rakhnā* to pay attention to, look after
नीचे *nīce* down, downstairs
पास में *pās mẽ* nearby
पिछला *pichlā* previous, last
प्रिय *priy* dear; 'Dear...' (in informal correspondence)
बरतन *bartan* m. dish, utensil
बाप रे बाप ! *bāp re bāp!* Oh God!
भिजवाना *bhijvānā* to have sent, to cause to be sent
मदद *madad* f. help; किसी की मदद करना *kisī kī madad karnā* to help someone
माँजना *mā̃jnā* f. to scour, clean
मुस्कराना *muskarānā* to smile
रात *rāt* f. night; रात का खाना *rāt kā khānā* m. dinner
लगना *lagnā* to seem
लाना *lānā* to bring
रोना *ronā* to cry, weep
लाना *lānā* to bring
सबसे *sabse* of all (in superlatives, e.g. सबसे अच्छा *sabse acchā* best, best of all)
सही *sahī* correct, true
सहेली *sahelī* f. female's female friend
हँसना *hãsnā* to laugh
हफ़्ता *haftā* m. week
होशियार hośiyār clever

09

भविष्य में
bhaviṣya
in the future

In this unit you will learn

- how to talk about the future
- how to use 'if' expressions
- how to express doubts and possibilities

Language points

- future tenses
- conditional clauses
- subjunctive mood

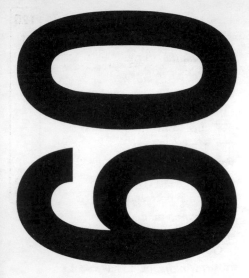

1 The future tense

The future is quite simple in Hindi. We'll begin with 'I will do' and 'you will do', which together will give lots of potential for practice. You already know that 'to do' is करना *karnā,* stem कर *kar* — now here are the future forms:

मैं करूँगा / करूँगी	*maĩ karũgā / karũgī*	I will do
आप करेंगे / करेंगी	*āp karẽge / karẽgī*	You will do

So the future ending for मैं *maĩ* is *-ũgā / -ũgī,* and the आप *āp* ending is *-ẽge / -ẽgī.*

What will you do tomorrow?

This pair of dialogues uses the future tense of the verbs रहना *rahnā* 'to stay' and जाना *jānā* 'to go'.

राजू कल आप क्या करेंगे ?
जावेद कल मैं काम करूँगा । आप क्या करेंगे ?
राजू मैं घर पर रहूँगा ।
जावेद आप घर पर क्यों रहेंगे ? काम पर नहीं जाएँगे ?
राजू नहीं, काम पर नहीं जाऊँगा । कल छुट्टी है ।

Rājū *kal āp kyā karẽge?*
Jāved *kal maĩ kām karũgā. āp kyā karẽge?*
Rājū *maĩ ghar par rahũgā.*
Jāved *āp ghar par kyõ rahẽge? kām par nahī̃ jāẽge?*
Rājū *nahī̃, kām par nahī̃ jāũgā. kal chuṭṭī hai.*

गीता कल आप क्या करेंगी ?
उषा कल मैं काम करूँगी । आप क्या करेंगी ?
गीता मैं घर पर रहूँगी ।
उषा आप घर पर क्यों रहेंगी ? काम पर नहीं जाएँगी ?
गीता नहीं, काम पर नहीं जाऊँगी । कल छुट्टी है ।

Gītā *kal āp kyā karẽgī?*
Uṣā *kal maĩ kām karũgī. āp kyā karẽgī?*
Gītā *maĩ ghar par rahũgī.*

Uṣā	*āp ghar par kyõ rahẽgī? kām par nahī̃ jāẽgī?*
Gītā	*nahī̃, kām par nahī̃ jāū̃gī. kal chuṭṭī hai.*

Raju/Geeta	What will you do tomorrow?
Javed/Usha	Tomorrow I'll work. What will you do?
Raju/Geeta	I shall stay at home.
Javed/Usha	Why will you stay at home? Won't you go to work?
Raju/Geeta	No, I won't go to work. Tomorrow's a holiday.

Practise what you've learnt

These questions are for you to answer:

१ आज रात को आप क्या खाएँगे / खाएँगी ? (खाना to eat)
āj rāt ko āp kyā khāẽge/khāẽgī? *khānā*

२ ... और क्या पिएँगे / पिएँगी ? (पीना to drink)
... aur kyā piẽge/piẽgī? *pīnā*

३ आज आप क्या करेंगे / करेंगी ? (करना to do)
āj āp kyā karẽge/karẽgī? *karnā*

४ कल सुबह आप कहाँ जाएँगे / जाएँगी ? (जाना to go)
kal subah āp kahā̃ jāẽge/jāẽgī? *jānā*

५ परसों आप किससे मिलेंगे / मिलेंगी ? (मिलना to meet)
parsõ āp kisse milẽge/milẽgī? *milnā*

The future with 'they' and 'we' is the same as with आप *āp* — it ends *-ẽge / -ẽgī.*

वे लोग खाना बनाएँगे ।
ve log khānā banāẽge. Those people will make food.

ये लोग बीयर लाएँगे ।
ye log bīyar lāẽge. These people will bring beer.

हम लोग सिर्फ़ खाएँगे और पियेंगे !
ham log sirf khāẽge aur piyẽge! We will just eat and drink!

The future tense with 'he, she, it' (and also तू *tū* 'you') has the ending *-ega / -egī* —

वह घर जाएगा ।
vah ghar jāegā. He will go home.

वह घर आएगी ।
vah ghar āegī. She will come home.

कल कौनसा दिन होगा ?
kal kaunsā din hogā? What day will it be tomorrow?

कल सोमवार होगा ।
kal somvār hogā. Tomorrow will be Monday.

Finally, the future with तुम *tum* has the ending *-oge / -ogī* —

राजू, तुम चाय पियोगे ?
Rājū, tum cāy piyoge? Raju, will you have tea?

गीता, तुम मेरे साथ चलोगी ?
Gītā, tum mere sāth calogī? Geeta, will you come with me?

So here's the future tense in all its glory, shown in the verb बोलना *bolnā* 'to speak'.

मैं बोलूँगा / बोलूँगी *maĩ bolū̃gā / bolū̃gī*	हम बोलेंगे / बोलेंगी *ham bolẽge / bolẽgī*
तू बोलेगा / बोलेगी *tū bolegā / bolegī*	तुम बोलोगे / बोलेगी *tum bologe / bologī*
	आप बोलेंगे / बोलेंगी *āp bolẽge / bolẽgī*
यह, वह बोलेगा / बोलेगी *yah, vah bolegā / bolegī*	ये, वे बोलेंगे / बोलेंगी *ye, ve bolẽge / bolẽgī*

Once you've become familiar with the form of बोलना *bolnā,* practise the future by using it in other everyday verbs.

Reported speech and 'would'

In 'reported speech', the future tense gives the sense 'would':

राजू कह रहा था कि वह नाश्ता तैयार करेगा ।
Rājū kah rahā thā ki vah nāśtā taiyār karega. Raju was saying that he would get breakfast ready.

गीता कह रही थी कि वह आराम करेगी ।
Gītā kah rahī thī ki vah ārām karegī. Geeta was saying that she would rest.

मनोज और राम कह रहे थे कि वे जल्दी नहीं उठेंगे ।
Manoj aur Rām kah rahe the ki ve jaldī nahī̃ uṭhẽge. Manoj and Ram were saying that they wouldn't get up early.

मोती सोच रहा था कि क्या मुझे भी नाश्ता मिलेगा?
Motī soc rahā thā ki kyā mujhe bhī nāśtā milegā? Moti was wondering if he'd get breakfast too.

The days ahead

Manoj is helping Pratap with his Hindi by asking about the coming week.

मनोज प्रताप, तुम हफ़्ते के दिनों के नाम बताओगे ?

प्रताप हाँ, ये हैं — सोमवार, मंगलवार, बुधवार, फिर ... फिर ...

मनोज गुरु...

प्रताप हाँ ! गुरुवार या बृहस्पतिवार, शुक्रवार, शनिवार, रविवार ।

मनोज शाबाश ! कल कौनसा दिन होगा ?

प्रताप कल मंगलवार होगा ।

मनोज परसों तुम क्या करोगे ?

प्रताप परसों, यानी बुधवार को, मैं पिताजी से मिलने जाऊँगा ।

मनोज गुरुवार को तुम कहाँ जाओगे ?

प्रताप गुरुवार को मैं घर पर रहूँगा ।

मनोज शुक्रवार को तुम क्या करोगे ?

प्रताप शुक्रवार को मैं अपनी पढ़ाई करूँगा ।

मनोज और शनिवार को तुम आराम करोगे ?

प्रताप नहीं, शनिवार को मैं बाहर जाऊँगा और मज़े करूँगा !

Manoj *Pratāp, tum hafte ke dinõ ke nām batāoge?*
Pratāp *hā̃, ye haĩ — somvār, mangalvār, budhvār, phir... phir...*
Manoj *guru...*
Pratāp *hā̃! guruvār yā bṛhaspativār, śukravār, śanivār, ravivār.*
Manoj *śābāś! kal kaunsā din hogā?*
Pratāp *kal mangalvār hogā.*

Manoj *parsõ tum kyā karoge?*

Pratāp *parsõ, yānī budhvār ko, maĩ pitājī se milne jāū̃gā.*

Manoj *guruvār ko tum kahā̃ jāoge?*

Pratāp *guruvār ko maĩ ghar par rahū̃gā.*

Manoj *śukravār ko tum kyā karoge?*

Pratāp *śukravār ko maĩ apnī paṛhāi karū̃gā.*

Manoj *aur śanivar ko tum ārām karoge?*

Pratāp *nahī̃, śanivār ko maĩ bāhar jāū̃gā aur maze karū̃gā!*

Manoj Pratap, will you tell [me] the names of the days of the week?

Pratap Yes, they are… *somvār, mangalvār, budhvār*, then... then...

Manoj *guru...*

Pratap Yes! *guruvār* or *bṛhaspativār, śukravār, śanivār, ravivār*.

Manoj Bravo! What day will it be tomorrow?

Pratap Tomorrow will be Tuesday.

Manoj What will you do the day after tomorrow?

Pratap The day after tomorrow, that is on Wednesday, I'll go to meet Father.

Manoj Where will you go on Thursday?

Pratap On Thursday I'll stay at home.

Manoj What will you do on Friday?

Pratap On Friday I'll do my studying.

Manoj And on Saturday you'll rest?

Pratap No, on Saturday I'll go out and enjoy myself!

▶ Geeta's diary

Your next task is to fill Geeta's appointment diary for the coming week, based on what she tells you below (notice that she sometimes uses abbreviation for the names of the days). Write the activity using an infinitive verb — Monday has already been completed as an example of the format to use.

आज सोम है; आज मैं घर पर रहूँगी । कल, यानी मंगल को, हम लोग दिल्ली जाएँगे । परसों, यानी बुध को, हम अपने मकान के लिए कुछ चीज़ें ख़रीदने जाएँगे । गरुवार को हम घर वापस आएँगे । शुक्रवार को मैं आराम करूँगी । शनिवार की रात को हम सीता के यहाँ जाएँगे । रविवार को मैं अगले हफ़्ते की तैयारियाँ करूँगी ।

āj som hai; āj maĩ ghar par rahū̃gī. kal, yānī mangal ko, ham log dillī jāẽge. parsõ, yānī budh ko, ham apne makān ke lie kuch cīzẽ <u>kh</u>arīdne jāẽge. guruvār ko ham ghar vāpas āẽge. śukravār ko maĩ ārām karū̃gī. śanivār kī rāt ko ham Sītā ke yahā̃ jāẽge. ravivār ko maĩ agle hafte kī taiyāriyā̃ karū̃gī.

Today is Monday; today I'll stay at home. Tomorrow, i.e. on Tuesday, we'll go to Delhi. The day after, i.e. on Wednesday, we'll go to buy some things for our house. On Thursday we'll come back home. On Friday I'll rest. On Saturday night we'll go to Sita's. On Sunday I'll get ready for next week.

सोमवार *somvār*	घर पर रहना ghar par rahnā
मंगलवार *mangalvār*	
बुधवार *budhvār*	
गुरुवार *guruvār*	
शुक्रवार *śukravār*	
शनिवार *śanivār*	
रविवार *ravivār*	

2 Ifs and maybes

The sentence आप घर जाएँगे *āp ghar jāẽge* means 'you'll go home'. It's a positive statement of something that is clear, certain, definite. But if we remove the last syllable of जाएँगे *jāẽge,* we are left with आप घर जाएँ *āp ghar jāẽ* — which means 'you should go home' (suggestion) or 'you might go home' (possibility) or even 'you may go home' (permission). We've cut off the *certainty* of the verb with its last syllable.

This form of the verb is called the 'subjunctive': it expresses a sense of uncertainty, possibility, permission, suggestion, and similar indefinite, imagined or tentative senses. As we've just seen, it's formed by lopping off the last syllable of the future tense; the distinction between masculine and feminine is lost as a result. You'll often find words like अगर *agar* 'if', शायद *śāyad* 'maybe, perhaps' or ज़रूर *zarūr* 'of course' lurking nearby. *All* the verbs in this next dialogue are in the subjunctive.

Javed calls on Raju

जावेद मैं अंदर आऊँ ?

राजू जी हाँ, जी हाँ, आप ज़रूर आएँ !

जावेद मैं कहाँ बैठूँ ?

राजू आप इधर बैठें । मैं चाय बनाऊँ ?

जावेद अगर आप चाहें । या हम बाहर जाएँ ?

राजू नहीं, हम घर पर ही रहें ।

Jāved *maĩ andar āū̃?*
Rājū *jī hā̃, jī hā̃, āp zarūr āẽ.*
Jāved *maĩ kahā̃ baiṭhū̃?*
Rājū *āp idhar baiṭhẽ. maĩ cāy banāū̃?*
Javed *agar āp cāhẽ. yā ham bāhar jāẽ?*
Rājū *nahĩ, ham ghar par hī rahẽ.*

Javed May I come in?
Raju Yes yes, of course you may come in! [Do come in!]
Javed Where should I sit?
Raju Please sit over here. Should I make tea?
Javed If you wish. Or should we go out?
Raju No, let's stay at home.

Sentences involving an 'if' are quite likely to use a subjunctive verb, but verb forms such as a future tense are also possible:

अगर वह "हाँ" कहे तो हम शादी करेंगे ।
agar vah 'hā̃' kahe to ham śādī karẽge. If she says 'yes', then we'll marry. (Subjunctive *kahe* — don't count on her agreement.)

अगर वह "हाँ" कहेगी तो हम शादी करेंगे ।

agar vah 'hā̃' kahegī to ham śādī karẽge. If she says 'yes', then we'll marry. (Future *kahegī* — book the photographer!)

These two sentences show how Hindi pairs an अगर *agar* clause with a तो *to* clause: 'If X, then Y'.

A suggestion or a command?

A subjunctive verb blurs the boundary between a suggestion and a command, offering a nicely diplomatic way of getting someone to comply with your wishes:

आप थोड़ी देर बैठे रहें ।

āp thoṛī der baiṭhe rahẽ. Kindly remain seated for a while.

कृपया गिलास में हाथ न धोएँ ।

kṛpayā gilās mẽ hāth na dhoẽ. Please do not wash your hands in the tumbler. (Restaurant sign.)

I want to... / I want *you* to...

Look closely at the difference between the following pair of sentences. How many people are involved in each one?

मैं कुछ कहना चाहता हूँ ।

maĩ kuch kahnā cāhtā hū̃. I want to say something.

मैं चाहता हूँ कि आप कुछ कहें ।

maĩ cāhtā hū̃ ki āp kuch kahẽ. I want *you* to say something.

The first sentence involves 'Person A' doing both the wanting and the speaking; the construction uses चाहना *cāhnā* 'to want' with an infinitive verb (here कहना *kahnā* 'to say'). The second involves 'Person A' wanting 'Person B' to do something: the construction uses चाहना *cāhnā* 'to want' with a subjunctive verb (here कहें *kahẽ*). The two clauses are linked by कि *ki* 'that'. Here are two more examples:

मैं चाहता हूँ कि वे यहाँ रहें ।

maĩ cāhtā hū̃ ki ve yahā̃ rahẽ. I want them to stay here.

वे चाहते हैं कि मैं यहाँ रहूँ ।

ve cāhte haĩ ki maĩ yahā̃ rahū̃. They want me to stay here.

Practise what you've learnt

Over to you. Make sentences by combining a phrase from the left-hand list with a phrase from the right-hand list, giving meanings such as 'I want you to rest'. All the verbs in the right-hand list are subjunctive.

मैं चाहता हूँ कि ...	... आप आराम करें ।
maĩ cāhtā hū̃ ki ...	*... āp ārām karẽ.*
हम चाहते थे कि ...	... तुम हमारे यहाँ ठहरो ।
ham cāhte haĩ ki ...	*... tum hamāre yahā̃ ṭhahro.*
वे चाहते हैं कि ...	... तुम्हारा दोस्त भी आए ।
ve cahte haĩ ki ...	*... tumhārā dost bhī āe.*
यह चाहता है कि ...	... तुम जाने की तैयारियाँ करो ।
vah cāhtā hai ki ...	*... tum jāne kī taiyāriyā̃ karo.*
मैं चाहती थी कि ...	... वह अपना काम करे ।
maĩ cāhtī thī ki ...	*... vah apnā kām kare.*
मेरी बहिन चाहती है कि ...	... तुम खाना बनाओ ।
merī bahin cāhtī hai ki ...	*... tum khānā banāo.*

3 So that, in order that

The conjunction (or 'linking word') ताकि *tāki* means 'so that, in order that', and is always followed by a subjunctive verb:

मैं उठूँगा ताकि दूसरे लोग बैठें ।

maĩ uṭhū̃gā tāki dūsre log baiṭhẽ. I'll get up so that others may sit.

अभी आइए ताकि हम काम शुरू करें ।

abhī āie tāki ham kām śurū karẽ. Come right now so that we can start work.

जल्दी उठो ताकि देरी न हो ।

jaldī uṭho tāki derī na ho. Get up early so that there won't be any delay.

हम धीरे धीरे बोलेंगे ताकि वे हमारी बात समझें ।

ham dhīre dhīre bolẽge tāki ve hamārī bāt samjhẽ. We'll speak slowly so that they understand what we say.

Did you know?

The official Indian name for India is भारत *bhārat* or भारतवर्ष *bhāratvarṣ*. Many people use हिन्दुस्तान *hindustān* instead, though this can sometimes be taken to imply 'northern India' only. The word हिन्द *hind* is now mostly limited to formulas such as जय हिन्द ! *jay hind!* ('Victory to India!' — once used as a nationalistic greeting) and to terms such as हिन्द महासागर *hind mahāsāgar* 'Indian Ocean'. Another common option is इंडिया *iṇḍiyā*, whose retroflex consonants show that it has been re-imported through English.

Words such as 'India', 'Hindi' and 'Hindu' all derive from the name of the Indus river; its Sanskrit name is सिंधु *sindhu*, but the Sanskrit 's' becomes 'h' in Persian. The word हिन्दी *hindī* is itself Persian in origin.

4 How long does it take?

To say 'how long something takes', Hindi uses the versatile verb लगना *lagnā*, here referring to the 'time taken':

एक घंटा लगता है ।

ek ghaṇṭā lagtā hai. It takes one hour.

दस मिनट लगते हैं ।

das minaṭ lagte haĩ. It takes ten minutes.

दो दिन लगेंगे ।

do din lagẽge. It'll take two days.

Notice how the verb agrees with the unit of time — 'one hour' (singular) 'ten minutes' (plural), etc. To specify the *action done* within the particular time frame, add an infinitive plus में *mẽ*, as in किताब लिखने में *kitāb likhne mẽ* 'in writing the book':

किताब लिखने में एक साल लगेगा ।

kitāb likhne mẽ ek sāl lagegā. It'll take a year to write the book.

घर जाने में दो घंटे लगते हैं ।

ghar jāne mẽ do ghaṇṭe lagte haĩ. It takes two hours to get home.

यह काम ख़त्म करने में मुझे डेढ़ घंटा लगेगा ।

yah kām <u>kh</u>atm karne mẽ mujhe ḍeṛh ghaṇṭā lagegā. It'll take me an hour and a half to finish this work.

Exercise 9a Match up the अगर *agar* (1–6) and तो *to* (A–F) clauses to make meaningful sentences, then translate them.

१ अगर सब्ज़ी-मंडी आज बंद हो ...
agar sabzī-maṇḍī āj band ho ...

२ अगर तुम्हें रास्ता नहीं मालूम ...
agar tumhẽ rāstā nahī̃ mālūm ...

३ अगर आप किसी शब्द का मतलब नहीं जानते ...
agar āp kisī śabd kā matlab nahī̃ jānte ...

४ अगर गोलचक्कर पर पुलिसवाला न मिले ...
agar golcakkar par pulisvālā na mile...

५ अगर होटल में कमरा न मिले ...
agar hoṭal mẽ kamrā na mile ...

६ अगर आप उस तंग गली में मुड़ेंगे ...
agar āp us tang galī mẽ muṛẽge ...

A ... तो आप मेरे यहाँ रहें ।
... to āp mere yahā̃ rahẽ.

B ... तो थाने पर जाओ ।
... to thāne par jāo.

C ... तो शब्दकोश में देखिए ।
... to śabdkoś mẽ dekhie.

D ... तो नक़्शा ख़रीदना ।
... to naqśā <u>kh</u>arīdnā.

E ... तो कल सुबह को सब्ज़ी लेना ।
... to kal subah ko sabzī lenā.

F ... तो बायें हाथ पर ढाबा दिखाई देगा ।
... to bāyẽ hāth par ḍhābā dikhāī degā.

Exercise 9b You have just arrived at a hotel where you will be staying for several days. Do as instructed:

7 Tell the hotel receptionist that you need a room for two people and that you will stay for three days.

8 Say that some friends will come to meet you this evening.

9 Ask what will be available for breakfast (नाश्ते में *nāśte mẽ*).

10 Ask whether dinner will be available as well.

11 Ask how long it will take to go on foot from the hotel to the cinema.

12 Tell the receptionist that you would like to phone London; ask if you can phone from your room.

13 Say that next week you will go to Agra and Delhi.

14 Ask if your friends can eat with you in the hotel tonight.

Exercise 9c Translate into Hindi:

15 Tomorrow is Saturday, so we'll go out.

16 We were thinking that we would go to the cinema.

17 My brother was saying that he would stay at home.

18 If you wish, come with us.

19 We'll go early so that we can get good seats [सीट *sīṭ* f.].

20 If it's raining we'll go by car.

Glossary

अगर *agar* if

आराम *ārām* m. rest; आराम करना *ārām karnā* to rest

इधर *idhar* here, over here; **इधर-उधर** *idhar-udhar* here and there, hither and thither

इमारत *imārat* f. building

उठना *uṭhnā* to get up, rise

उधर *udhar* there, over there

कृपया *kṛpayā* please (formal)

ओर *or* f. side, direction

के चारों तरफ़ *ke cārõ taraf* all around

के सामने *ke sāmne* opposite

गली *galī* f. lane, narrow street

गिलास *gilās* m. tumbler

गुरुवार *guruvār* m. Thursday

गोलचक्कर *golcakkar* m. roundabout

घंटा *ghaṇṭā* m. hour

ठंड *ṭhaṇḍ* f. cold; ठंड लगना *ṭhaṇḍ lagnā* to feel cold

ठहरना *ṭhaharnā* to stay, remain

ताकि *tāki* so that, in order that

तैयारी *taiyārī* f. preparation

देरी *derī* f. delay

नक़्शा *naqśā* m. map, plan

नाश्ता *nāśtā* m. breakfast

पढ़ाई *paṛhāī* f. studies, studying

परसों *parsõ* two days away (day after tomorrow; day before yesterday)

पहुँचना *pahũcnā* to reach, arrive

पुलिसवाला *pulisvālā m.* policeman

बंद *band* closed, shut

बीयर *bīyar* f. beer

बुधवार *budhvar* m. Wednesday

बेहतर *behtar* better

मंगलवार *maṅgalvār* f. Tuesday

मज़ा *mazā* m. enjoyment, fun; मज़े करना *maze karnā* to enjoy oneself, have fun

मतलब *matlab* m. meaning

मुड़ना *muṛnā* to turn

रविवार *ravivār* m. Sunday

लगना *lagnā* time to be taken; घर जाने में १० मिनट लगते हैं / एक घंटा लगता है *ghar jāne mẽ 10 minaṭ lagte haĩ / ek ghaṇṭā lagtā hai* It takes 10 minutes / one hour to get home

वापस *vāpas* 'back' in वापस आना/जाना/देना *vāpas ānā/jānā/denā* to come/go/give back

शनिवार *śanivār* m. Saturday

शब्द *śabd* m word

शब्दकोश *śabdkoś* m. dictionary

शादी *śādī* f. wedding, marriage; शादी करना *śādī karnā* to marry

शाबाश *śābāś* bravo

शुक्रवार *śukravār* m. Friday

सब्ज़ी *sabzī* f. vegetable(s); सब्ज़ी मंडी *sabzī maṇḍī* f. vegetable market

सब्ज़ीवाला *sabzīvālā* m. vegetable seller

सुबह *subah f. morning*

10

क्या हुआ ?
kyā huā?
what happened?

In this unit you will learn
- how to describe past events
- how to link connected actions in a sequence

Language points
- perfective tenses
- transitivity
- absolutives

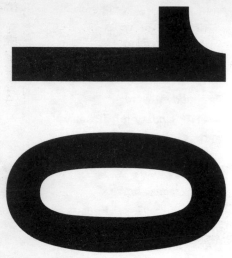

1 The past tense

So far we've seen two kinds of past tense: 'imperfective' (describing *routine or habitual events* of the 'I used to' type), and 'continuous' (describing *actions in progress* of the 'I was doing' type). Here's an example of each to remind you:

मैं दौड़ता था ।

maĩ dauṛtā thā. I used to run.

मैं दौड़ रहा था ।

maĩ dauṛ rahā thā. I was running.

The new tense we're going to look at now is this:

मैं दौड़ा ।

maĩ dauṛā. I ran.

This describes a *completed* action in the past, and is called the 'perfective' tense. It uses a 'perfective participle' consisting of verb stem plus *-ā / -e / -ī / -ī̃.* Thus दौड़ा *dauṛā* 'ran', बोला *bolā* 'spoke', हँसा *hãsā* 'laughed', उठा *uṭhā* 'got up', पहुँचा *pahũcā* 'arrived', and so on.

Look carefully at the verb endings in the following three sentences, making sure you can see how they agree with their subjects (for example, the first one is feminine singular to agree with 'Meena'):

मीना घर पहुँची ।

Mīnā ghar pahũncī. Meena arrived home.

फिर मनोज और राजू पहुँचे ।

phir Manoj aur Rājū pahũce. Then Manoj and Raju arrived.

बाद में गीता और सीता पहुँचीं ।

bād mẽ Gītā aur Sītā pahũcī̃. Later Geeta and Sita arrived.

Before going any further, practise using the verbs बोलना *bolnā* and उठना *uṭhnā* (or any others given above) with a range of different subjects, paying attention to the agreements of gender and number.

Coming and going

You're probably thinking this is all too easy. And you're right: it's time to introduce an exception! The participle from जाना *jānā* 'to go' is गया / गए / गई / गईं — *gayā / gae / gaī / gaī̃.* (Don't confuse this with गाया *gāyā* etc., from गाना *gānā* to sing.)

मीना स्कूल गई, मनोज बाहर गया, राजू और राम बाज़ार गए, गीता और सीता सिनेमा गईं ।

Mīnā skūl gaī, Manoj bāhar gayā, Rājū aur Rām bāzār gae, Gītā aur Sītā sinemā gaī̃. Meena went to school, Manoj went out, Raju and Ram went to the market, Geeta and Sita went to the cinema.

Participles for the verb आना *ānā* 'to come' are आया, आए, आई, आईं *āyā, āe, āī, āī̃.* Notice how the masculine singular आया *āyā* has a 'y' between the stem and the ending. All verbs with *-ā* stems do this.

What happened then?

The perfective from होना *honā* 'to be, to happen' is हुआ, हुए, हुई, हुईं *huā, hue, huī, huī̃,* 'happened'.

तब क्या हुआ ?

tab kyā huā ? What happened then?

एक दुर्घटना हुई ।

ek durghaṭnā huī. An accident happened. (There was an accident.)

Practise what you've learnt

This is all quite easy to understand, but you'll only really learn it when you use it. So make up some short subject-plus-verb sentences using Meena and anyone else (as in the long sentence at the top of this page) as subjects, combined with the following verbs:

आना	*ānā*	to come
जाना	*jānā*	to go
उठना	*uṭhnā*	to get up
दौड़ना	*dauṛnā*	to run
पहुँचना	*pahũcnā*	to arrive
हँसना	*hãsnā*	to laugh

Now answer these questions with the data supplied on the right:

१	मनोज कहाँ गया ?	घर
	Manoj kahā̃ gayā?	*ghar*
२	राजू और राम कहाँ गए ?	बाहर
	Rājū aur Rām kahā̃ gae?	*bāhar*

३ सीता कहाँ गई ? दिल्ली
Sītā kahā̃ gaī? *dillī*

४ क्या हुआ ? कुछ नहीं
kyā huā? *kuch nahī̃*

५ मीना कब पहुँची ? कल
Mīnā kab pahucī? *kal*

६ दादीजी कब आईं ? परसों
dādījī kab āī̃? *parsõ*

७ मनोज कब आया ? मंगलवार को
Manoj kab āyā? *mangalvār ko*

2 Transitivity

In the perfective, Hindi verbs follow two different patterns depending on whether they are 'intransitive' or 'transitive'. A transitive verb describes an action done to an object, as in 'We drank coffee' (in which the drinking was a process done by us to the coffee). We can test its transitivity by asking a question about the object: '*What* did we drink?'. By contrast, an *in*transitive verb simply describes an action occurring, with no object being involved, as in 'we arrived', or 'I got up'; here we can't make questions like 'What did we arrive' or 'What did I get up', so these verbs don't pass the transitivity test.

The Hindi verbs we've used so far in this unit have all been intransitive; but it's time now to move on transitive verbs, which behave differently in the past tense. Look very closely at the constructions of the following four sentences (a hint: किताब *kitāb* is feminine, अख़बार *akhbār* is masculine).

राजू ने किताब पढ़ी ।
Rājū ne kitāb paṛhī. Raju read a book.

राजू ने दोनों किताबें पढ़ीं ।
Rājū ne donõ kitābẽ paṛhī̃. Raju read both books.

गीता ने अख़बार पढ़ा ।
Gītā ne akhbār paṛhā. Geeta read a newsaper.

गीता ने दोनों अख़बार पढ़े ।
Gītā ne donõ akhbār paṛhe. Geeta read both newsapers.

Well, you should have noticed that the verbs agree with the 'book/books' and 'newspaper/newspapers' rather than with their readers! And also that the readers have sprouted an untranslatable postposition, ने *ne*. This is how transitive verbs always operate in the perfective. A verb that has no object for the verb to agree with stays in the masculine singular:

राम ने खाया । मीनू ने खाया ।

Rām ne khāyā. *Mīnū ne khāyā.* Ram ate. Meenu ate.

Because we're not told *what* they ate, the verb stays as खाया *khāyā*.

What happened at the party?

There was a party at the Sharmas' house. Complete the sentences with the appropriate form of the verb supplied on the right. The agreement of the verb will be with the *subject* if there's no ने *ne* construction, but with the *object* if there *is* a ने *ne* construction. Answers below.

१	गीता ने बढ़िया खाना ... *Gītā ne baṛhiyā khānā ...*	बनाना to make *banānā*
२	मीना की दो सहेलियाँ पार्टी में ... *Mīnā kī do saheliyā̃ pārṭī mẽ ...*	आना to come *ānā*
३	मनोज के कई दोस्त भी ... *Manoj ke kaī dost bhī ...*	आना to come *ānā*
४	गीता की सहेली ने सितार ... *Gītā kī sahelī ne sitār...*	बजाना to play *bajānā*
५	फिर मोती ज़ोर से ... *phir Moti zor se ...*	भौंकना to bark *bhaũknā*
६	राजू ने पाँच समोसे ... *Rājū ne pā̃c samose ...*	खाना to eat *khānā*
७	सब लोग बड़ी देर तक ... *sab log baṛī der tak ...*	रहना to stay *rahnā*
८	दूसरे दिन बच्चे देर से ... *dūsre din bacce der se ...*	उठना to get up *uṭhnā*

Answers: 1 बनाया *banāyā*; 2 आईं *āī̃*; 3 आए *āe*; 4 बजाया *bajāyā*; 5 भौंका *bhaũkā*; 6 खाए *khāe*; 7 रहे *rahe*; 8 उठे *uṭhe*.

How many did you see?

Make up sentences on the model of मैंने एक मकान देखा *maĩne ek makān dekhā* 'I saw one house', to reflect the following objects:

1
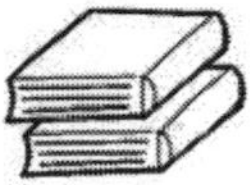

2

3

4

5

6

7

8
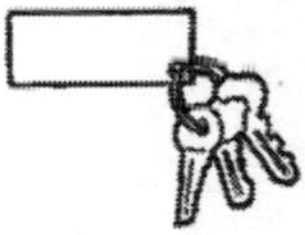

9

10

11

12

13

14

15
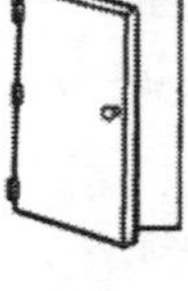

16

Check the back of the book for the answers.

Some special pronouns...

Some pronouns have special oblique forms for the ने *ne* construction:

PRONOUN	USUAL OBLIQUE	SPECIAL FORM + ने *ne*
मैं *maĩ*	मुझ *mujh*	मैंने *maĩne*
तू *tū*	तुझ *tujh*	तूने *tūne*
ये *ye*	इन *in*	इन्होंने *inhõne*
वे *ve*	उन *un*	उन्होंने *unhõne*

And some special verbs

Some very common verbs have irregular participles:

करना *karnā* 'to do': किया, किए, की, कीं *kiyā, kie, kī, kī̃* 'did'

देना *denā* 'to give': दिया, दिए, दी, दीं *diyā, die, dī, dī̃* 'gave'

लेना *lenā* 'to take': लिया, लिए, ली, लीं *liyā, lie, lī, lī̃* 'took'

पीना *pīnā* 'to drink': पिया, पिए, पी, पीं *piyā, pie, pī, pī̃* 'drank'

What did Geeta see?

Now answer the questions using the data supplied on the right (with which the verb must agree!):

१	गीता ने क्या देखा ? *Gītā ne kyā dekhā?*	एक नई फ़िल्म *ek naī film*
२	राजू ने क्या ख़रीदा ? *Rājū ne kyā <u>kh</u>arīdā?*	दो अख़बार *do a<u>kh</u>bār*
३	मोती ने क्या खाया ? *Motī ne kyā khāyā?*	दस चपातियाँ *das capātiyā̃*
४	मीना ने क्या पढ़ा ? *Mīnā ne kyā paṛhā?*	दो कहानियाँ *do kahāniyā̃*
५	हमने कितने कुरते ख़रीदे ? *hamne kitne kurte <u>kh</u>arīde?*	चार *cār*
६	उन्होंने मेज़ पर क्या रखा ? *unhõne mez par kyā rakhā?*	कुछ किताबें *kuch kitābẽ*
७	आपने दीवार पर क्या लिखा ? *āpne dīvar par kyā likhā?*	अपना नाम *apnā nam*

८ तुमने क्या सुना ? कई बातें
tumne kyā sunā? *kaī bātẽ*

९ तुमने कितनी भाषाएँ सीखीं ? एक ही
tumne kitnī bhāṣāẽ sīkhī̃? *ek hī*

All verbs that take the ने *ne* construction are shown with N in the English–Hindi glossary (e.g. देखना *dekhnā* N) at the end of the book. The construction itself may take some time to digest — like Moti's ten chapatties.

A *particular* object

Back in section 7.2 we saw that को *ko* is often added to an object that's particularized in some way. (Turn back to 7.2 now if you've forgotten this.) If को *ko* is added to the object of a ने *ne* verb, then the verb reverts to a masculine singular.

राम ने चपाती को खाया ।
Rām ne capātī ko khāyā. Ram ate the chapatti.

मैंने उनके बच्चों को देखा ।
maĩne unke baccõ ko dekhā. I saw their children.

उसने किताबों को पढ़ा ।
usne kitābõ ko paṛhā. He/she read the books.

The verbs in these three sentences all end in -ā (खाया *khāyā*, देखा *dekhā*, पढ़ा *paṛhā*) because in each one the presence of को *ko* insulates the verb from its object.

3 Other perfective tenses

In English we differentiate time frames by saying 'I wrote, have written, had written, will have written' etc. Similarly in Hindi, all three kinds of perfective verbs can be used in different time frames by adding auxiliary verbs (है *hai*, था *thā* etc.):

A राजू ने चिट्ठी लिखी ।
Rājū ne ciṭṭhī likhī. Raju wrote a letter.

B राजू ने चिट्ठी लिखी है ।
Rājū ne ciṭṭhī likhī hai. Raju has written a letter.

C राजू ने चिट्ठी लिखी थी ।
Rājū ne ciṭṭhī likhī thī. Raju had written a letter (or wrote it some time ago).

D राजू ने चिट्ठी लिखी होगी ।
Rājū ne ciṭṭhī likhī hogī. Raju will have written a letter.

E राजू ने चिट्ठी लिखी हो ।
Rājū ne ciṭṭhī likhī ho. Raju may have written a letter.

COMMENTARY

A लिखी *likhī*, no auxiliary verb; it's the simple past.

B लिखी है *likhī hai*, 'has written' (है *hai* is singular because चिट्ठी *ciṭṭhī* is singular), suggesting that the effect of the writing is still felt in the present.

C लिखी थी *likhī thī* (both words are feminine singular, to agree with चिट्ठी *ciṭṭhī*), suggesting that the action happened some time earlier.

D लिखी होगी *likhī hogī* 'will have written', either referring to some future time (such as 'Raju will have written a letter by Monday'), or making an assumption about the present (such as 'Presumably Raju will have written a letter by now').

E लिखी हो *likhī ho* 'may have written', in which the subjunctive हो *ho* shows that the matter is open to some doubt.

The same range can be used with any perfective verb:

पिताजी मिठाई लाए हैं/ थे ।
pitājī miṭhāī lāe haĩ/ the. Father has/had brought sweets.

पिताजी मिठाई लाए होंगे/ हों ।
pitājī miṭhāī lāe hõge. Father will/may have brought sweets.

In the above, the verbs agree with पिताजी *pitājī* (masculine honorific plural) because लाना *lānā*, though transitive, is *not* a ने *ne* verb.

मोती ने दस चपातियाँ खाई हैं/ थीं ।
Motī ne das capātiyā̃ khāī haĩ/ thī̃. Moti has/had eaten ten chapatties.

मोती ने दस चपातियाँ खाई होंगी/हों ।
Motī ne das capātiyā̃ khāī hõgī/ hõ. Moti will/may have eaten ten chapatties.

Raju's version of the morning

Here's Raju's account of his morning, following an evening when he and Geeta had been to see a Hindi film starring Shahrukh Khan. Make sure you can understand all the verb agreements!

आज सुबह मैं पाँच बजे उठा । थोड़ी देर के लिए मैं आँगन में बैठा । कल शाम को जब हम शाहरुख़ खाँ की नई फिल्म देखने सिनेमा गए तो बारिश हुई थी लेकिन आज मैंने देखा कि आकाश साफ़ है ।* सुबह के समय चारों ओर शान्ति होती है । मुझे सुबह का समय बहुत पसंद है ।

मैंने अपने लिए चाय बनाई । चाय पीने के बाद मैंने अपनी पत्नी को जगाया । चाय बनाना तो दो मिनट का काम है लेकिन मेमसाहब को जगाना दूसरी बात है । आख़िर में जब वह नीचे आई तो मैंने उसका नाश्ता तैयार किया । मैं तो नाश्ता कभी नहीं खाता, लेकिन गीता ज़रूर खाती है । मैंने उसके लिए दो टोस्ट बनाए । उसने चाय पी, आधा केला भी खाया । उसने शिकायत की कि चाय में चीनी ज़्यादा है ।* मैंने कहा कि तुम्हारी जिन्दगी में थोड़ी मिठास की ज़रूरत है ।*

āj subah maĩ pā̃c baje uṭhā. thoṛī der ke lie maĩ ā̃gan mẽ baiṭhā. kal śām ko jab ham Śāhrukh Khā̃ kī naī film dekhne sinemā gae to bāriś huī thī lekin āj maĩne dekhā ki ākāś sāf hai. subah ke samay cārõ or śānti hotī hai. mujhe subah kā samay bahut pasand hai.*

maĩne apne lie cāy banāī. cāy pīne ke bād maĩne apnī patnī ko jagāyā. cāy banāna to do minaṭ kā kām hai lekin memsāhib ko jagānā dūsrī bāt hai. ākhir mẽ jab vah nīce āī to maĩne uskā nāśtā taiyār kiyā. maĩ to nāśtā kabhī nahī̃ khātā, lekin Gītā zarūr khātī hai. maĩne uske lie do ṭosṭ banāe. usne cāy pī, ādhā kelā bhī khāyā. usne śikāyat kī ki cāy mẽ cīnī zyādā hai. maĩne kahā ki tumhārī zindagī mẽ thoṛī miṭhās kī zarūrat hai.**

This morning I got up at five o'clock. For a little while I sat in the courtyard. Yesterday evening when we went to the cinema to see Shahrukh Khan's new film it had rained; but today I saw that the sky was clear.* In the mornings it's peaceful all around. I'm very fond of the morning time.
I made tea for myself. After having tea I woke up my wife. Making tea is two minutes' work but waking up the memsahib is another matter. Finally, when she came down I got her breakfast ready. Me, I never eat breakfast, but Geeta does of course. I made two pieces of toast for her. She had tea and ate half a banana too. She complained that there was too much sugar in the tea.* I said that she needed a bit of sweetness in her life.*

*These three sentences show the use of 'reported speech' in Hindi. Literally, they translate as 'Today I saw that the sky is clear'; 'She complained that "There's too much sugar in the tea"'; and 'I said, "In your life a bit of sweetness is needed"'.

Practise what you've learnt

Time for you to try your hand at the past tenses. Translate the following:

1 I got up early today.
2 My father woke me up at six o'clock.
3 He prepared breakfast for me.
4 Then I went out to buy a newspaper.
5 Near the shop I saw my uncle's car.
6 My uncle had gone into the shop.
7 My uncle saw me and asked me how I was.
8 He came home with me and I made coffee for him.
9 My father asked me where the newspaper was.
10 I said I hadn't brought the newspaper, I'd brought uncle.

▶ Geeta's version of the morning

आम तौर पर राजू मुझे देर से जगाता है लेकिन आज उसने मुझे जल्दी ही जगाया । मैं आराम से सो रही थी और शाहरुख़ खाँ का सपना देख रही थी । इतना मीठा सपना था ! जब मैंने अपने पति की आवाज़ सुनी तो मैंने सोचा कि शाहरुख़ ही मुझे जगाने आया है । लेकिन यह तो सपना ही था । मैं नीचे रसोई में गई । मेरे पति

ने मेरे लिए दो टोस्ट बनाए थे । मैंने उसे कितनी बार बताया है कि मुझे टोस्ट पसंद नहीं लेकिन वह तो सुनता ही नहीं । चाय में उसने बहुत ज़्यादा चीनी डाली थी । मेरे सिर में दर्द था इसलिए मैंने दो गोलियाँ खाईं । राजू ने मुझे जगाने से पहले ही नाश्ता किया होगा क्योंकि मेरे साथ तो उसने कुछ नहीं खाया । मैंने उससे पूछा कि तुमने मुझे इतनी जल्दी क्यों जगाया, लेकिन उसने कोई जवाब नहीं दिया । शाहरुख़, तू कहाँ है ?

ām taur par Rājū mujhe der se jagātā hai lekin āj usne mujhe jaldī hī jagāyā. maĩ ārām se so rahī thī aur Śāhrukh Khā̃ kā sapnā dekh rahī thī. itnā mīṭhā sapnā thā! jab maĩne apne pati kī āvāz sunī to maĩne socā ki Śāhrukh hī mujhe jagāne āyā hai. lekin yah to sapnā hī thā. maĩ nīce rasoī mẽ gaī. mere pati ne mere lie do ṭosṭ banāe the. maĩne use kitnī bār batāyā hai ki mujhe ṭosṭ pasand nahī̃ lekin vah to suntā hī nahī̃. cāy mẽ usne bahut zyadā cīnī ḍālī thī. mere sir mẽ dard thā islie maĩne do goliyā̃ khāī̃. Rājū ne mujhe jagāne se pahle hī nāśtā kiyā hogā kyõki mere sāth to usne kuch nahī̃ khāyā. maĩne usse pūchā ki tumne mujhe itnī jaldī kyõ jagāyā, lekin usne koī javāb nahī̃ diyā. Śāhrukh, tū kahā̃ hai?

Usually Raju wakes me late but today he woke me very early. I was sleeping peacefully and dreaming about Shahrukh Khan [an actor]. It was such a sweet dream! When I heard my husband's voice I thought Shahrukh himself had come to wake me. But this was just a dream. I went down into the kitchen. My husband had made two pieces of toast for me. How many times have I told him that I don't like toast, but him, he doesn't listen. He'd put far too much sugar in the tea. I had a headache so I took two pills. Raju must have had breakfast before waking me because he didn't eat anything with me. I asked him why he woke me up so early but he didn't answer. Shahrukh, where art thou?

And here are some questions about the two accounts:

१ सबसे पहले कौन उठा ?
sabse pahle kaun uṭhā?

२ किसने किसके लिए नाश्ता तैयार किया ?
kisne kiske lie nāśtā taiyār kiyā?

३ गीता को जगाने से पहले राजू ने क्या क्या किया ?
Gītā ko jagāne se pahle Rājū ne kyā kyā kiyā?

४ चाय के बारे में गीता की क्या शिकायत थी ?
cāy ke bare mẽ Gītā kī kyā śikāyat thī?

५ गीता ने नाश्ता कहाँ किया ?
Gītā ne nāśtā kahā̃ kiyā?

६ किसने गोलियाँ खाईं, और क्यों ?
kisne goliyā̃ khāī̃, aur kyõ?

७ क्या राजू और गीता को जल्दी उठना पसंद है ?
kyā Rājū aur Gīta ko jaldī uṭhnā pasand hai?

८ जब गीता ने राजू की आवाज़ सुनी तो उसने क्या सोचा ?
jab Gītā ne Rājū kī āvāz sunī to usne kyā socā?

९ क्या शाहरुख़ ने गीता के साथ चाय पी ?
kyā Śāhrukh ne Gītā ke sāth cāy pī?

4 Sit and rest — linking two actions

English often links two successive actions with 'and', as in 'sit and rest'. But Hindi has a neat short cut for this. Instead of saying बैठो और आराम करो *baiṭho aur ārām karo* we can say बैठकर आराम करो *baiṭhkar ārām karo,* in which बैठकर *baiṭhkar* means literally 'having sat'.

This short verb form has a long name — the 'absolutive'. (The name means that the construction is complete in itself, and has no impact on the surrounding grammar.) It consists of the stem + कर *kar*; thus जाकर *jākar* 'having gone', देखकर *dekhkar* 'having seen', etc.

हाथ धोकर खाओ ।
hāth dhokar khāo. Wash your hands and eat.

बैठकर आराम करो ।
baiṭhkar ārām karo. Sit and rest.

सोचकर बोलो ।
sockar bolo. Think before you speak.

चाय पीकर जाइए ।
cāy pīkar jāie. Have some tea before you go.

A colloquial form of the absolutive has -के *-ke* instead of -कर *-kar* (आके *āke,* जाके *jāke,* देखके *dekhke,* बुलाके *bulāke*). The verb करना *karnā* always uses this -के *-ke* form: करके *karke* 'having done'.

हाथ धोके खाओ ।

hāth dhoke khāo. Wash your hands and eat.

अपना काम ख़त्म करके घर जाओ ।

apnā kām <u>kh</u>atm karke ghar jāo. Finish your work and go home.

What *really* happened that morning

Here's a third-person account of Raju and Geeta's morning. It contains several 'absolutive' expressions — how many can you spot?

आज उठकर राजू नीचे गया । फिर चाय बनाकर वह आँगन में बैठने गया । चाय पीकर वह अपने सपनों के बारे में सोचने लगा । सपने में उसने शाहरुख़ ख़ाँ को देखा था । दरवाज़े को तोड़कर शाहरुख़ घर में घुसा था, लेकिन राजू ने मेज़ पर से एक भारी शब्दकोश को उठाकर शाहरुख़ को ख़ूब पीटा था ।

सात बजे राजू ने गीता का नाम पुकारकर उसे जगाने की कोशिश की लेकिन गीता तो घोड़े बेचकर सो रही थी । तब राजू ने ख़ुद चार-पाँच टोस्ट बनाकर खाए । फिर तीन-चार संतरे खाए । आठ बजे उसने गीता के कंधे को हिलाकर उसे जगाया । फिर उसके लिए चाय बनाकर दो टोस्ट भी बनाए । जँभाई लेकर गीता ने कहा कि "संतरा देना" तो राजू ने हँसकर कहा कि "मनोज ने जल्दी उठके सारे संतरे खाए होंगे, उसे तो संतरे बहुत पसंद हैं" ।

āj uṭhkar Rājū nīce gayā. phir cāy banākar vah ā̃gan mẽ baiṭhne gayā. cāy pīkar vah apne sapnõ ke bāre mẽ socne lagā. sapne mẽ usne Śāhru<u>kh</u> <u>Kh</u>ā̃ ko dekhā thā. darvāze ko toṛkar Śāhru<u>kh</u> ghar mẽ ghusā thā, lekin Rājū ne mez par se ek bhārī śabdkoś ko uṭhākar Śāhru<u>kh</u> ko <u>kh</u>ūb pīṭā thā.

sāt baje Rājū ne Gītā kā nām pukārkar use jagāne kī kośiś kī lekin Gītā to ghoṛe beckar so rahī thī. tab Rājū ne <u>kh</u>ud cār-pā̃c ṭosṭ banākar khāe. phir tīn-cār santare khāe. āṭh baje usne Gītā ke kandhe ko hilākar use jagāyā. phir uske lie cāy banākar do ṭosṭ bhī banāe. jā̃bhāī lekar Gītā ne kahā ki 'santarā denā' to Rājū ne hā̃skar kahā ki 'Manoj ne jaldī uṭhke sāre santare khāe hõge, use to santare bahut pasand haĩ!'

Today Raju got up and went downstairs. Then he made tea and went to sit in the courtyard. After drinking his tea he began to think about his dreams. He had dreamed of Shahrukh Khan. Shahrukh had broken down the door and come into the room, but Raju had picked up a heavy dictionary from on the table and had given Shahrukh a good thrashing.

At seven o'clock Raju called out Gita's name and tried to wake her, but she was sleeping deeply. Raju himself made four or five pieces of toast and ate them. Then he ate three or four oranges. At eight o'clock he shook Geeta's shoulder and woke her. Then he made tea for her, and two pieces of toast as well. Geeta yawned and said 'Give me an orange', and Raju laughed and said, 'Manoj must have got up early and eaten all the oranges, he loves oranges!'

Exercise 10a Link the paired sentences about Raju and Javed, following the model shown. Remember that whether ने *ne* is used will depend on the main verb: in the model sentence, ने *ne* is used when the main verb is पीना *pīnā*, but not when it's जाना *jānā*.

मैंने चाय पी । मैं घर गया । > मैं चाय पीकर घर गया ।
maĩne cāy pī. maĩ ghar gayā. > maĩ cāy pīkar ghar gayā.

१ जावेद ने मुझे फ़ोन किया । उसने कहा कि तबियत ख़राब है ।
Jāved ne mujhe fon kiyā. usne kahā ki tabiyat <u>kh</u>arāb hai.

२ मैं जावेद के घर गया । मैं उसके कमरे में गया ।
maĩ Jāved ke ghar gayā. maĩ uske kamre mẽ gayā.

३ मैंने जावेद का हाल देखा । मैंने डाक्टर को बुलाया ।
maĩne Jāved kā hāl dekhā. maĩne ḍākṭar ko bulāyā.

४ थोड़ी देर में डाक्टर आए । उन्होंने कहा कि जावेद बहुत ही कमज़ोर है ।
thoṛī der mẽ ḍākṭar āe. unhõne kahā ki Jāved bahut hī kamzor hai.

५ डाक्टर ने जावेद को कुछ गोलियाँ दीं । उन्होंने उससे कहा कि रोज़ दो गोलियाँ लेना ।
ḍākṭar ne Jāved ko kuch goliyā̃ dī̃. unhõne usse kahā ki roz do goliyā̃ lenā.

६ जावेद मुस्कराया । उसने डाक्टर से धन्यवाद कहा ।
Jāved muskarāyā. usne ḍākṭar se dhanyavād kahā.

७ डाक्टर ने मेरी तरफ़ देखा। उन्होंने कहा कि "अच्छा, तो मैं चलता हूँ"।

ḍākṭar ne merī taraf dekhā. unhõne kahā ki 'acchā, to maĩ caltā hū̃'.

८ मैं ने कहा कि चाय पीजिए। फिर जाइए।

maĩne kahā ki cāy pījie. phir jāie.

९ डाक्टर हँसे। उन्होंने कहा कि मैं चाय नहीं लूँगा, अपनी फ़ीस लूँगा!

ḍākṭar hãse. unhõne kahā ki maĩ cāy nahī̃ lū̃gā, apnī fīs lū̃gā!

Exercise 10b Translate into Hindi. (This is a longish piece; you may want to do it in two parts. You'll find the new vocabulary in the glossary on the following pages.)

Yesterday morning I got up at six o'clock. After having breakfast I phoned my brother. He was sleeping. When he heard my voice he said, 'Why did you wake me up so early?' I said, 'Don't you remember? Today we are going to Jaipur [जयपुर *jaypur*]!' He asked, 'What time are we going?' I answered, 'We'll catch the ten o'clock train. Get ready quickly!' He yawned and said that he'd had a dream in the night. In the dream an old woman had said to him, 'Don't go anywhere today! Stay right at home!' I laughed and said, 'This was just a dream! Get up, won't you! Get ready.'

The train moved out of the station at exactly ten o'clock. But after twenty or twenty-five minutes it stopped. The engine had broken down. It was a desolate place; there was no village or house nearby. In the July heat everyone got down from the train and waited for several hours in the shade of some small trees. The heat was terrible. At three o'clock another train came and stopped. This second train had come to bring the passengers back to Delhi.

We heard the story of the train on the radio. We'd taken that old woman's advice! We'll go to Jaipur tomorrow…

Glossary

अकेलापन *akelāpan* m. loneliness
आकाश *ākāś* m. sky
आम [1] *ām* m. mango
आम [2] *ām* ordinary; आम तौर पर *ām taur par* usually
आराम से *ārām se* comfortably, easily
इंजन *injan* m. engine (train)
इंतज़ार *intazār* m. waiting, *expecting*; का इंतज़ार करना *kā intazār karnā* to wait for
इतना *itnā* so much, so
उठाना *uṭhānā* to pick up, raise
कंधा *kandhā* m. shoulder
कमज़ोर *kamzor* weak
कहीं *kahī̃* anywhere
कुरता *kurtā* m. kurta, loose shirt
केला *kelā* m. banana
ख़त्म *khatm* finished; ख़त्म करना *khatm karnā* to finish
ख़राब हो जाना *kharāb ho jānā* to break down
ख़ुद *khud* oneself (myself etc.)
गाँव *gā̃v* m. village
गोली *golī* f. tablet, pill; bullet
घुसना *ghusnā* to enter, sneak in, break in
घोड़ा *ghoṛā* m. horse; घोड़े बेचकर सोना *ghoṛe beckar sonā* to sleep like a log
चपाती *capātī* f. chapati
चारों ओर *cārõ or* all around
चिट्ठी *ciṭṭhī* f. letter, note
चीनी *cīnī* f. sugar
जँभाई *jā̃bhāī* f. yawn
जगाना *jagānā* to awaken
जल्दी *jaldī* quickly, early; f. hurry
जीतना *jītnā* to win, conquer
टोस्ट *ṭosṭ* m. toast, piece of toast
ठीख *ṭhīk* exactly
डालना *ḍālnā* to put, pour
तकलीफ़ *taklīf* f. suffering, pain, discomfort, inconvenience, trouble
तब *tab* then
तैयार *taiyār* ready, prepared; तैयार हो जाना *taiyār ho jānā* to get ready
तोड़ना *toṛnā* to break, smash
दर्द *dard* m. pain
दाल *dāl* f. daal, lentil
दीवार *dīvār,* दीवाल *dīvāl* f. wall
दुर्घटना *durghaṭnā* f. accident
देर *der* f. a while, length of time; delay; देर से *der se* late
नहाना *nahānā* to bathe
पकड़ना *pakaṛnā* to catch
पार्टी *pārṭī* f. party
पीटना *pīṭnā* to beat, thrash
पुकारना *pukārnā* to call out
पेट *peṭ* m. stomach
प्यास *pyās* f. thirst; प्यास लगना *pyās lagnā* (thirst to strike) to feel thirsty
फ़ीस *fīs* f. fee, fees
बढ़िया *baṛhiyā* (invariable -*ā*) excellent, really good, fine
बत्ती *battī* f. light, lamp
बस *bas* f. bus

बाज़ार *bāzār* m. market, bazaar
बार *bār* f. time, occasion; इस बार *is bār* this time; कितनी बार *kitnī bār* how many times?; कई बार *kaī bār* several times
बारिश *bāriś* f. rain; बारिश होना *bāriś honā* to rain
बुलाना *bulānā* to call, invite, summon
बोतल *botal* f. bottle
भयंकर *bhayankar* terrible
भूख *bhūkh* f. hunger; भूख लगना *bhukh lagnā* (hunger to strike) to feel hungry
महसूस करना *mahsūs karnā* to feel
मिठाई *miṭhāī* f. sweet, sweetmeat
मिठास *miṭhās* f. sweetness
मीठा *mīṭhā* sweet
मेमसाहब *memsāhab* f. memsahib
यात्री *yātrī* m. traveller, passenger
रसोई *rasoī* f. kitchen
लौटना *lauṭnā* to return
शांति *śānti* f. peace
शिकायत *śikāyat* f. complaint; शिकायत करना *śikāyat karnā* to complain
संतरा *santarā* m. orange
सलाह *salāh* f. advice
साया *sāyā* m. shade, shadow
सिर *sir* m. head
सुनसान *sunsān* desolate, empty
हिलाना *hilānā* to move, shake
हुआ *huā* [past tense of होना *honā*] 'happened'

11

कहा जाता है कि …

kahā jātā hai ki …

it is said that…

In this unit you will learn

- how to say 'should' and 'must'
- how to describe things *being done*
- how to give directions

Language points

- obligation expressions
- passive verbs

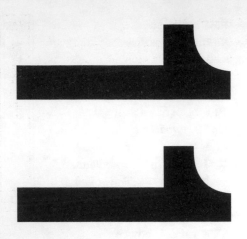

1 A verb with many meanings

The verb लगना *lagnā* (literally 'to strike') carries a variety of meanings. Many of these relate to the experiencing of sensations such as heat or cold, hunger or thirst, which 'strike' or impinge on the person; but the range of usages is very wide. Here are some of them:

'To seem':

लगता है कि वह नहीं आएगी ।

lagtā hai ki vah nahī̃ āegī. It seems she won't come.

तुम बहुत ख़ुश नहीं लगते ।

tum bahut <u>kh</u>uś nahī̃ lagte. You don't seem too happy.

'Thirst/hunger/cold (etc.) to strike':

हमें गरमी/ठंड लग रही है ।

hamẽ garmī/ṭhaṇḍ lag rahī hai. We're feeling hot/cold.

मुझे प्यास/भूख लगी है ।

mujhe pyās/bhūkh lagī hai. I'm feeling thirsty/hungry.

'To strike one as good/bad etc.':

यह जगह मुझे बहुत अच्छी लगती है ।

yah jagah mujhe bahut acchī lagtī hai. I really like this place.

उनकी बातें हमें बुरी लगीं ।

unkī bātẽ hamẽ burī lagī̃. We were hurt by what they said.

'To begin' (here it follows an oblique infinitive such as होने *hone*):

बारिश होने लगी ।

bāriś hone lagī. It began raining.

मैं सोचने लगा कि अब तो वह नहीं आएगी ।

maĩ socne lagī ki ab to vah nahī̃ āegī. I began to think that she wouldn't come now.

'Time to be taken' (already seen in Unit 9; here the *unit of time* is the subject):

सितार सीखने में सात साल लगेंगे ।

sitār sīkhne mẽ sāt sāl lagẽge. Learning the sitar will take seven years.

2 Finding the way in Vilaspur

In this section we'll look at expressions that are useful for finding your way. Your first task is to familiarize yourself with the new words relating to 'directions' in the chapter glossary.

Then come with the Sharmas to the town of Vilaspur, shown in the map opposite; they're are going to stay at the Madhuban Hotel and have been given some directions for getting there from the station:

स्टेशन से निकलकर दाहिने मुड़िए । थोड़ी दूरी पर बायें हाथ पर एक तंग गली आएगी । इस गली में मुड़ना । आगे चलकर एक चौड़ी सड़क आएगी जिसे "चंद्रशेखर आज़ाद रोड" कहते हैं । बाएँ मुड़कर और सड़क को पार करके आप चलते जाएँ । दाहिने हाथ पर स्कूल दिखाई देगा । इसके बाद आप दाहिने मुड़िए । इस सड़क का नाम मुझे याद नहीं लेकिन बायें हाथ पर सिनेमा दिखाई देगा । फिर थोड़ी दूर जाकर एक दूसरी बड़ी सड़क आएगी जिसे शायद "नई सड़क" कहते हैं । बाएँ मुड़िए । फिर गोलचक्कर आएगा । गोलचक्कर के उस पार आपका मधुबन होटल दिखाई देगा ।

स्टेशन से मधुबन होटल ज़्यादा दूर नहीं है । मुश्किल से आठ-दस मिनट का रास्ता है । अगर आपके पास बहुत सामान हो तो बेहतर है कि आप रिक्शा लें । रिक्शेवाले से कहें कि होटल "एम० जी० रोड" पर है । वह बीस-पच्चीस रुपये लेगा । आप उसे पच्चीस से ज़्यादा न दें ।

sṭeśan se nikalkar dāhine muṛie. thoṛī dūrī par bāyẽ hāth par ek taṅg galī āegī. is galī mẽ muṛnā. āge calkar ek cauṛī saṛak āegī jise 'Candraśekhar Āzād roḍ' kahte haĩ. bāyẽ muṛkar aur saṛak ko pār karke āp calte jāẽ. dāhine hāth par skūl dikhāī degā. iske bād āp dāhine muṛie. is saṛak kā nām mujhe yād nahī̃ lekin bāyẽ hāth par sinemā dikhāī degā. phir thoṛī dūr jākar ek dūsrī baṛī saṛak āegī jise śāyad 'naī saṛak' kahte haĩ. bāyẽ muṛie. phir golcakkar āegā. golcakkar ke us pār āpkā madhuban hoṭal dikhāī degā.

sṭeśan se madhuban hoṭal zyādā dūr nahī̃ hai. muśkil se āṭh-das minaṭ kā rāstā hai. agar āpke pās bahut sāmān ho to behtar hai ki āp rikśā lẽ. rikśevāle se kahẽ ki hoṭal 'em. jī. roḍ' par hai. vah bīs-paccīs rupaye legā. āp use paccīs se zyādā na dẽ.

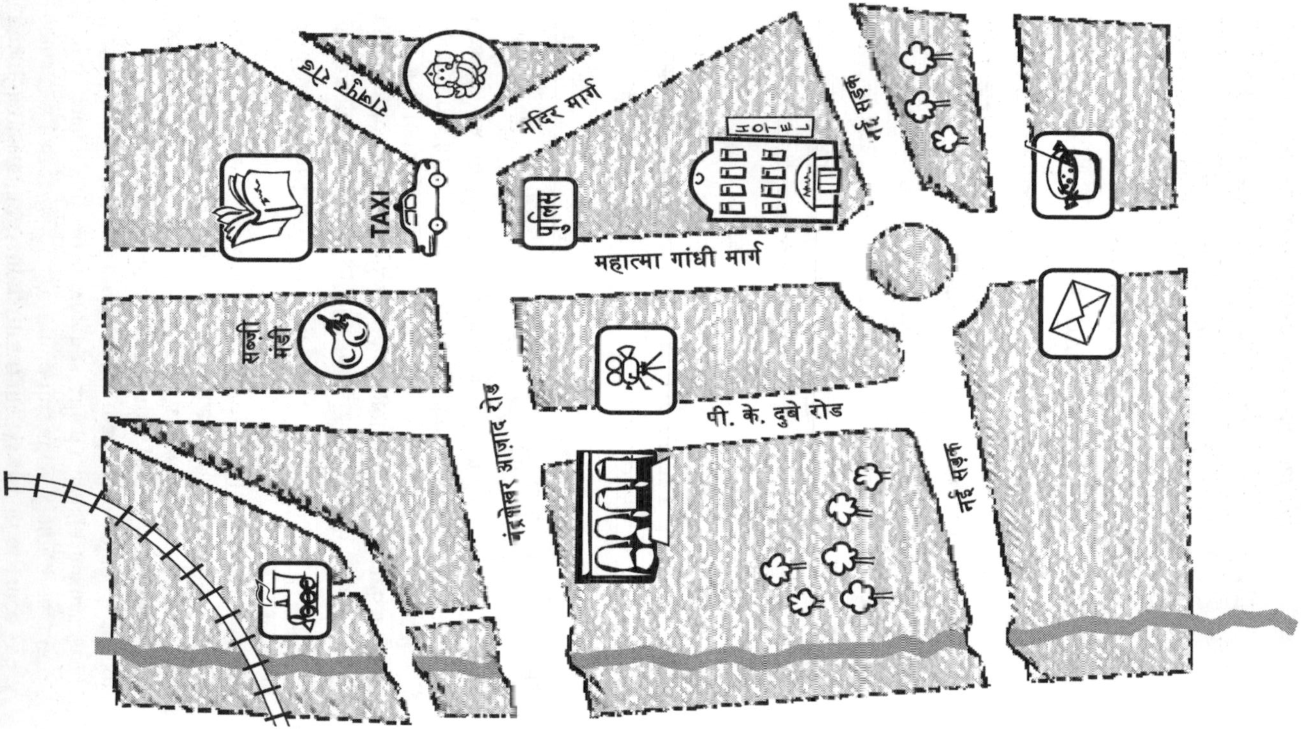
राजपुर रोड
मंदिर मार्ग
TAXI
पुलिस
HOTEL
नई सड़क
सब्ज़ी
मंडी
महात्मा गांधी मार्ग
चंद्रशेखर आज़ाद रोड
पी. के. दुबे रोड
नई सड़क

Emerging from the station, turn right. At a short distance you'll come to a narrow alley. Turn into this alley. Going straight on you'll reach a wide road which is called Chandrashekhar Azad Road. Turning left and crossing the road, keep going. A school will be seen on the right. After this turn right. I don't remember the name of this road but you'll see a cinema on your left. Then a little further on you'll come to another big road which is called maybe 'Nai Sarak' [New Road]. Turn left. Then you'll come to a roundabout. On the other side of the roundabout you'll see your Madhuban Hotel.

The Madhuban Hotel isn't far from the station. It's barely an eight- or ten-minute trip. If you've got a lot of luggage it would be better to take a rickshaw. Tell the rickshaw driver that the hotel is on 'M.G. Road'. The rickshaw driver will take 20 or 25 rupees. You shouldn't give him more than 25.

Play around with the map, describing journeys from place to place. Then...

True or false?

Are these statements right (सही *sahī*) or wrong (ग़लत *galat*)? Answers below.

		सही *sahī*	ग़लत *galat*
१	मधुबन होटल के सामने एक स्कूल है । *madhuban hoṭal ke sāmne ek skūl hai.*	☐	☐
२	सिनेमा थाने की बग़ल में है । *sinemā thāne kī bagal mẽ hai.*	☐	☐
३	विलासपुर में तीन छोटे-से पुल हैं । *vilāspur mẽ tīn choṭe-se pul haĩ.*	☐	☐
४	डाकघर के सामने एक ढाबा है । *ḍākghar ke sāmne ek ḍhābā hai.*	☐	☐
५	सिनेमा गोल-चक्कर के बहुत पास है । *sinemā golcakkar ke bahut pās hai.*	☐	☐
६	नई सड़क को "एम. जी. रोड" भी कहते हैं । *naī saṛak ko 'em. jī. roḍ' bhī kahte haĩ.*	☐	☐

७ इस नक़्शे में कुछ पेड़ दिखाई देते हैं । ☐ ☐
is naqśe mẽ kuch peṛ dikhāī dete haĩ.

८ गणेश मंदिर पश्चिम की तरफ़ है । ☐ ☐
Gaṇeś mandir paścim kī taraf hai.

९ स्टेशन से पुस्तकालय तक एक घंटे का रास्ता है । ☐ ☐
sṭeśan se pustakālay tak ek ghaṇṭe kā rāstā hai.

१० स्टेशन से गणेश मंदिर पहुँचने में छह-सात मिनट से ज़्यादा नहीं लगेंगे । ☐ ☐
sṭeśan se Gaṇeś mandir pahũcne mẽ chah-sāt minaṭ se zyādā nahī̃ lagẽge.

Answers: 2, 3, 4, 5, 7 and 10 are right.

3 It is said that... the passive is easy

A passive verb is one that concentrates on *what is done*, rather than the person who does it. In other words, its focus is the action, not the doer of the action. Thus 'we give money' is active, and 'money is given' is passive. 'Money is given by the government' is also passive, but it identifies the doer of the action with a 'by' phrase.

The passive is based on the perfective participle (e.g. दिया *diyā* 'given'). But whereas English forms its passive with 'to be', Hindi uses जाना *jānā* — literally 'to go':

करना	*karnā*	*to do*	किया जाना	*kiyā jānā*	to be done
देना	*denā*	to give	दिया जाना	*diyā jānā*	to be given
रखना	*rakhnā*	*to put*	रखा जाना	*rakhā jānā*	to be put

होटल का इंतज़ाम किया जा रहा है ।
hoṭal kā intazām kiyā jā rahā hai. Arrangements for a hotel are being made.

आपको एक अच्छा कमरा दिया जाएगा ।
āpko ek acchā kamrā diyā jāegā. You will be given a good room.

आपका सामान टैक्सी में रखा गया है ।
āpkā sāmān ṭaiksī mẽ rakhā gayā hai. Your luggage has been put into the taxi.

India: states and languages

This map of northern India shows the ten states (shaded) where Hindi is the primary language.

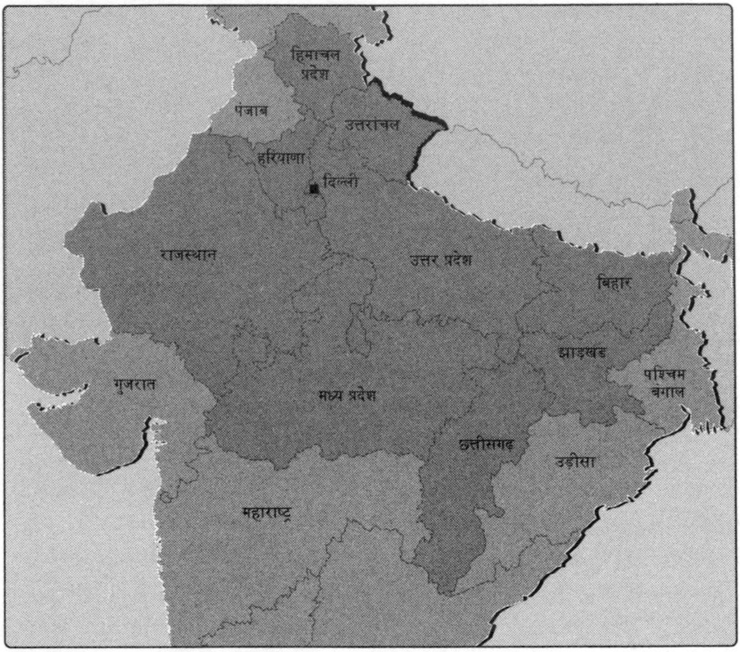

Hindi is closely related to its neighbouring languages, such as Marathi (spoken in Maharashtra), Gujarati (Gujarat), Punjabi (Punjab), Bengali (West Bengal and Bangladesh), and so on. All these languages derive from Sanskrit, and share much vocabulary.

In South India — not shown here — are the four major languages of the 'Dravidian' family: Tamil (spoken in Tamil Nadu), Malayalam (Kerala), Kannada (Karnataka) and Telugu (Andhra Pradesh).

Now you have all the information you need to answer a few questions that involve passive verbs:

१ तमिल कहाँ बोली जाती है?
tamil kahā̃ bolī jātī hai?

२ मराठी कहाँ बोली जाती है?
marāṭhī kahā̃ bolī jātī hai?

३ केरल में कौनसी भाषा बोली जाती है?
keral mẽ kaunsī bhāṣā bolī jātī hai?

४ हिन्दी कितने प्रदेशों में बोली जाती है?
hindī kitne pradeśõ mẽ bolī jātī hai?

५ दिल्ली और बिहार के बीच कौनसा प्रदेश पाया जाता है?
dillī aur bihār ke bīc kaunsā pradeś pāyā jātā hai?

Practise what you've learnt

Work out the passive infinitives of the following verbs (example: बनाना *banānā* to make, बनाया जाना *banāyā jānā* to be made).

खाना *khānā* to eat	डालना *ḍālnā* to pour
पीना *pīnā* to drink	बताना *batānā* to tell
लाना *lānā* to bring	लेना *lenā* to take
लिखना *likhnā* to write	कहना *kahnā* to say

(Answers: खाया जाना *khāyā jānā*, डाला जाना *ḍālā jānā*, पिया जाना *piyā jānā*, बताया जाना *batāyā jānā*, लाया जाना *lāyā jānā*, लिया जाना *liyā jānā*, लिखा जाना *likhā jānā*, कहा जाना *kahā jānā*.)

Now make up a sentence using each of these passive verbs!

Agreement all round

Notice how *all* parts of the verb (the participle, e.g. दिया *diyā*, the form of जाना *jānā*, and the auxiliary होना *honā*) must agree with the subject. The subject is shown here in **bold**:

उनको **पैसा** दिया जाता है ।
unko ***paisā*** *diyā jātā hai.* Money is given to them.

उनको अच्छी **सलाह** दी जाती है ।
unko acchī ***salāh*** *dī jātī hai.* Good advice is given to them.

उनको **कपड़े** दिए जाते हैं ।
unko ***kapṛe*** *die jāte haĩ.* Clothes are given to them.

Any tense can have a passive verb

The passive can be used with all tenses etc.:

उनको पैसा दिया जाता है । [Present imperfective]
unko paisā diyā jātā hai. Money is given to them.

उनको पैसा दिया जा रहा है । [Present continuous]
unko paisā diyā jā rahā hai. Money is being given to them.

उनको पैसा दिया गया ।   [Perfective]
unko paisā diyā gayā. Money was given to them.

उनको पैसा दिया जाएगा ।   [Future]
unko paisā diyā jāegā. Money will be given to them.

उनको पैसा दिया जाए ।   [Subjunctive]
unko paisā diyā jāe. Money should be given to them.

The person *by whom* an action is done can be identified with से *se* (or, in more formal Hindi, with के द्वारा *ke dvārā*):

पैसा सरकार से (सरकार के द्वारा) दिया जाता है ।
paisā sarkār se (sarkār ke dvārā) diyā jātā hai. Money is given by the government.

What's the passive *for*?

We use a passive verb when the main focus is on the *action done* rather than the *person doing it.* In saying 'this money was found under the chair', we're more concerned with the *act of finding* than with the person who found it; if it had been the other way round, we would have said 'So-and-so found this money under the chair'. In other words, passives offer a way of making 'impersonal statements': instead of saying 'we use the passive' at the beginning of this paragraph, I could have adopted a more impersonal tone by saying 'the passive is used...'. The passive is used a lot in Hindi.

Sharma ji in his shop

Read the passage about Sharma ji in his shop, then answer the questions.

शर्मा जी अपनी दुकान में बैठकर सोच रहे थे । उन्होंने गोपाल को बुलाकर कहा, "बेटा, यह सारा सामान छोटे कमरे में रखो । फिर दुकान की सफ़ाई करो । मैं बहुत थका हूँ, थोड़ी देर के लिए घर जाकर सोऊँगा । आठ बजे दुकान को बंद करना । फिर बीस रुपये लो और धोबी के पास जाकर मेरे साफ़ कपड़े लाओ ।" पर गोपाल से कुछ नहीं सुना गया क्योंकि वह रेडियो को सुन रहा था ।

Śarmā jī apnī dukān mẽ baiṭhkar soc rahe the. unhõne Gopāl ko bulākar kahā, 'beṭā, yah sārā sāmān choṭe kamre mẽ rakho. phir dukān kī safāī karo. maĩ bahut thakā hū̃, thoṛī der ke lie ghar jākar soū̃gā. āṭh baje dukān ko band karnā. phir bīs rupaye lo aur dhobī ke pās jākar mere sāf kapṛe lāo.' par Gopāl se kuch nahī̃ sunā gayā kyõki vah reḍiyo ko sun rahā thā.

Sharma ji was sitting in his shop thinking. He called Gopal and said, 'Son, put this new stuff in the little room. Then clean the shop. I'm very tired, I'll go home and sleep for a little while. Close the shop at eight o'clock. Then take twenty rupees and go to the dhobi and bring my clean clothes.' But none of this was heard by Gopal because he was listening to the radio.

१ गोपाल को किससे बुलाया गया ?
Gopāl ko kisse ['by whom'] *bulāyā gayā?*

२ सामान कहाँ रखा जाएगा ?
sāmān kahā̃ rakhā jāegā?

३ कमरे की सफ़ाई किससे की जाएगी ?
kamre kī safāī kisse kī jāegī?

४ दुकान को कितने बजे बंद किया जाएगा ?
dukān ko kitne baje band kiyā jāega?

५ शर्मा जी के साफ़ कपड़े कहाँ से लाए जाएँगे ?
Śarmā jī ke sāf kapṛe kahā̃ se lāe jāẽge?

६ गोपाल से शर्मा जी की बातें क्यों नहीं सुनी गईं ?
Gopāl se Śarmā jī kī bātẽ kyõ nahī̃ sunī gaī̃?

Did you know?

Why is it that some Hindi words resemble their English equivalents so closely? There are various reasons: words can be 'borrowed' by one language from another one, or similar words from two different languages may share a common origin. A few examples may help make this clearer. Some words (such as बूट *būṭ* 'boot') have been borrowed by Hindi from English; others (such as 'loot' लूट *lūṭ*) have been borrowed by English from Hindi; others again, such as नाम *nām* 'name', or कटना *kaṭnā* 'to be cut', sound similar in the two languages because they have a shared ancestry going far back into the history of the Indo-European language family.

4 You should read this — obligations

Way back in Unit 5 we saw that चाहिए *cāhie*, used with को *ko*, meant 'wanted, needed'. This construction relates to things, objects — 'I want a newspaper', and so on:

आपको क्या चाहिए ?

āpko kyā cāhie? What do you need/want?

मुझे (मुझको) आज का अख़बार चाहिए ।

mujhe (mujhko) āj kā akhbār cāhie. I want today's newspaper.

When चाहिए *cāhie* follows an infinitive verb (such as जाना *jānā* 'to go') it has a completely different meaning: it means 'should, ought to'. Though the meaning of चाहिए *cāhie* has changed here, the word को *ko* remains an essential part of the construction

मुझको घर जाना चाहिए ।

mujhko ghar jānā cāhie. I should go home.

आपको ध्यान से सुनना चाहिए ।

āpko dhyān se sunnā cāhie. You should listen carefully.

उनको समझना चाहिए ।

unko samajhnā cāhie. They should understand.

हमको चलना चाहिए ।

hamko calnā cāhie. We should be on our way.

तुमको यहाँ रहना चाहिए ।

tumko yahā̃ rahnā cāhie. You should stay here.

If there's a direct object involved, the infinitive verb agrees with it. In the next two sentences, the verbs बोलना *bolnā* 'to speak' and सीखना *sīkhnā* 'to learn' have to agree with its feminine object, उर्दू *urdū* —

तुमको उर्दू बोलनी चाहिए ।

tumko urdū bolnī cāhie. You should speak Urdu.

हमको थोड़ी उर्दू सीखनी चाहिए ।

hamko thoṛī urdū sīkhnī cāhie. We should learn a little Urdu.

You'll notice similar agreements in the following:

उन्हें मेरी बात सुननी चाहिए ।

unhẽ merī bāt sunnī cāhie. They should listen to what I say.

ड्राइवर को नक़्शा ख़रीदना चाहिए ।

ḍrāivar ko naqśā <u>kh</u>arīdnā cāhie. The driver should buy a map.

राजू को ये ख़त पढ़ने चाहिए ।

Rājū ko ye <u>kh</u>at paṛhne cāhie. Raju should read these letters.

आपको उनकी सलाह लेनी चाहिए ।

āpko unkī salāh lenī cāhie. You should take their advice.

Before going further, read the last four sentences again and make sure you understand what the infinitive verbs (सुननी *sunnī*, ख़रीदना *<u>kh</u>arīdnā*, पढ़ने *paṛhne* and लेनी *lenī* respectively) agree with.

When we were doing the ने *ne* construction in Unit 10, we saw that the postposition को *ko* 'insulates' the verb, preventing agreement — हमने चिट्ठियाँ पढ़ीं *hamne ciṭṭhiyā̃ paṛhī̃*, but हमने चिट्ठियों को पढ़ा *hamne ciṭṭhiyõ ko paṛhā*, both meaning 'we read the letters'). Similarly with obligation expressions, the verb reverts to masculine singular when the direct object takes को *ko*. Confused? Look at the examples:

हमें चिट्ठियाँ पढ़नी चाहिए ।

hamẽ ciṭṭhiyā̃ paṛhnī cāhie. We should read the letters.

becomes…

हमें चिट्ठियों को पढ़ना चाहिए ।

hamẽ ciṭṭhiyõ ko paṛhnā cāhie. We should read the letters.

उन्हें मेरी बात सुननी चाहिए ।

unhẽ merī bāt sunnī cāhie. They should listen to what I say.

becomes…

उन्हें मेरी बात को सुनना चाहिए ।

unhẽ merī bāt ko sunnā cāhie. They should listen to what I say.

Finally, using चाहिए *cāhie* in the past is simplicity itself. Just add था, थे, थी, थीं *thā, the, thī, thī̃.*

हमको ये चिट्ठियाँ पढ़नी चाहिए थीं ।

hamko ciṭṭhiyā̃ paṛhnī cāhie thī̃. We should have read these letters.

उन्हें मेरी बात सुननी चाहिए थी ।

unhẽ merī bāt sunnī cāhie thī. They should have listened to what I said.

Your help is needed

The Sharmas need your advice on various matters. Please respond:

१ गीता बहुत थकी है। उसको क्या करना चाहिए ?
Gītā bahut thakī hai. usko kyā karnā cāhie?

२ मनोज के सिर में दर्द है। उसे क्या करना चाहिए ?
Manoj ke sir mẽ dard hai. use kyā karnā cāhie?

३ राजू ने देखा है कि फ़र्श गंदी है। उसको क्या करना चाहिए ?
Rājū ne dekhā hai ki farś gandī hai. usko kyā karnā cāhie?

४ मीना को भूख लगी है। उसको क्या करना चाहिए ?
Mīnā ko bhūkh lagī hai. usko kyā karnā cāhie?

५ शर्मा परिवार का घर बहुत छोटा है। उन लोगों को क्या करना चाहिए ?
Śarmā parivār kā ghar bahut choṭā hai. un logõ ko kyā karnā cāhie?

5 You *must* read this — stronger obligations

When 'I should' gives way to 'I have to' or 'I must', चाहिए *cāhie* gives way to stronger expressions. The first of these involves using the infinitive verb with है *hai*, as in मुझे जाना है *mujhe jānā hai* 'I have to go' or 'I am to go'.

Let us imagine that Raju's agenda for the day includes writing some letters, talking to Javed, and meeting his brother Mohan. He'd say:

मुझे पाँच ख़त लिखने हैं।
mujhe pā̃c khat likhne haĩ. I have to write five letters.

मुझे जावेद से कुछ बातें कहनी हैं।
mujhe Jāved se kuch bātẽ kahnī haĩ. I have to say some things to Javed.

मुझे मोहन से मिलना है।
mujhe Mohan se milnā hai. I have to meet Mohan.

The sense of compulsion here isn't very strong: these are just ordinary things that are to be done in the normal course of events. The verb agreement follows the pattern of the चाहिए *cāhie* usage: लिखने हैं *likhne haĩ* agrees with पाँच ख़त *pā̃c khat*, etc.

What's on today

The Sharma children have several things to do today. Taking as your model the sentence मनोज को जल्दी उठना है *Manoj ko jaldī uṭhnā hai* 'Manoj has to get up early', go through their lists.

MANOJ	MEENA	RAM
get up early	make breakfast	read a story
read the paper	do some studying	write a letter
go to the shops	write two letters	make a picture
phone Nani ji	rest	sleep at 9 o'clock

A stronger sense of compulsion involves the verb पड़ना *paṛnā*, literally meaning 'to fall' but here meaning 'to be compelled to' , 'to really *have to*'. It's used when circumstances beyond your control make the action essential — as when the children have broken their father's radio...

हमें पिताजी को बताना पड़ेगा ।

hamẽ pitājī ko batānā paṛegā. We'll have to tell father.

हमें नया रेडियो ख़रीदना पड़ेगा ।

hamẽ nayā reḍiyo kharīdnā paṛegā. We'll have to buy a new radio.

पिताजी को हमें पैसे देने पड़ेंगे ।

pitājī ko hamẽ paise dene paṛẽge. Father will have to give us the money.

In the imperfective (पड़ता है *paṛtā hai*, or पड़ता था *paṛtā thā*), this same construction implies a compulsion that occurs *regularly* —

हमें रोज़ काम करना पड़ता है ।

hamẽ roz kām karnā paṛtā hai. We have to work every day.

मुझे सात बजे उठना पड़ता था ।

mujhe sāt baje uṭhnā paṛtā thā. I [always] had to get up at seven.

क्या तुम्हें अपने कपड़े ख़ुद धोने पड़ते हैं ?

kyā tumhẽ apne kapṛe khud dhone paṛte haĩ? Do you have to wash your own clothes?

In the perfective (पड़ा *paṛā*), this same construction implies an *unexpected* compulsion, such as some kind of unforeseen event or emergency, as on discovering that Meena's car was stolen — complete with the children's toys! Keep an eye on the agreements: watch पड़ा *paṛā* changing to पड़ी *paṛī* or पड़े *paṛe* to match the object.

मुझे पुलिस को फ़ोन करना पड़ा ।
mujhe pulis ko fon karnā paṛā. I had to phone the police.

घर जाने के लिए हमें टैक्सी लेनी पड़ी ।
ghar jāne ke lie hamẽ ṭaiksī lenī paṛī. We had to take a taxi to get home.

मुझे बच्चों के लिए नए खिलौने ख़रीदने पड़े ।
mujhe baccõ ke lie nae khilaune kharīdne paṛe. I had to buy new toys for the children.

Exercise 11a Someone's having a party on Sunday. Translate:

1 About thirty people will be invited.
2 The house will be cleaned on Saturday.
3 The food will be made on Sunday morning.
4 In the afternoon some relatives will be fetched from the station.
5 Presents will be given to the children.
6 Lamps will be lit in the garden at night.
7 Music will be played too.
8 The neighbours will also be invited.

Exercise 11b Things haven't gone too well at the Madhuban Hotel, and you need to get the following points across to the long-suffering receptionist. Use passive verbs for the parts in bold print.

9 Today's food wasn't fresh — it seems it was **made** yesterday.
10 Your friends came to visit you last night, but you were not **told** that they had come.
11 Someone's dirty clothes were **put** in your room.
12 This evening you saw that the door of your room hadn't been **closed** properly...
13 .....and your luggage had been **opened**.
14 You were not **given** hot water for bathing.
15 You gave clothes for washing two days ago but they have not been **given back**.

16 Your driver was **told** that he would [say 'will'] have to sleep in the car.

Exercise 11c Enjoy (and translate) the receptionist's thoughts.

ये लोग मुझे क्यों तंग करते हैं ? वे हर रोज़ किसी चीज़ की शिकायत करते हैं । लगता है उनको शिकायत करना बहुत पसंद है । मालूम नहीं वे किस देश से आए हैं । मेरे ख़याल से हमारे देश में आकर लोगों को हर चीज़ की शिकायत नहीं करनी चाहिए । उनको इस देश का आदर करना चाहिए । सच है कि उनके सामान को खोला नहीं जाना चाहिए था, लेकिन सारी दूसरी बातें तो मामूली-सी थीं । मुझे मैनेजर ['manager'] को इसके बारे में बताना चाहिए पर मैं उन्हें बताना नहीं चाहता । नहीं बताऊँगा । ये लोग भाड़ में जाएँ !

ye log mujhe kyõ tang karte haĩ? ve har roz kisī cīz kī śikāyat karte haĩ. lagtā hai unko śikāyat karnā bahut pasand hai. mālūm nahī̃ ve kis deś se āe haĩ. mere khyāl se hamāre deś mẽ ākar logõ ko har cīz kī śikāyat nahī̃ karnī cāhie. unko is deś kā ādar karnā cāhie. sac hai ki unke sāmān ko kholā nahī̃ jānā cāhie thā, lekin sārī dūsrī bātẽ to māmūlī-sī thī̃. mujhe mainejar ko iske bāre mẽ batānā cāhie par maĩ unhẽ batānā nahī̃ cāhtā. nahī̃ batāū̃gā. ye log bhāṛ mẽ jāẽ!

Glossary

आगे *āge* ahead
आदर *ādar* m. respect
इमारत *imārat* f. building
उत्तर *uttar* north
उर्दू *urdū* f. Urdu
कहानी *kahānī* f. story
के द्वारा *ke dvārā* by (in formal passive sentences)
ख़याल *khyāl*, m. opinion, thought, idea
खिलौना *khilaunā* m. toy
गरम *garam* hot, warm
चलते जाना *calte jānā* to keep going
चौड़ा *cauṛā* wide, broad
जलाना *jalānā* to light
टैक्सी *ṭaiksī* f. taxi
तंग *tang* narrow
तंग करना *tang karnā* to annoy, harass
तोहफ़ा *tohfā* m. gift, present
थकना *thaknā* to get tired

थाना *thānā* m. police station
दक्षिण *dakṣiṇ* south
दवाख़ाना *davākhānā* m. pharmacy, chemist's shop
दाहिना *dāhinā* right (not left)
देश *deś* m. country
धोबी *dhobī* m. washerman
नक़्शा *naqśā* m. map
निकलना *nikalnā* to emerge, come/go out
पचास *pacās* fifty
पड़ना *paṛnā* to fall; to have to (with preceding infinitive — मुझे जाना पड़ेगा *mujhe jānā paṛegā* 'I'll have to go')
पश्चिम *paścim* west
पार *pār* across; पार करना *pār karnā* to cross; उस पार *us pār* on the other side (of, के *ke*)
पुलिस *pulis* f. police
पुस्तकालय *pustakālay* m. library
पूर्व *pūrv* east
प्रदेश *prades* m. state, region
बजे *baje* o'clock
बटुआ *baṭuā* m. purse, wallet
बायाँ *bāyā̃* left (direction)
बुरा *burā* bad
भाड़ में जाए *bhāṛ mẽ jāe* '(he/she) can go to hell' (भाड़ *bhāṛ* m. grain-parching oven)
मंदिर *mandir* m. temple
मराठी *marāṭhī* f. Marathi, language of Maharashtra
माफ़ी *māfī* f. forgiveness; माफ़ी माँगना *māfī mā̃gnā* to apologize
मामूली *māmūlī* ordinary
मार्ग *mārg* m. road, street (used in street names)
मैला *mailā* dirty
रिक्शेवाला *rikśevālā* m. rickshaw driver
रिश्तेदार *riśtedār* m. relation, relative
लगना *lagnā* to seem; to be felt (of hunger, thirst etc.); to take (time); to have an effect; to begin (following an oblique infinitive)
सरकार *sarkār* f. government
सामान *sāmān* m. goods, furniture, luggage

12

तबियत और शैली
tabiyat
health and style

In this unit you will learn

- how to talk about getting things done by others
- ways of adding nuance to what you say
- terms for health matters

Language points

- relative clauses
- causative verbs
- compound verbs

1 'J-words' and relative clauses

Earlier we saw a set of 'question-words' beginning with *k-*.

कब *kab* when? कहाँ *kahā̃* where? कौन *kaun* who?

Now we meet a similar set of words, this time beginning with *j-*. These are used in 'relative clauses', where they introduce one clause that is 'related' or linked to a second one. Here are three members of this set:

जब *jab* when जहाँ *jahā̃* where जो *jo* who

जब *jab* is often partnered by तो *to* (or तब *tab* 'then') which ushers in a paired clause:

जब मैं छोटा था तो मुझे संगीत का बहुत शौक़ था ।
jab maĩ choṭā thā to mujhe sangīt kā bahut śauq thā. When I was little I was very fond of music.

जब लता जी गाती थीं तब पिताजी भी सुनते थे ।
jab Latā jī gātī thī̃ tab pitājī bhī sunte the. When Lata ji sang, even Father used to listen.

जब संगीत शुरू होता था तो सब लोग नाचने लगते थे ।
jab sangīt śurū hotā thā to sab log nācne lagte the. When the music started everyone would begin to dance.

जहाँ *jahā̃* is often partnered by वहाँ *vahā̃* 'there':

जहाँ मैं रहता हूँ वहाँ कोई सिनेमा नहीं है ।
jahā̃ maĩ rahtā hū̃, vahā̃ koī sinemā nahī̃ hai. Where I live, there's no cinema.

जहाँ सिनेमा पहले था वहाँ एक होटल बन रहा है ।
jahā̃ sinemā pahle thā vahā̃ ek hoṭal ban rahā hai. Where the cinema was previously, a hotel is being built.

जहाँ लोग सो रहे हों वहाँ रेडियो मत बजाना ।
jahā̃ log so rahe hõ vahā̃ reḍiyo mat bajānā. Don't play the radio where people may be sleeping.

जो *jo* 'who/which/what' is often partnered by वह / वे *vah / ve*:

जो आदमी रेडियो में गाना गाता है वह सामने रहता है ।
jo ādmī reḍiyo mẽ gānā gātā hai vah sāmne rahtā hai. The man who sings on the radio lives opposite.

जो गाना तुमने गाया, वह हमें बहुत पसंद आया ।
jo gānā tumne gāyā, vah hamẽ bahut pasand āyā. We really liked the song you sang. ('The song you sang, it pleased us...')

जो लोग गाना सीखना चाहते हैं उनको यह गाना सुनना चाहिए ।
jo log gānā sīkhnā cāhte haĩ unko yah gānā sunnā cāhie. People who want to learn to sing should listen to this song.

जो *jo* has the oblique जिस *jis* (singular) and जिन *jin* (plural):

जिसने यह फ़िल्म बनाई वह मेरा पुराना दोस्त है ।
jisne yah film banāī vah mera purānā dost hai. The person who made this film is my old friend.

जिस फ़िल्म में यह गाना आता है वह काफ़ी पुरानी है ।
jis film mẽ yah gānā ātā hai vah kāfī purānī hai. The film in which this song comes is quite old.

जिन लोगों ने "शोले" फ़िल्म देखी है वे उसे कभी नहीं भूलेंगे ।
jin logõ ne 'śole' film dekhī hai ve use kabhī nahī̃ bhūlẽge. People who have seen the film 'Sholay' will never forget it.

Hiralal helps us out

Now a narrative about Hiralal the rickshaw driver helps us get used to relative clauses. In addition to a couple of English words used here ('artist', 'seat'), you will need these new words:

शानदार *śāndār* splendid
हीरा *hīrā* m. diamond
चमकना *camaknā* to shine
सवारी *savārī* f. passenger, rider
जेब *jeb* f. pocket
थक जाना *thak jānā* to get tired
मुफ़्त (का) *muft (kā)* cost-free
बारिश *bāriś* f. rain
ग़रीब *garīb* poor
मौसम *mausam* m. weather
पहाड़ *pahāṛ* m. hill
चढ़ाव *caṛhāv* m. rise, incline

भारी *bhārī* heavy
चढ़ना *caṛhnā* to climb, get into vehicle
वज़न *vazan* m. weight
हो जाना *ho jānā* to become
उतरना *utarnā,* उतर जाना *utar jānā* to get down, alight
लेटना *leṭnā* to lie down

यह हीरालाल है, जो आगरे में रहता है। हीरालाल रिक्शेवाला है। जो रिक्शा हीरालाल चलाता है वह बहुत शानदार है। वह हीरे की तरह चमकता है! जिसने यह रिक्शा बनाया हो[1] वह बहुत बड़ा आर्टिस्ट होगा।[2]

जहाँ हीरालाल रहता है वहाँ बहुत-से दूसरे रिक्शेवाले भी रहते हैं। रिक्शे तो बहुत हैं लेकिन सवारियाँ कम आती हैं।[3] जब एक भी सवारी नहीं आती तब हीरालाल की जेब ख़ाली रहती है। जब जेब ख़ाली रहती है तो पेट भी ख़ाली रहता है। मुफ़्त का खाना कहाँ मिलता है?[4] और जब बारिश होती है तब भी हीरालाल को काम करना पड़ता है। जो लोग ग़रीब हैं उनको हर मौसम में काम करना पड़ता है।

जहाँ पहाड़ या चढ़ाव हो वहाँ रिक्शा चलाना बहुत ही मुश्किल है। जब दो मोटे लोग अपने भारी सामान को लेकर[5] रिक्शे में चढ़ते हैं तो वज़न बहुत ज़्यादा हो जाता है। जब सवारियाँ उतर जाती हैं तो हीरालाल अपने रिक्शे की सीट पर लेटकर सोता है। जो लोग रिक्शे चलाते हैं उन्हें बहुत मेहनत करनी पड़ती है।

yah Hīrālāl hai, jo āgre mẽ rahtā hai. Hīrālāl rikśevālā hai. jo rikśā Hīrālāl calātā hai vah bahut śāndār hai. vah hīre kī tarah camaktā hai! jisne yah rikśā banāyā ho[1] *vah bahut baṛā ārṭisṭ hogā.*[2]

jahā̃ Hīrālāl rahtā hai vahā̃ bahut-se dūsre rikśevale bhī rahte haĩ. rikśe to bahut haĩ lekin savāriyā̃ kam ātī haĩ. [3] *jab ek bhī* *savārī nahī̃ ātī tab Hīrālāl kī jeb <u>kh</u>ālī rahtī hai. jab jeb <u>kh</u>ālī rahtī hai to peṭ bhī <u>kh</u>ālī rahtā hai. muft kā khānā kahā̃ miltā hai?* [4] *aur jab bāriś hotī hai tab bhī Hīrālāl ko kām karnā paṛtā hai. jo log garīb haĩ unko har mausam mẽ kām karnā paṛtā hai.*

jahā̃ pahāṛ yā caṛhāv ho vahā̃ rikśā calānā bahut hī muśkil hai. jab do moṭe log apne bhārī sāmān ko lekar [5] *rikśe mẽ caṛhte haĩ to vazan bahut zyādā ho jātā hai. jab savāriyā̃ utar jātī haĩ to Hīrālāl apne rikśe kī sīṭ par leṭkar sotā hai. jo log rikśe calāte haĩ unhẽ bahut mehnat karnī paṛtī hai.*

This is Hiralal, who lives in Agra. Hiralal is a rickshaw driver. The rickshaw that Hiralal drives is very fine. It shines like a diamond! Whoever made this rickshaw [1] must be a very great artist. [2]

Where Hiralal lives many other rickshaw-drivers live too. There are lots of rickshaws but few passengers come. [3] When not a single passenger comes, Hiralal's pocket remains empty. When the pocket remains empty the stomach also remains empty. Where can one get free food? [4] And when it rains, even then Hiralal has to work. People who are poor have to work in all weathers ['in every weather'].

Where there's a hill or a slope it's very difficult to drive a rickshaw. When two fat people get onto the rickshaw with their heavy luggage [5] the weight gets too much. When the passengers get down Hiralal lies down on the seat of his rickshaw and sleeps. People who drive rickshaws have to work very hard.

1 जिसने यह रिक्शा बनाया हो *jisne ya rikśā banāyā ho* — 'the person who made this rickshaw'; हो *ho* is subjunctive (see 9.2) to reflect the fact that the identity of the person is vague or unknown.

2 Remember that the future can express an assumption — 'he must be a very great artist' (lit. 'he will be…').

3 The noun सवारी *savārī* is feminine, even if the 'passenger' described is male.

4 मुफ़्त का खाना कहाँ मिलता है? *muft kā khānā kahā̃ miltā hai?* 'Where can you get food for free?' It's a rhetorical question — you can't get free food anywhere.

5 भारी सामान को लेकर *bhārī sāmān ko lekar* 'taking heavy luggage' i.e. having heavy luggage with them.

True or false?

Are these statements right (सही *sahī*) or wrong (ग़लत *galat*)? Answers below.

		सही *sahī*	ग़लत *galat*
१	हीरालाल दिल्ली से है । *Hīrālāl dillī se hai.*	☐	☐
२	उसके पास बहुत पैसा है । *uske pās bahut paisā hai.*	☐	☐
३	हीरालाल का रिक्शा काफ़ी सुंदर है । *Hīrālāl kā rikśā kāfī sundar hai.*	☐	☐
४	हीरालाल के घर के पास कोई दूसरा रिक्शेवाला नहीं रहता । *Hīrālāl ke ghar ke pās koī dūsrā rikśevālā nahī̃ rahtā.*	☐	☐
५	सवारियों की कोई कमी नहीं है । *savāriyõ kī koī kamī nahī̃ hai.*	☐	☐
६	बारिश के मौसम में हीरालाल काम नहीं करता । *bāriś ke mausam mẽ Hīrālāl kām nahī̃ kartā.*	☐	☐
७	हीरालाल को खाना मुफ़्त में मिलता है । *Hīrālāl ko khānā muft mẽ miltā hai.*	☐	☐
८	जब हीरालाल थक जाता है तो वह सोता है । *jab Hīrālāl thak jātā hai to vah sotā hai.*	☐	☐

Answers: Only 3 and 8 are right.

A crossword puzzle

And now for something completely different: a crossword puzzle. Because the basic unit of the Devanagari script is the *syllable* (and not the individual letter, as in roman-script languages), each square will contain a complete syllable: so the word सोमवार *somvar* 'Monday' would split up into four component units, सो | म | वा | र (*so* | *m* | *va* | *r*). You will need to look up one or two words in the English–Hindi vocabulary.

ACROSS

1 brave
5 political party, group
6 teacher (female)
8 Madhuban (hotel name)
9 always (archaic/formal)
10 then
11 Tuesday
12 newspaper seller
17 don't...!
18 ashtray
20 an Indian epic poem
22 straight
25 to bathe
26 singer

DOWN

1 ugly
2 condition, state
3 enemy
4 shopkeeper
6 now
7 concentration, attention
9 question
11 temple
12 American
13 danger
14 ancient city on Ganges
15 100,000
16 that is to say
19 lentils
21 to hit
23 thread
24 one

2 Getting things done – causatives

As you know, the Hindi for 'to make' is बनाना *banānā* (हम चाय बनाएँगे *ham cāy banāẽge* 'we'll make tea'). Extend this to बनवाना *banvānā* and you have a verb that means 'to get made, to cause to be made'.

हम चाय बनवाएँगे ।

ham cāy banvāẽge. We'll get tea made.

हम नौकर से चाय बनवाएँगे ।

ham naukar se cāy banvāẽge. We'll get tea made by the servant.

These verbs with -वा- *-vā-* extensions are called 'causatives'. The word से *se* conveys the sense 'by': नौकर से *naukar se* 'by the servant'.

Some causatives are less obviously connected to their base verb. For example, धोना *dhonā* 'to wash' yields the causative धुलवाना *dhulvānā* 'to get washed', and सीना *sīnā* 'to sew' has सिलवाना *silvānā* 'to get sewn'.

How many causatives can you spot in the following, in which Geeta talks about her annual preparations for Diwali?

सबसे पहले मैं दरज़ी से नए कपड़े सिलवाती हूँ । फिर धोबी को बुलवाकर मैं उससे सारे गंदे कपड़े धुलवाती हूँ । जो कपड़े मैंने ख़ुद धोए हों उनको मैं धोबी से प्रेस ['press'] करवाती हूँ । फिर घर को अच्छी तरह से साफ़ करवाती हूँ और रात का खाना बनवाती हूँ । रात को हम दिये जलाते हैं, या उनको बच्चों से जलवाते हैं ।

sabse pahle maĩ darzī se nae kapṛe silvātī hū̃. phir dhobī ko bulvākar maĩ usse sāre gande kapṛe dhulvātī hū̃. jo kapṛe maĩne <u>kh</u>ud dhoe hõ unko maĩ dhobī se pres ['press'] *karvātī hū̃. phir ghar ko acchī tarah se sāf karvātī hū̃ aur rāt kā khānā banvātī hū̃. rāt ko ham diye jalāte haĩ, yā unko baccõ se jalvāte haĩ.*

First of all I get new clothes sewn by the tailor. Then I have the dhobi called and I get all the dirty clothes washed by him ['get him to wash…']. Whatever clothes I've washed myself I get ironed by him. Then I get the house cleaned thoroughly and I get dinner made. At night we light lamps, or get them lit by the children ['get the children to light them'].

There are *seven* causatives here (including two appearances of करवाना *karvānā* 'to get done, cause to be done'):

सिलवाना *silvānā* to get sewn (सीना *sīnā* to sew)

बुलवाना *bulvānā* to get called, to summon (बुलाना *bulānā* to call)

धुलवाना *dhulvānā* to get washed (धोना *dhonā* to wash)

प्रेस करवाना *pres karvānā* to get pressed, ironed (प्रेस करना *pres karnā* to press, iron)

साफ़ करवाना *sāf karvānā* to get cleaned (साफ़ करना *sāf karnā* to clean)

बनवाना *banvānā* to get made (बनाना *banānā* to make)

जलवाना *jalvānā* to get lit (जलाना *jalānā* to light)

Verb triplets

You'll often find triplets of related verbs like these sets:

बनना *bannā* to be made	बनाना *banānā* to make	बनवाना *banvānā* to get made
बोलना *bolna* to speak	बुलाना *bulānā* to call	बुलवाना *bulvānā* to summon
धुलना *dhulnā* to be washed	धोना *dhonā* to wash	धुलवाना *dhulvānā* to get washed
जलना *jalnā* to burn	जलाना *jalānā* to light	जलवाना *jalvānā* to get lit

Practise what you've learnt

Now it's your turn to use causatives. Translate these sentences using the verbs provided.

1 We'll have the children taught Hindi by Sharma ji.
(सिखवाना *sikhvānā* to have taught)

2 I got some food prepared by the servants.
(तैयार करवाना *taiyār karvānā* to get prepared)

3 We have to get the car fixed.
(ठीक करवाना *ṭhīk karvānā* to get fixed)

4 I want to get some kurtas sewn by Masterji.
(सिलवाना *silvānā* to get sewn)

5 I got these letters written by someone.
(लिखवाना *likhvānā* to get written)

Did you know?

The popular Hindi film from Bombay brings a knowledge of the language to millions of people outside the Hindi-speaking area. Despite its nickname of 'Bollywood', the Hindi film industry has its own conventions — quite different from those of Hollywood.

A visit to the doctor

Sadly, Raju has been feeling unwell. Can the doctor help?

डाक्टर आइए, आइए। क्या तकलीफ़ है आपको ?

राजू डाक्टर साहब, मेरा सारा शरीर दर्द कर रहा है।[1]

डाक्टर आपकी तबियत कब से ख़राब है ?

राजू दो दिन से। परसों मैं काम पर जानेवाला था[2] कि[3] सिर में दर्द होने लगा।

डाक्टर लगता है आपको फ़्लू हो गया है।[4]

राजू तो मुझे क्या करना चाहिए ?

डाक्टर सिर्फ़ आराम करना चाहिए।

राजू कोई दवा या गोली तो दीजिए !

डाक्टर आपको किसी गोली-वोली[5] की ज़रूरत नहीं है। आराम ही इलाज है।

ḍākṭar *āie, āie. kyā taklīf hai āpko?*

Rājū *ḍākṭar sāhab, merā sārā śarīr dard kar rahā hai.*[1]

ḍākṭar *āpkī tabiyat kab se kharāb hai?*

Rājū *do din se. parsõ maĩ kām par jānevālā thā*[2] *ki*[3] *sir mẽ dard hone lagā.*

ḍākṭar *lagtā hai āpko flū ho gayā hai.*[4]

Rājū *to mujhe kyā karnā cāhie?*

ḍākṭar *sirf ārām karnā cāhie.*

Rājū	*koī davā yā golī dījie.*
ḍākṭar	*āpko kisī golī-volī* [5] *kī zarūrat nahī̃ hai. ārām hī ilāj hai.*

Doctor	Come in, come in. What's your complaint?
Raju	Doctor sahib, my whole body is aching.
Doctor	How long has your health been bad?
Raju	For two days. The day before yesterday I was just about to go to work when my head started to ache.
Doctor	It seems you've caught flu.
Raju	So what should I do?
Doctor	You should just rest.
Raju	Please give [me] some medicine or tablet!
Doctor	You don't need any tablet or anything like that. Rest itself is the cure.

1 दर्द करना *dard karnā* 'to hurt'; also दर्द होना *dard honā* 'to have a pain' (मेरे सिर में दर्द हो रहा है *mere sir mẽ dard ho rahā hai* 'I have a headache').

2 मैं जानेवाला था *maĩ jānevālā thā* 'I was about to go'; -वाला *-vālā* added to a verb ending in *-ne* means 'about to'. गीता अभी जानेवाली है *Gītā abhī jānevālī hai* 'Geeta's just about to go', मैं अभी आपको फ़ोन करनेवाला था *maĩ abhī āpko fon karnevālā thā* 'I was just about to phone you'.

3 कि *ki* here means 'when, when suddenly' in this construction with -वाला *-vālā* (see note 2).

4 हो जाना *ho jānā* is the simplest way of saying 'to get' an illness etc. The patient takes को *ko*.

6 गोली-वोली *golī-volī* 'tablet or anything like that' — वोली *volī* is a meaningless echo-word. Echo-words, usually beginning *v-*, generalize the sense of the preceding word, opening out the range of meaning from something specific (here, medicine) to a broader category (here, any kind of medication). Compare the following: चाय-वाय *cāy-vāy* 'tea etc.', खाना-वाना *khānā-vānā* 'food, something to eat', पानी-वानी *pānī-vānī* 'water, something to drink'. The doctor's remark here has a disparaging touch: 'You don't need any tablet or any such nonsense!'

3 Parts of the body

In order to explain feelings of pain and sickness etc. you need to know the main parts of the body. Ram has helpfully agreed to pose for us (for a substantial fee):

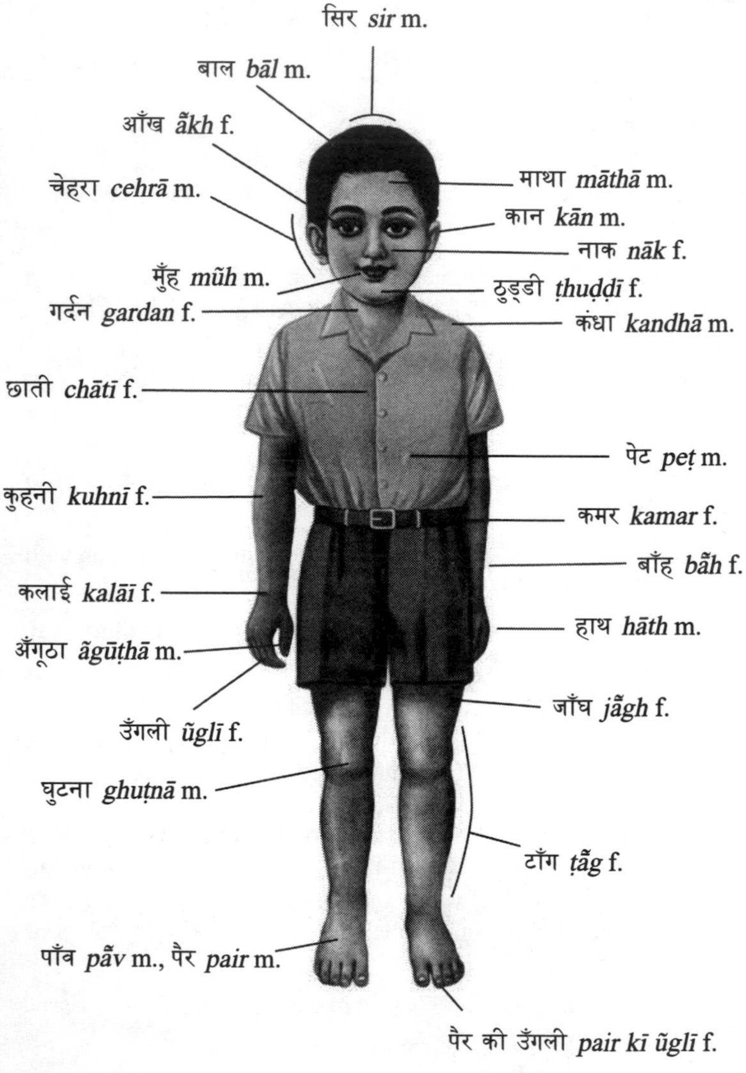

▶ The doctor asks *you* some questions

Role play: you go to the doctor because you've had a stomach ache, sickness and diarrhoea for two days. You have a headache but your temperature is normal. Your alcohol consumption is moderate; you usually sleep OK. You have been careful about your food, and the only water you drink is bottled water (बोतल का पानी *botal kā pānī*). Now, answer the doctor's questions:

१ आपकी तबियत कब से ख़राब है ?

āpkī tabiyat kab se kharāb hai? How long has your health been bad?

२ आपको बुख़ार तो नहीं है ?

āpko bukhār to nahī̃ hai? You don't have fever, do you?

३ क्या सिर में दर्द है ?

kyā sir mẽ dard hai? Do you have a headache?

४ आप बाहर का खाना खाते/खाती हैं, बाज़ार में ?

āp bāhar kā khānā khāte/khātī haĩ, bāzār mẽ ? Do you eat food from outside, in the market?

५ आप नल का पानी पीते/पीती हैं ?

āp nal kā pānī pīte/pītī haĩ? Do you drink tap water?

६ उलटी हो रही है ?

ulṭī ho rahī hai? [Are you] Having vomiting attacks?

७ दस्त भी हैं ?

dast bhī hai? Is there diarrhoea too?

८ क्या आप शराब पीते/पीती हैं ?

kyā āp śarāb pīte/pītī haĩ? Do you drink alcohol?

९ क्या आपको नींद ठीक से आती है ?

kyā āpko nī̃d ṭhīk se ātī hai? Do you sleep properly?

१० आप कितने बजे सोते/सोती हैं ?

āp kitne baje sote/sotī haĩ? What time do you sleep?

११ कितने घंटे सोते/सोती हैं ?

kitne ghaṇṭe sote/sotī haĩ? How many hours do you sleep?

१२ और कोई तकलीफ़ है आपको ?

aur koī taklīf hai āpko? Do you have any other symptoms?

4 Shades of meaning

Different languages have different ways of adding shades of meaning to a statement. In English, for example, the basic verb 'to write' underlies the variations 'write down, write up, write out, write in' and so on. In Hindi, shades of meaning are often conveyed by a *pairing of two verbs.* Think of it being a bit like making lassi, the yoghurt drink: the first verb is the yoghurt that gives the basic meaning, while the second verb is the choice of sugar or salt that adds the flavouring. Here's an example with लिखना *likhnā* 'to write' as first verb, and लेना *lenā* 'to take' or देना *denā* 'to give' as second verb:

मेरा पता लिख लो ।

merā patā likh lo. Write down my address.

नहीं, तुम लिख दो ।

nahī̃, tum likh do. No, you write [it] out.

लिख लो *likh lo* — this combines the basic sense of लिखना likhnā 'to write' with a shade of meaning from लेना *lenā* 'to take'; लेना *lenā* here suggests that the action is a 'taking' one — something done *for the benefit of the person who does the action.* So the implied meaning is 'Take down my address [for your own use]'.

लिख दो *likh do* — this combines the basic sense of लिखना *likhnā* with a shade of meaning from देना *denā* 'to give'; देना *denā* here suggests that the action is a 'giving' one — something done *for the benefit of someone else.* So the implied meaning is 'Write it out for me'.

As well as लेना *lenā* and देना *denā,* another verb commonly used in this construction is जाना *jānā,* literally 'to go'. In harmony with its literal meaning of movement from one place to another, it colours a preceding verb with a sense of *completed action,* or a *change of state*:

अरे ! बिजली बंद हो गई !

are! bijlī band ho gaī! Hey! The electricity's gone off!

अच्छा ? मैं तो सो गया था ।

acchā? maĩ to so gayā thā. Really? I'd gone to sleep.

बिजली बंद हो गई *bijlī band ho gaī* — the main verb होना *honā* 'to be' changes to हो जाना *ho jānā* 'to become', because a *change of state* has taken place.

मैं सो गया था *maĩ so gayā thā* — the verb सोना *sonā* 'to sleep' changes to सो जाना *so jānā* 'to go to sleep', with the sense of 'go' very similar in both English and Hindi.

Verbs of this kind are called 'compound verbs'. (Hindi has a better name for them — रंजक क्रिया *ranjak kriyā* 'colouring verbs'.) There are many more combinations, some of which are given in the Grammar Summary, but लेना *lenā*, देना *denā* and जाना *jānā* are by far the most common.

The ने *ne* construction is only used with compound verbs if *both* verbs in the compound are ने *ne* verbs (i.e. ones that are marked with N in the glossary at the end of the book).

Finally, a word of warning: compound verbs give a specific sense of the way in which a *particular* action is done. It therefore follows that *a sentence that's negative or general won't use them*; if no one drinks the lassi, its taste is irrelevant! Look closely at the use of a compound verb in the first of these two sentences, then at the *dropping* of the compound in the second (which is negative):

राजू — मैंने खाना खा लिया है ।

Rājū — maĩne khānā khā liyā hai. I've had my meal.

गीता — अच्छा? मैंने तो नहीं खाया है ।

Gītā — acchā? maĩne to nahĩ khāyā hai. Really? I haven't.

Raju stresses that he's had (and enjoyed or benefited from) his meal, a sense given by लेना *lenā*. But Geeta hasn't eaten yet, so her reply has no scope for the implication that लेना *lenā* brings.

▶ I've already done this

The verb चुकना *cuknā* means 'to have finished doing, to have already done', and it's used in a structure identical to the one we've just been looking at — it follows the stem of the main verb:

मीना जा चुकी है ।

Mīnā jā cukī hai. Meena has already gone.

राम अपना काम कर चुका है ।

Rām apnā kām kar cukā hai. Ram has already done his work.

मनोज अपनी किताब पढ़ चुका है ।

Manoj apnī kitāb paṛh cukā hai. Manoj has already read (or 'finished reading') his book.

राजू और गीता खाना खा चुके हैं ।

Rājū aur Gītā khānā khā cuke haĩ. Raju and Geeta have already eaten (or 'have finished eating').

You'll be glad to hear that the ने *ne* construction is *never* used here!

Did you manage to do this?

The same structure is used again with the verb पाना *pānā.* This literally means 'to find, obtain', but here it gives the meaning 'to manage to, to be able to' (compare सकना *saknā*, met in Unit 6).

कल मैं नहीं जा पाया ।

kal maĩ nahĩ jā pāyā. I didn't manage to go yesterday.

गीता टिकट नहीं ख़रीद पाई ।

Gītā ṭikaṭ nahĩ <u>kh</u>arīd pāī. Geeta wasn't able to buy a ticket.

क्या तुम यह काम अकेले कर पाओगे ?

kyā tum yah kām akele kar pāoge? Will you manage to do this work alone?

5 Style in Hindi

The language used in this book reflects ordinary unselfconscious speech. But like all languages, Hindi has a variety of styles — formal, informal, colloquial and so on. Formal Hindi uses a lot of loanwords from Sanskrit (India's main classical language) just as formal English uses words from Latin and Greek. For example, formal Hindi would use the Sanskrit loanword सहायता *sahāytā* 'assistance' rather than the informal मदद *madad* 'help'; which is a loanword from Arabic and which has an entirely natural place in informal Hindi. Many Arabic and some Turkish words came to India as part of the Persian language, from about the 11th century onwards — they are far from being newcomers!

The formal style of the language is called शुद्ध हिन्दी *śuddh hindī* — 'pure Hindi'; but as this example of सहायता *sahāytā* shows, it is itself dependent on Sanskrit loanwords, which means that any claims to linguistic 'purity' have to be taken with a pinch of salt. In formal Hindi, especially in the written language but also in some people's preferred speaking style also, one 'requires assistance', one does not 'need help'! When you start reading Hindi books and newspapers, you'll have to start adding Sanskritic vocabulary to the colloquial base you're learning here. But be careful about using it too much in everyday conversational contexts, because it could make your Hindi sound very bookish. People who learn Hindi from grammar books alone, especially those of the traditional variety, end up 'requiring assistance'!

Today, informal Hindi uses words from a rich variety of sources, especially English, whose relentless spread throughout the world can be seen as a threat to so many languages. Go shopping with Geeta and you'll hear *lots* of familiar words. Here we catch up with her buying shoes in a shop in 'fashionable' South Extension, Delhi:

गीता आपके पास ग्रीन कलर का जूता है ?

दुकानदार हाँ मैडम, देखिए, ये शूज़ ग्रीन कलर के हैं । और बहुत ही रीज़नेबुल हैं ।

गीता नहीं, यह स्टाइल मैं लाइक नहीं करती ।

दुकानदार पर इसकी लेदर बहुत ही सॉफ़्ट है ! और क्वालिटी भी देखिए इसकी ! ट्राई तो कीजिए !

Gītā *āpke pās grīn kalar kā jūtā hai?*

dukāndār *hā̃ maiḍam, dekhie, ye śūz grīn kalar ke haĩ. aur bahut hī rīzanebul haĩ.*

Gītā *nahī̃, yah sṭāil maĩ lāik nahī̃ kartī.*

dukāndār *par iskī ledar bahut hī sāfṭ hai! aur kvāliṭī bhī dekhie iskī! ṭrāī to kījie!*

Geeta Do you have a green colour shoe?

Shopkeeper Yes madam, please look, these shoes are green. And they're very reasonable.

Geeta No, I don't like this style.

Shopkeeper But its leather is very soft. And see its quality too! Try it at least!

... and so on! As a learner of Hindi, you may find it rather depressing that it has allowed itself to be so heavily influenced by a language that is so foreign to its own character. But between the two extremes of heavily Sanskritized and heavily Anglicized versions of the language, Hindi remains a superbly subtle and vibrant language, full of expressiveness and life!

6 Numbers

Here are the cardinal numbers. You'll find it easier to get familiar with the higher ones (above 20) if you read them in 'decade' sequences such as 21, 31, 41 etc.

० शून्य *śūnya*

१ एक	११ ग्यारह	२१ इक्कीस	३१ इकत्तीस	४१ इकतालीस
1 ek	*11 gyārah*	*21 ikkīs*	*31 ikattīs*	*41 iktālīs*
२ दो	१२ बारह	२२ बाईस	३२ बत्तीस	४२ बयालीस
2 do	*12 bārah*	*13 bāīs*	*33 battīs*	*43 bayālīs*
३ तीन	१३ तेरह	२३ तेईस	३३ तैंतीस	४३ तैंतालीस
3 tīn	*13 terah*	*23 teīs*	*33 taĩtīs*	*43 taĩtālīs*
४ चार	१४ चौदह	२४ चौबीस	३४ चौंतीस	४४ चवालीस
4 cār	*14 caudah*	*24 caubīs*	*34 caũtīs*	*44 cavālīs*
५ पाँच	१५ पंद्रह	२५ पच्चीस	३५ पैंतीस	४५ पैंतालीस
5 pā̃c	*15 pandrah*	*25 paccīs*	*35 paĩtīs*	*45 paĩtālīs*
६ छह	१६ सोलह	२६ छब्बीस	३६ छत्तीस	४६ छियालीस
6 chah	*16 solah*	*26 chabbīs*	*36 chattīs*	*46 chiyālīs*
७ सात	१७ सत्रह	२७ सत्ताईस	३७ सैंतीस	४७ सैंतालीस
7 sāt	*17 satrah*	*27 sattāīs*	*37 saĩtīs*	*47 saĩtālīs*
८ आठ	१८ अठारह	२८ अट्ठाईस	३८ अड़तीस	४८ अड़तालीस
8 āṭh	*18 aṭhārah*	*28 aṭṭhāīs*	*38 aṛtīs*	*48 aṛtālīs*
९ नौ	१९ उन्नीस	२९ उनतीस	३९ उनतालीस	४९ उनचास
9 nau	*19 unnīs*	*29 untīs*	*39 untālīs*	*41 uncās*
१० दस	२० बीस	३० तीस	४० चालीस	५० पचास
10 das	*20 bīs*	*30 tīs*	*40 cālīs*	*50 pacās*

५१ इक्यावन	६१ इकसठ	७१ इकहत्तर	८१ इक्यासी	९१ इक्यानवे
51 ikyāvan	*61 iksaṭh*	*71 ik'hattar*	*81 ikyāsī*	*91 ikyānve*
५२ बावन	६२ बासठ	७२ बहत्तर	८२ बयासी	९२ बानवे
52 bāvan	*62 bāsaṭh*	*72 bahattar*	*82 bayāsī*	*92 bānve*
५३ तिरपन	६३ तिरसठ	७३ तिहत्तर	८३ तिरासी	९३ तिरानवे
53 tirpan	*63 tirsaṭh*	*73 tihattar*	*83 tirāsī*	*93 tirānve*

५४ चौवन	६४ चौंसठ	७४ चौहत्तर	८४ चौरासी	९४ चौरानवे
54 cauvan	*64 caũsaṭh*	*74 cauhattar*	*84 caurāsī*	*94 caurānve*
५५ पचपन	६५ पैंसठ	७५ पचहत्तर	८५ पचासी	९५ पचानवे
55 pacpan	*65 paĩsaṭh*	*75 pac'hattar*	*85 pacāsī*	*95 pacānv̀*
५६ छप्पन	६६ छियासठ	७६ छिहत्तर	८६ छियासी	९६ छियानवे
56 chappan	*66 chiyāsaṭh*	*76 chihattar*	*86 chiyāsī*	*96 chiyānve*
५७ सत्तावन	६७ सरसठ	७७ सतहत्तर	८७ सत्तासी	९७ सत्तानवे
57 sattāvan	*67 sarsaṭh*	*77 sat'hattar*	*87 sattāsī*	*97 sattānve*
५८ अट्ठावन	६८ अड़सठ	७८ अठहत्तर	८८ अट्ठासी	९८ अट्ठानवे
58 aṭṭāvan	*68 aṛsaṭh*	*78 aṭhhattar*	*88 aṭṭhāsī*	*98 aṭṭhānve*
५९ उनसठ	६९ उनहत्तर	७९ उन्यासी	८९ नवासी	९९ निन्यानवे
59 unsaṭh	*69 unhattar*	*79 unyāsī*	*89 navāsī*	*99 innyānve*
६० साठ	७० सत्तर	८० अस्सी	९० नब्बे	१०० सौ
60 sāṭh	*70 sattar*	*80 assī*	*90 nabbe*	*100 sau*

1.5	डेढ़ *ḍeṛh*
2.5	ढाई *ḍhāī*
1000	हज़ार *hazār*
100,000	लाख *lākh*
10,000,000	करोड़ *karoṛ* (100 lakh, written 100,00,000)
150	डेढ़ सौ *ḍeṛh sau*
1500	डेढ़ हज़ार *ḍeṛh hazār*
150,000	डेढ़ लाख *ḍeṛh lākh*
250	ढाई सौ *ḍhāī sau*
2500	ढाई हज़ार *ḍhāī hazār*
250,000	ढाई लाख *ḍhāī lākh*

7 Time

Telling the time involves the following words:

बजे *baje* o'clock

बजना *bajnā* to chime, resound

डेढ़ *ḍeṛh* one and a half

ढाई *ḍhāī* two and a half

पौन, पौना *paun, paune* three quarters

सवा *savā* one and a quarter

साढ़े *sāṛhe* plus a half (with 3 and upwards)

पौन बजा है । *paun bajā hai.* It's a quarter to one.

एक बजा है । *ek bajā hai.* It's one o'clock.

डेढ़ बजा है । *ḍeṛh bajā hai.* It's half past one.

दो बजे हैं । *do baje haĩ.* It's two o'clock.

ढाई बजे हैं । *ḍhāī baje haĩ* It's half past two.

सवा सात बजे हैं । *savā sāt baje haĩ.* It's a quarter to seven.

पौने दस बजे हैं । *paune das baje haĩ.* It's a quarter to ten.

साढ़े ग्यारह बजे हैं । *sāṛhe gyārah baje haĩ.* It's half past eleven.

हम दो बजे मिलेंगे । *ham do baje milẽge.* We'll meet at two o'clock.

मैं डेढ़ बजे तक आऊँगा । *maĩ ḍeṛh baje tak āũgā.* I'll come by half past one.

दस बज रहे हैं । *das baj rahe haĩ.* It's just ten (ten is striking).

दस बजनेवाले हैं । *das bajnevāle haĩ.* It's nearly ten (ten's about to strike).

Minutes before and after the hour are expressed by बजने में *bajne mẽ* and बजकर *bajkar* respectively.

एक बजनें में बीस मिनट हैं । *ek bajne mẽ bīs minaṭ haĩ.* It's 12.40.

आठ बजकर बीस मिनट हैं । *āṭh bajkar bīs minaṭ haĩ.* It's 8.20.

What's the time?

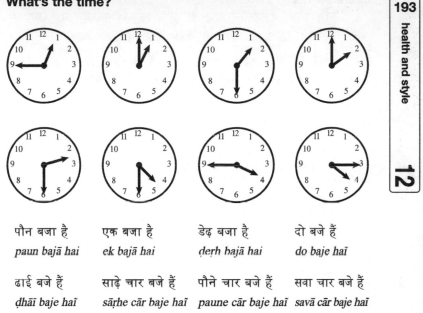

पौन बजा है	एक बजा है	डेढ़ बजा है	दो बजे हैं
paun bajā hai	*ek bajā hai*	*ḍeṛh bajā hai*	*do baje haĩ*
ढाई बजे हैं	साढ़े चार बजे हैं	पौने चार बजे हैं	सवा चार बजे हैं
ḍhāī baje haĩ	*sāṛhe cār baje haĩ*	*paune cār baje haĩ*	*savā cār baje haĩ*

Months

India still uses its traditional calendar (with lunar months) for festival dates, and you can find plenty of web-based information on this by typing 'Hindu Calendar' into a search engine. But the 'western' (or global) calendar is usually preferred for mundane functions.

The month names are spelt in Hindi with dental consonants: this reflects their Portuguese ancestry (words from English being generally spelt with retroflexes).

जनवरी	फ़रवरी	मार्च	अप्रैल	मई	जून
janvarī	*farvarī*	*mārc*	*aprail*	*maī*	*jūn*
जुलाई	अगस्त	सितंबर	अक्तूबर	नवंबर	दिसंबर
julāī	*agast*	*sitambar*	*aktūbar*	*navambar*	*disambar*

Exercise 12a Answer the questions about Hiralal:

१ जो रिक्शा हीरालाल चलाता है, उसको किसने बनाया होगा ?
jo rikśā Hīrālāl calātā hai, usko kisne banāyā hogā?

२ जहाँ हीरालाल रहता है वहाँ और कौन रहता है ?
jahā̃ Hīrālāl rahtā hai vahā̃ aur kaun rahtā hai?

३ जिस शहर में हीरालाल रहता है, उसका नाम क्या है ?
jis śahar mẽ Hīrālāl rahtā hai, uskā nām kyā hai?

४ जब बारिश होती है तो क्या हीरालाल घर जाता है ?
jab bāriś hotī hai to kyā Hīrālāl ghar jātā hai?

५ रिक्शे का वज़न कब बहुत ज़्यादा हो जाता है ?
rikśe kā vazan kab bahut zyādā ho jātā hai?

६ हीरालाल की जेब कब ख़ाली रहती है ?
Hīrālāl kī jeb kab <u>kh</u>ālī rahtī hai?

७ जो लोग रिक्शे चलाते हैं उनकी ज़िन्दगी कैसी होती है ?
jo log rikśe calāte haĩ unkī zindagī kaisī hotī hai?

Exercise 12b Complete the sentences meaningfully:

८ जो लोग भारत के बारे में कुछ सीखना चाहते हैं, उनको ...
jo log bhārat ke bāre mẽ kuch sīkhnā cāhte haĩ, unko…

९ जब मैंने पहली बार ताज महल को देखा, मैंने सोचा कि ...
jab maĩne pahlī bār tāj mahal ko dekhā, maĩne socā ki…

१० जहाँ मेरे रिश्तेदार रहते हैं, वहाँ ...
jahā̃ mere riśtedār rahte haĩ, vahā̃…

११ जो आदमी मेरे साथ काम करता है उसकी ...
jo ādmī mere sāth kām kartā hai uskī…

१२ जो आदमी मेरे घर के सामने रहता है वह ...
jo ādmī mere ghar ke sāmne rahtā hai vah…

१३ जिन लोगों के पास बहुत पैसा है, वे ...
jin logõ ke pās bahut paisā hai, ve…

१४ जो कपड़े मैंने कल ख़रीदे ...
jo kapṛe maĩne kal <u>kh</u>arīde…

Exercise 12c Translate:

15 When I go to Agra I often stay at Raju's place.
16 The man who teaches us Hindi is Raju's brother.
17 The present I gave to Ram today was quite cheap.
18 When I gave it to him he showed it to his mother.
19 When Raju's mother saw my present she began to laugh.
20 I'll never forget the question she asked Raju about me.
21 The answer Raju gave will always remain in my memory.

Exercise 12d Here's a short letter to Manoj from a friend in the USA. Translate it, keeping an eye out the compound verbs.

प्रिय मनोज,

तुम्हारा ख़त मिल गया, शुक्रिया । एक साल से कोई ख़त नहीं आया था तो मैं सोचने लगा था कि मेरे दोस्त मनोज को क्या हो गया है ?

यहाँ सब ठीक है । मेरे भाई की शादी हो गई है । उसने दिल्ली में एक छोटा-सा मकान किराये पर लिया है ।

मेरे पिताजी कहते हैं कि अब तुम भी शादी कर लो । पर मैंने उनको साफ़ बता दिया है कि मैं अभी शादी नहीं करूँगा । अभी जवान हूँ । जब तीस साल का हो जाऊँगा तो शायद इन बातों के बारे में सोचना शुरू करूँगा । लेकिन पिताजी मेरी बात नहीं सुनना चाहते । अभी थोड़ी देर पहले वे फिर से शादी के बारे में बात करने लगे । मैं थोड़ा नाराज़ हो गया । मैंने कहा, "हाँ पापा, मैं ने सुन लिया !"

अपना ई-मेल का पता मुझे बता देना ।

तुम्हारा

मोटू

priy Manoj,
tumhārā <u>kh</u>at mil gayā, śukriyā. ek sāl se koī khat nahī̃ āyā thā to maĩ socne lagā thā ki mere dost Manoj ko kyā ho gayā hai?
yahā̃ sab ṭhīk hai. mere bhāī kī śādī ho gaī hai. usne dillī mẽ ek choṭa-sā makān kirāye par liyā hai.
mere pitājī kahte haĩ ki ab tum bhī śādī kar lo. par maĩne unko sāf kah diyā hai ki maĩ abhī śādī nahī̃ karū̃gā. abhī javān hū̃. jab tīs sāl kā ho jāū̃gā to śāyad in bātõ ke bāre mẽ

socnā śurū karū̃gā. lekin pitājī merī bāt nahī̃ sunna cāhte.
abhī thoṛī der pahle ve phir se śādī ke bāre mẽ bāt karne lage.
maĩ thoṛā nārāz ho gayā. maĩne kahā, 'hā̃ pāpā, maĩne sun liyā!'
apnā ī-mel ka patā mujhe batā denā.
tumhārā
Moṭū.

Glossary

अँगूठा *ãgūṭhā m.* thumb
आँख *ā̃kh f.* eye
उँगली *ũglī* f. finger
उगना *ugnā* to grow (of plants)
उतरना, उतर जाना *utarnā, utar jānā* to get down, alight
उलटी *ulṭī* f. vomiting, sickness
कटना *kaṭnā* to be cut
कमर *kamar* f. waist
कलाई *kalāī* f. wrist
करवाना *karvānā* to cause to be done, to get done
कान *kān* m. ear
कि *ki* when, when suddenly; or
कुहनी *kuhnī* f. elbow
खेल *khel* m. game
ग़रीब *garīb* poor
गर्दन *gardan* f. neck
गाल *gāl* f. cheek
घास *ghās* f. grass
घुटना *ghuṭnā* m. knee
चढ़ना *caṛhnā* to climb; to get into vehicle
चढ़ाव *caṛhāv* m. rise, incline
चमकना *camaknā* to shine
चुकना *cuknā* to have already done (with verb stem: वह जा चुका है *vah jā cukā hai* 'He's already gone')
छाती *chātī* f. chest
जब *jab* when
जलना *jalnā* to burn
जलवाना *jalvānā* to cause to burn
जवान *javān* young
जहाँ *jahā̃* where
जाँघ *jā̃gh* f. high
जेब *jeb* f. pocket
जैसा... वैसा *jaisā... vaisā* as [one thing], so [another]
टाँग *ṭā̃g* f. leg
टूटना *ṭūṭnā* to break
ठुड्डी *ṭhuḍḍī* f. chin
ताज महल *tāj mahal* m. Taj Mahal
दस्त *dast* m. diarrhoea; दस्त आना *dast ānā* to have diarrhoea
दाँत *dā̃t* m. tooth
दिया *diyā* m. lamp
दिल *dil* m. heart
धुलना *dhulnā* to be washed
धुलवाना *dhulvānā* to cause to be washed
नल *nal* m. tap, pipe
नाक *nāk* f. nose
नींद *nī̃d* f. sleep; नींद आना *nī̃d ānā* (sleep to come) to get to sleep
नौकर *naukar* m. servant
पता *patā* m. address; whereabouts

पहाड़ *pahāṛ* m. hill
पाँव *pā̃v* m. foot, leg
पाना *pānā* to find, obtain; to be able, to manage to (with verb stem: मैं नहीं जा पाया *maĩ nahī̃ jā pāyā* 'I didn't manage to go')
पैर *pair* m. foot; पैर की उँगली *pair kī ũglī* f. toe
प्रेस करना *pres karnā* to iron
बनवाना *banvānā* to cause to be made
बहुत ज़्यादा *bahut zyādā* very great, too much
बाँह *bā̃h* f. arm, upper arm
बाल *bāl* m. hair
बुलवाना *bulvānā* to cause to be called
भरना *bharnā* to be filled
भारी *bhārī* heavy
माथा *māthā* m. forehead
मुफ़्त (का) *muft (kā)* free; मुफ़्त में *muft mẽ* for nothing, free
मुँह *mũh* m. mouth; face
मौसम *mausam* m. weather
रिक्शा *rikśā* m. rickshaw
लेटना *leṭnā* to lie down
वज़न *vazan* m. weight
विदेश *videś* abroad; विदेशी *videśī* m. foreigner; adj. foreign
शरीर *śarīr* m. body
शानदार *śāndār* splendid, magnificent
शुद्ध *śuddh* pure
शोला *śolā* m. flame; शोले *śole* 'Sholay', the title of a cult Hindi film (1975)
सवारी *savārī* f. passenger, rider
सहायता *sahāytā* f. assistance
सामने *sāmne* opposite
सिखवाना *sikhvānā* to cause to be taught
सिलवाना *silvānā* to cause to be sewn
सीना *sīnā* to sew
हर *har* every, each
हराम *harām* forbidden
हीरा *hīrā* m. diamond
हो जाना *ho jānā* to become

key to the exercises

Bear in mind that there will often be several possible ways of answering questions and translating sentences! In the case of questions addressed to the reader, sample answers are given.

Unit 1

What's this?

१ जी नहीं, मोती बिल्ली नहीं, कुत्ता है ।
jī nahī̃, Motī billī nahī̃, kuttā hai.

२ जी हाँ, गीता डाक्टर है ।
jī hā̃, Gītā ḍākṭar hai.

३ जी नहीं, मैं डाक्टर नहीं, अध्यापक हूँ ।
jī nahī̃, maĩ ḍākṭar nahī̃, adhyāpak hū̃.

४ जी हाँ, राजू और गीता हिन्दुस्तानी हैं ।
jī hā̃, Rājū aur Gītā hindustānī haĩ.

५ जी हाँ, हिन्दी बहुत आसान है !
jī hā̃, hindī bahut āsān hai!

1a

जावेद यह क्या है ? *Jāved: yah kyā hai?*

मनोज यह मेरा रेडियो है । *Manoj: yah merā reḍiyo hai.*

जावेद वह लड़का कौन है ? *Jāved: vah laṛkā kaun hai?*

मनोज वह मेरा भाई है । *Manoj: vah merā bhāī hai.*

जावेद उसका नाम क्या है ? *Jāved: uskā nām kyā hai?*

मनोज उसका नाम राम है । *Manoj: uskā nām Rām hai.*

जावेद वह लड़की कौन है ? *Jāved: vah laṛkī kaun hai?*

मनोज उसका नाम मीना है । *Manoj: uskā nām Mīnā hai.*

जावेद क्या वह बीमार है ? *Jāved: kyā vah bīmār hai?*

मनोज जी नहीं, वह बीमार नहीं है, वह ठीक है । *Manoj: jī nahī̃, vah bīmār nahī̃ hai, vah ṭhīk hai.*

1b

१ जी नहीं, सुरेश शादी-शुदा नहीं है ।
jī nahī̃, Sureś śādī-śudā nahī̃ hai.

२ जी हाँ, वह हिन्दुस्तानी है ।
jī hā̃, vah hindustānī hai.

३ जी नहीं, वह अध्यापक नहीं है, विद्यार्थी है ।
jī nahī̃, vah adhyāpak nahī̃ hai, vidyārthī hai.

४ उसका पूरा नाम सुरेश खन्ना है ।
uskā pūrā nām Suresh Khannā hai.

५ जी हाँ, उमा हिन्दुस्तानी है ।
jī hā̃, Umā hindustānī hai.

६ जी नहीं, वह डाक्टर नहीं है, वह अध्यापक है ।
jī nahī̃, vah ḍākṭar nahī̃ hai, vah adhyāpak hai.

७ जी नहीं, वह शादी-शुदा नहीं है ।
jī nahī̃, vah śādī-śudā nahī̃ hai.

८ जी हाँ, वह सुखी है ।
jī hā̃, vah sukhī hai.

९ जी नहीं, विनोद अँग्रेज़ नहीं है, वह अमरीकन है ।
jī nahī̃, Vinod ā̃grez nahī̃ hai, vah amrīkan hai.

१० जी नहीं, वह अध्यापक नहीं है, वह डाक्टर है ।
jī nahī̃, vah adhyāpak nahī̃ hai, vah ḍākṭar hai.

११ उसका पूरा नाम विनोद कुमार है ।
uskā pūrā nām Vinod Kumār hai.

१२ जी हाँ, वह शादी-शुदा है ।
jī hā̃, vah śādī-śudā hai.

१३ जी नहीं, सुरेश हिन्दुस्तानी है लेकिन विनोद अमरीकन है ।
jī nahī̃, Sureś hindustānī hai lekin Vinod amrīkan hai.

१४ जी नहीं, विनोद शादी-शुदा है लेकिन उमा शादी-सुदा नहीं है ।
jī nahī̃, Vinod śādī-śudā hai lekin Umā śādī-śudā nahī̃ hai.

१५ जी नहीं, उमा अध्यापक है लेकिन सुरेश विद्यार्थी है ।
jī nahī̃, umā adhyāpak hai lekin Sureś vidyārthī hai.

Unit 2

Role play

१ जी हाँ, मैं गीता हूँ । *jī hā̃, maĩ Gītā hū̃.*

२ मेरा पूरा नाम गीता शर्मा है । *merā pūrā nām Gītā Śarmā hai.*

३ जी हाँ, मैं शादी-शुदा हूँ । *jī hā̃, maĩ śādī-śudā hū̃.*

४ राकेश मेरा भाई है । *Rākeś merā bhāī hai.*

५ सीता मेरी बहिन है । *Sītā merī bahin hai.*

६ जी नहीं, मेरी बहिन बीमार है । *jī nahī̃, merī bahin bīmār hai.*

७ जी नहीं, मेरा भाई ठीक है । *jī nahī̃, merā bhāī ṭhīk hai.*

८ जी नहीं, मैं बीमार नहीं हूँ, मैं ठीक हूँ । *jī nahī̃, maĩ bīmār nahī̃ hū̃, maĩ ṭhīk hū̃.*

Ordinal numbers quiz

१ जी हाँ, पहला लड़का मोटा है ।
jī hā̃, pahlā laṛkā moṭā hai.

२ पहला लड़का गणेश है ।
pahlā laṛkā Gaṇeś hai.

३ जी नहीं, तीसरा लड़का ख़ुश नहीं है ।
jī nahī̃, tīsrā laṛkā <u>kh</u>uś nahī̃ hai.

४ पाँचवाँ लड़का राजेश है ।
pā̃cvā̃ laṛkā Rājeś hai.

५ जी हाँ, चौथा लड़का बहुत पतला है ।
jī hā̃, cauthā laṛkā bahut patlā hai.

६ चौथा लड़का दिनेश है ।
cauthā laṛkā Dineś hai.

५ जी नहीं, दूसरा लड़का महेश नहीं, सुरेश है ।
jī nahī̃, dūsrā laṛka Maheś nahī̃, Sureś hai.

2a

१ मेरा नाम मनोज है । राजू और गीता शर्मा मेरे माता-पिता हैं ।
merā nām Manoj hai. Rājū aur Gītā Śarmā mere mātā-pitā haĩ.

२ मीना मेरी छोटी बहिन है और राम मेरा छोटा भाई है ।
Mīnā merī choṭī bahin hai aur Rām merā choṭā bhāī hai.

३ मोती हमारा कुत्ता है । वह बहुत प्यारा है ।
Motī hamārā kuttā hai. vah bahut pyārā hai.

४ यह मीना है । यह ठीक है । यह छोटी है ।
yah Mīnā hai. yah ṭhīk hai. yah choṭī hai.

५ हमारा मकान बहुत बड़ा नहीं है । सिर्फ़ पाँच कमरे हैं ।
hamārā makān bahut baṛā nahī̃ hai. sirf pā̃c kamre haĩ.

६ वह लड़का मेरा दोस्त है । उसका नाम प्रताप है ।
vah laṛkā merā dost hai. uskā nām Pratāp hai.

७ जावेद साहब हमारे पड़ोसी हैं ।
Jāved sāhab hamāre paṛosī haĩ.

2b

८ ये लड़के बहुत प्यारे हैं । *ye laṛke bahut pyāre haĩ.*

९ ये कुत्ते हमारे नहीं हैं । *ye kutte hamāre nahī̃ haĩ.*

१० वे लड़के कौन हैं ? *ve laṛke kaun haĩ?*

११ ये आदमी कौन हैं ? *ye ādmī kaun haĩ?*

१२ मेरे दोस्त पंजाबी हैं । *mere dost panjābī haĩ.*

१३ क्या ये कुत्ते आपके हैं ? *kyā ye kutte āpke haĩ?*

१४ वे औरतें कौन हैं ? *ve auratẽ kaun haĩ?*

१५ हमारे बेटे अच्छे लड़के हैं । *hamāre beṭe acche laṛke haĩ.*

१६ मेरी बेटियाँ बीमार हैं । *merī beṭiyā̃ bīmār haĩ.*

१७ क्या ये किताबें महँगी हैं ? *kyā ye kitābẽ mahãgī haĩ?*

१८ ये मेज़ें गंदी हैं । *ye mezẽ gandī haĩ.*

2c

१९ आप कौन हैं ? *āp kaun haĩ?*

२० आपका नाम क्या है ? *āpkā nām kyā hai?*

२१ आपके माता-पिता बहुत अच्छे लोग हैं । *āpke mātā-pitā bahut acche log haĩ.*

२२ आपका भाई सुंदर नहीं है । *āpkā bhāī sundar nahī̃ hai.*

२३ आप दोनों लड़के लंबे हैं । *āp donõ laṛke lambe haĩ.*

२४ आप कैसे हैं ? *āp kaise haĩ?*

२५ तुम्हारा नाम क्या है ? *tumhārā nām kyā hai?*

२६ क्या तुम ठीक हो ? *kyā tum ṭhīk ho?*

२७ तुम नाराज़ नहीं हो ? *tum nārāz nahī̃ ho?*

२८ तुम कैसी हो ? *tum kaisī ho?*

Unit 3

Some questions for you

१ सिर्फ़ एक आदमी है । *sirf ek ādmī hai.*

२ यह लंबा आदमी है । *yah lambā ādmī hai.*

३ मेज़ छोटी है । *mez choṭī hai.*

४ दो लड़कियाँ हैं । *do laṛkiyā̃ haĩ.*

५ कुल मिलाकर तीन लोग हैं । *kul milākar tīn log haĩ.*

६ जी नहीं, एक लड़की लंबी है, दूसरी छोटी है । *jī nahī̃, ek laṛkī lambī hai, dūsrī choṭī hai.*

७ दो चूहे हैं । *do cūhe haĩ.*

८ सिर्फ़ एक कुरसी है । *sirf ek kursī hai.*

९ जी नहीं, चूहे छोटे हैं । *jī nahī̃, cūhe choṭe haĩ.*

१० सिर्फ़ एक तोता है । *sirf ek totā hai.*

Where's the cat?

१ बिल्ली बड़ी कुरसी पर है । *billī baṛī kursī par hai.*

२ कुत्ता छोटी कुरसी पर है । *kuttā choṭī kursī par hai.*

३ तस्वीर में दो कुरसियाँ हैं । *tasvīr mẽ do kursiyā̃ haĩ.*

४ तस्वीर में सिर्फ़ एक बिल्ली है । *tasvīr mẽ sirf ek billī hai.*

५ छोटी कुरसी पर कुत्ता है । *choṭī kursī par kuttā hai.*

६ बड़ी कुरसी पर बिल्ली है । *baṛī kursī par billī hai.*

७ मेज़ पर कुछ किताबें हैं । *mez par kuch kitābẽ haĩ.*

८ जी हाँ, दोनों बहुत प्यारे हैं ! *jī hā̃, donõ bahut pyāre haĩ!*

House for rent

१ घर आगरे में है ।
ghar āgre mẽ hai.

२ नहीं, वह नया है ।
nahī̃, vah nayā hai.

३ चार कमरे हैं -- दो बड़े और दो छोटे ।
cār kamre haĩ — do baṛe aur do choṭe.

४ हाँ, सब कमरों में खिड़कियाँ हैं ।
hā̃, sab kamrõ mẽ khiṛkiyā̃ haĩ.

५ बड़े कमरों में पंखे हैं ।
baṛe kamrõ mẽ pankhe haĩ.

६ बाहर बग़ीचा है । बग़ीचे में कुछ पेड़ हैं ।
bāhar bagīcā hai. bagīce mẽ kuch peṛ haĩ.

७ नहीं, दुकानें पास में हैं ।
nahī̃, dukānẽ pās mẽ haĩ.

८ किराया ५००० रुपये है ?
kirāyā 5000 hai.

Two tasks for you

१ गीता वाराणसी से है । *Gītā vārāṇasī se hai.*

२ जी हाँ, गीता शादी-शुदा है । *jī hā̃, Gītā śādī-śudā hai.*

३ जी हाँ, राजू दिल्ली से है । *jī hā̃, Rājū dillī se hai.*

४ जी नहीं, राजू डाक्टर नहीं, अध्यापक है । *jī nahī̃, Rājū ḍākṭar nahī̃, adhyāpak hai.*

५ जी नहीं, यह घर दिल्ली में नहीं, आगरे में है । *jī nahī̃, yah ghar dillī mẽ nahī̃, āgre mẽ hai.*

६ घर में पाँच कमरे हैं । *ghar mẽ pā̃c kamre haĩ.*

७ बड़े कमरे में एक मेज़ है । *baṛe kamre mẽ ek mez hai.*

८ कम्प्यूटर मेज़ पर है । *kampyūṭar mez par hai.*

९ किताबें फ़र्श पर हैं । *kitābẽ farś par haĩ.*

१० बग़ीचे में कुछ लंबे पेड़ हैं । *bag̱īce mẽ kuch lambe peṛ haĩ.*

3a

१ मेरी किताबें मेज़ पर पड़ी हैं ।
merī kitābẽ mez par paṛī haĩ.

२ आपका भाई बग़ीचे में बैठा है ।
āpkā bhāī bag̱īce mẽ baiṭhā hai.

३ मैं बड़े कमरे में खड़ा हूँ ।
maĩ baṛe kamre mẽ khaṛā hū̃.

४ आपकी किताबें छोटी अलमारी में हैं ।
āpkī kitābẽ choṭī almārī mẽ haĩ.

५ उसका मकान यहाँ से दूर नहीं है ।
uskā makān yahā̃ se dūr nahī̃ hai.

६ आपके परिवार में कितने लोग हैं ?
āpke parivār mẽ kitne log haĩ?

७ आपके पति के पास कितना पैसा है ?
āpke pati ke pās kitnā paisā hai?

८ आज आपकी पत्नी कैसी हैं ? और आप कैसे हैं ?
āj āpkī patnī kaisī haĩ? aur āp kaise haĩ?

९ बच्चे घर पर नहीं हैं, स्कूल पर हैं ।
bacce ghar par nahī̃ haĩ, skūl par haĩ.

१० क्या यह छोटी लड़की तुम्हारी बहिन है ?
kyā yah choṭī laṛkī tumhārī bahin hai?

3b

११ मेरा पूरा नाम श्रीमती गीता शर्मा है ।
merā pūrā nām śrīmatī Gītā Śarmā hai.

१२ जी हाँ, मैं डाक्टर हूँ ।
jī hā̃, maĩ ḍākṭar hū̃.

१३ जी नहीं, मेरे पति अध्यापक हैं ।
jī nahī̃, mere pati adhyāpak haĩ.

१४ जी हाँ, वे घर पर हैं । *jī hā̃, ve ghar par haĩ.*

१५ मेरे पति दिल्ली से हैं, लेकिन मैं वाराणसी से हूँ ।
mere pati dillī se haĩ, lekin maĩ vārāṇasī se hū̃.

१६ हमारे मकान में पाँच कमरे हैं ।
hamāre makān mẽ pā̃c kamre haĩ.

१७ हमारे परिवार में तीन बच्चे हैं ।
hamāre parivār mẽ tīn bacce haĩ.

१८ जी नहीं, वह बग़ीचे में है ।
jī nahī̃, vah bag̲īce mẽ hai.

१९ जी नहीं, उसका स्कूल यहाँ से दूर नहीं है ।
jī nahī̃, uskā skūl yahā̃ se dūr nahī̃ hai.

२० दूसरे बच्चे भी बग़ीचे में हैं ।
dūsre bacce bhī bag̲īce mẽ haĩ.

२१ जी हाँ, कुत्ता हमारा है ।
jī hā̃, kuttā hamārā hai.

२२ उसका नाम मोती है ।
uskā nām Motī hai.

२३ जी हाँ, हमारे पास गाड़ी है ।
jī hā̃, hamāre pās gāṛī hai.

२४ जी हाँ, मेरे पास कम्प्यूटर है ।
jī hā̃, mere pās kampyūṭar hai.

Unit 4

Practise what you've learnt

१ मत जाओ । आओ, बैठो ।
mat jāo! āo, baiṭho.

२ बताओ, तुम कैसे हो ?
batāo, tum kaise ho?

३ समोसा खाओ, पानी पियो ।
samosā khāo, pānī piyo.

४ यह दूसरा समोसा भी लो ।
yah dūsrā samosā bhī lo.

५ मोती को समोसा न दो ।
Motī ko samosā na do.

६ और खाओ !
aur khāo!

७ ख़ाली प्लेट मेज़ पर रखो ।
<u>kh</u>ālī pleṭ mez par rakho.

८ अरे ! सिग्रेट न पियो !
are! sigreṭ na piyo!

९ और चाय लो ।
aur cāy lo.

4a

१ घर में शराब मत पियो / पीजिए ।
ghar mẽ śarāb mat piyo / pījie.

२ ध्यान से सुनो / सुनिए ।
dhyān se suno / sunie.

३ यह पत्र मनोज को भेजो / भेजिए ।
yah patr Manoj ko bhejo / bhejie.

४ घर जाओ / जाइए ।
ghar jāo / jāie.

५ मुझको उसका नाम बताओ / बताइए ।
mujhko uskā nām batāo / batāie.

६ ये दो समोसे खाओ / खाइए ।
ye do samose khāo / khāie.

७ सितार बजाओ / बजाइए ।
sitār bajāo / bajāie.

८ मेरे पड़ोसी से पूछो / पूछिए ।
mere paṛosī se pūcho / pūchie.

९ यह पैसा मेरी पत्नी को दो / दीजिए ।
yah paisā merī patnī ko do / dījie.

१० आज गाड़ी मत चलाओ / चलाइए ।
āj gāṛī mat calāo / calāie.

११ धीरे धीरे बोलो / बोलिए ।
dhīre dhīre bolo / bolie.

4b

१२ राम से पूछिए । *Rām se pūchie.* Ask Ram.

१३ बच्चों को मत बताना । *baccõ ko mat batānā.* Don't tell the children.

१४ चाचा जी से हिन्दी बोलो । *cācā jī se hindī bolo.* Speak Hindi with uncle.

१५ मनोज से बात कीजिए । *Manoj se bāt kījie.* Talk to Manoj.

१६ गीता से पैसा माँगना । *Gītā se paisā mā̃gnā.* Ask Gita for money.

4c

१७ मेरा भाई दिल्ली में रहता है । मेरी बहिन दिल्ली में रहती है ।
merā bhāī dillī mẽ rahtā hai. merī bahin dillī mẽ rahtī hai.

१८ मैं हिन्दी समझता हूँ । हम हिन्दी समझते हैं ।
maĩ hindī samajhtā hū̃. ham hindī samajhte haĩ.

१९ लड़का गाड़ी बहुत तेज़ चलाता है । लड़की गाड़ी बहुत तेज़ चलाती है ।
laṛkā gāṛī bahut tez calātā hai. laṛkī gāṛī bahut tez calātī hai.

२० मेरा पति हिन्दी बोलता है । मेरी पत्नी हिन्दी बोलती है ।
merā pati hindī boltā hai. merī patnī hindī boltī hai.

२१ कौन अँग्रेज़ी बोलता है ? कौन अँग्रेज़ी बोलती है ?
kaun ā̃grezī boltā hai? kaun ā̃grezī boltī hai?

Unit 5

5a (sample answers)

१ बहुत अच्छी है, धन्यवाद ।
bahut acchī hai, dhanyavād.

२ जी हाँ, घर में सब लोग ठीक हैं ।
jī hā̃, ghar mẽ sab log ṭhīk haĩ.

३ मुझको चावल चाहिए ।
mujhko cāval cāhie.

४ पाँच किलो दीजिए ।
pā̃c kilo dījie.

५ चीनी भी चाहिए । दो किलो देना ।
cīnī bhī cāhie. do kilo denā.

६ हाँ, एक टिकिया साबुन ।
hā̃, ek ṭikiyā sābun.

७ नहीं, वह सब नहीं चाहिए ।
nahī̃, vah sab nahī̃ cāhie.

८ यहाँ से काफ़ी दूर है, लेकिन मेरे पास गाड़ी है ।
yahā̃ se kāfī dūr hai, lekin mere pās gāṛī hai.

९ जी नहीं, ये मेरी नहीं हैं ।
jī nahī̃, ye merī nahī̃ haĩ.

१० जी नहीं, गाड़ी दुकान के बहुत पास खड़ी है ।
jī nahī̃, gāṛī dukān ke bahut pās khaṛī hai.

5b

११ मुझको तीन समोसे चाहिए ।
mujhko tīn samose cāhie.

१२ उनको यह मकान पसंद नहीं है, छोटा मकान पसंद है ।
unko yah makān pasand nahī̃ hai, choṭā makān pasand hai.

१३ मुझको यह कमरा पसंद नहीं है, कोई दूसरा कमरा दिखाइए ।
mujhko yah kamrā pasand nahī̃ hai, koī dūsrā kamrā dikhāie.

१४ आप कहाँ रहते हैं ? हम पुरानी दिल्ली में रहते हैं ।
āp kahā̃ rahte haĩ? ham purānī dillī mẽ rahte haĩ.

१५ आपका मकान मेरे मकान से बहुत दूर नहीं है । कल आना ।
āpkā makān hamāre makān se bahut dūr nahī̃ hai. kal ānā.

१६ मुझको मालूम है कि मेरे अध्यापक यहाँ नहीं रहते ।
mujhko mālūm hai ki mere adhyāpak yahā̃ nahī̃ rahte.

१७ मुझको मालूम है कि आपके अध्यापक कहाँ रहते हैं ।
mujhko mālūm hai ki āpke adhyāpak kahā̃ rahte haĩ.

१८ दिल्ली में मकान बहुत महँगे होते हैं ।
dillī mẽ makān bahut mahãge hote haĩ.

१९ दादा जी बहुत सुन्दर हिन्दी बोलते हैं ।
Dādā jī bahut sundar hindī bolte haĩ.

२० हमको ये काले जूते नहीं चाहिए ।
hamko ye kāle jūte nahī̃ cāhie.

Unit 6

You can go

१ हम सिनेमा जा सकते हैं ।
ham sinemā jā sakte haĩ.

२ चाचा जी घर पर रह सकते हैं ।
cācā jī ghar par rah sakte haĩ.

३ मैं अध्यापक से पूछ सकता हूँ ।
maĩ adhyāpak se pūch saktā hū̃.

४ बच्चे बग़ीचे में खेल सकते हैं ।
bacce bag̱īce mẽ khel sakte haĩ.

५ मैं अख़बार पढ़ सकती हूँ ।
maĩ a<u>kh</u>bār paṛh saktī hū̃.

६ हम बच्चों को सब कुछ बता सकते हैं ।
ham baccõ ko sab kuch batā sakte haĩ.

७ तुम शराब नहीं पी सकते हो ।
tum śarāb nahī̃ pī sakte ho.

८ वह कुछ नहीं कह सकता है ।
vah kuch nahī̃ kah saktā hai.

Turning 'I want' into 'let me'

१ मुझको अमरीका जाने दीजिए ।
mujhko amrīkā jāne dījie.

२ मुझको गाड़ी चलाने दीजिए ।
mujhko gāṛī calāne dījie.

३ मुझको खाना खाने दीजिए ।
mujhko khānā khāne dījie.

४ मुझको काम करने दीजिए ।
mujhko kām karne dījie.

५ मुझको आपसे बात करने दीजिए ।
mujhko āpse bāt kare dījie.

६ उसको सिगरेट पीने दीजिए ।
usko sigreṭ pīne dījie.

७ हमको अध्यापक से कुछ कहने दीजिए ।
hamko adhyāpak se kuch kahne dījie.

८ उसको हिन्दी सीखने दीजिए ।
usko hindī sīkhne dījie.

९ बच्चों को समोसे खाने दीजिए ।
baccõ ko samose khāne dījie.

१० हमको यहाँ रहने दीजिए ।
hamko yahā̃ rahne dījie.

6a

१ फलवाला फल बेचता है !
phalvālā phal bectā hai!

२ अख़बारवाला अख़बार बेचता है !
akhbārvālā akhbār bectā hai!

३ दूधवाला दूध बेचता है !
dūdhvālā dūdh bectā hai!

४ अध्यापक पढ़ाता है ।
adhyāpak paṛhātā hai.

५ स्कूल में बच्चे पढ़ते हैं ।
skūl mẽ bacce paṛhte haĩ.

६ घर पर बच्चे खेलते हैं ।
ghar par bacce khelte haĩ.

७ ड्राइवर गाड़ी चलाता है ।
ḍrāivar gāṛī calātā hai.

८ दुकानदार माल बेचता है ।
dukāndār māl bectā hai.

6b (sample answers)

९ मैं लन्दन में रहता हूँ। *maĩ landan mẽ rahtā hū̃.*

१० मैं हिन्दी पढ़ाता हूँ। *maĩ hindī paṛhātā hū̃.*

११ जी नहीं, मैं सितार नहीं बजाता, सिर्फ़ सुनता हूँ! *jī nahī̃, maĩ sitār nahī̃ bajātā, sirf suntā hū̃!*

१२ मैं कई अख़बार पढ़ता हूँ। *maĩ kaī a<u>kh</u>bār paṛhtā hū̃.*

१३ मैं चार भाषाएँ बोलता हूँ। *maĩ cār bhāṣāẽ boltā hū̃.*

6c

१४ जगदीश मनोज का अख़बार पढ़ता है।
Jagdīś Manoj kā akhbār paṛhtā hai.

१५ मेरे दो भाई एक बड़े दफ़्तर में काम करते हैं।
mere do bhāī ek baṛe daftar mẽ kām karte haĩ.

१६ मेरी बहिन मेरे भाई की गाड़ी चलाती है।
merī bahin mere bhāī kī gāṛī calātī hai.

१७ वह सिर्फ़ हिन्दी बोलता है, अँग्रेज़ी नहीं बोलता।
vah sirf hindī boltā hai, ãgrezī nahī̃ boltā.

१८ हमारे अध्यापक तीन भाषाएँ बोलते हैं।
hamāre adhyāpak tīn bhāṣāẽ bolte haĩ.

१९ उसके बच्चे बग़ीचे में क्रिकेट खेलते हैं।
uske bacce bagīce mẽ kriket khelte haĩ.

२० हमारे माता-पिता गोश्त नहीं खाते हैं।
hamāre mātā-pitā gośt nahī̃ khāte haĩ.

२१ आप कहाँ काम करते हैं? आप कहाँ रहते हैं?
āp kahā̃ kām karte haĩ? āp kahā̃ rahte haĩ?

२२ आपका छोटा भाई क्या करता है?
āpka choṭā bhāī kyā kartā hai?

२३ आपकी माता जी कितनी भाषाएँ बोलती हैं?
āpkī mātā jī kitnī bhāṣāẽ boltī haĩ?

Unit 7

Some questions about Jagdish's memories

१ जगदीश जी वाराणसी में रहते थे ।
Jagdīś jī vārāṇasī mẽ rahte the.

२ उनके परिवार में सात बच्चे थे ।
unke parivār mẽ sāt bacce the.

३ उनकी बहिनें स्कूल जाना चाहती थीं, लेकिन उस ज़माने में बहुत कम लड़कियाँ स्कूल जाती थीं ।
unkī bahinẽ skūl jānā cāhtī thī̃, lekin us zamāne mẽ bahut kam laṛkiyā̃ skūl jātī thī̃.

४ उनका स्कूल उनके घर से काफ़ी दूर था ।
unkā skūl unke ghar se kāfī dūr thā.

५ जी नहीं, वे पैदल नहीं जाते थे, साइकिल से जाते थे ।
jī nahī̃, ve paidal nahī̃ jāte the, sāikil se jāte the.

7a

१ जगदीश मनोज का अख़बार पढ़ता था ।
Jagdīś Manoj kā a<u>kh</u>bār paṛhtā thā.

२ मेरे दो भाई एक बड़े दफ़्तर में काम करते थे ।
mere do bhāī ek baṛe daftar mẽ kām karte the.

३ मेरी बहिन मेरे भाई की गाड़ी चलाती थी ।
merī bahin mere bhāī kī gāṛī calātī thī.

४ वह सिर्फ़ हिन्दी बोलता था, अँग्रेज़ी नहीं बोलता था ।
vah sirf hindī boltā thā, ā̃grezī nahī̃ boltā thā.

५ हमारे अध्यापक तीन भाषाएँ बोलते थे ।
hamāre adhyāpak tīn bhāṣāẽ bolte the.

६ उसके बच्चे बग़ीचे में क्रिकेट खेलते थे ।
uske bacce bag̱īce mẽ kriket̩ khelte the.

७ हमारे माता-पिता गोश्त नहीं खाते थे ।
hamāre mātā-pitā gośt nahī̃ khāte the.

८ आप कहाँ काम करते थे ? आप कहाँ रहते थे ?
āp kahā̃ kām karte the? āp kahā̃ rahte the?

९ आपका छोटा भाई क्या करता था ?
āpka choṭā bhāī kyā kartā thā?

१० आपकी माता जी कितनी भाषाएँ बोलती थीं ?
āpkī mātā jī kitnī bhāṣāẽ boltī thī̃?

7b

11 In Jagdish's family only the boys used to go to school.
12 His school was *very* far from his house.
13 At school everyone called him 'Master ji', not just the children.
14 In his job the actual pay wasn't very good.
15 Jagdish's mother only spoke Hindi.
16 In those days the children, at least, were very happy.
17 There wasn't actually a garden, but there were lots of places for playing in.
18 As for the children, they used to sleep on the roof.
19 In his *childhood*, Raju was very fond of writing letters.
20 The Prime Minister was kind, but he used to have a lot of work.

7c

हम लोग वाराणसी के पास एक छोटे गाँव में रहते थे । मेरे पिताजी स्कूल में अध्यापक थे । लेकिन वे नता बनना चाहते थे । वे प्रधान मंत्री बनने के सपने देखते थे । मेरी माँ उनको "प्रधान मंत्री जी" ही कहती थीं । हमारा घर गंगा के निकारे पर था । हम नदी के किनारे बहुत खेलते थे ।

उस ज़माने में हम हमेशा बड़े शहरों के बारे में बात करते थे । मैं अपने भाइयों और दोस्तों से कहता था कि बड़े लोग बड़े शहरों में ही रहते हैं । मैं भी बड़ा आदमी बनना चाहता था, मैं भी बड़े शहर में रहना चाहता था । मैं अब लंदन में रहता हूँ और मुझे मालूम है कि बड़े शहर की ज़िन्दगी कैसी होती है ... मैं एक छोटे गाँव में रहना चाहता हूँ !

ham log vārāṇasī ke pās ek choṭe gā̃v mẽ rahte the. mere pitājī skūl mẽ adhyāpak the. lekin ve netā bannā cāhte the. ve pradhān mantrī banne ke sapne dekhte the. merī mā̃ unko 'pradhān mantrī jī' hī kahtī thī̃. hamārā ghar gangā ke kināre par thā. ham nadī ke kināre bahut khelte the.

us zamāne mẽ ham hameśā baṛe śaharõ ke bāre mẽ bāt karte the. maĩ apne bhāiyõ aur dostõ se kahtā thā ki baṛe log baṛe śaharõ mẽ hī rahte haĩ. maĩ bhī baṛā ādmī bannā cāhtā thā, maĩ bhī baṛe śahar mẽ rahnā cāhtā thā. maĩ ab landan mẽ rahtā hū̃ aur mujhe mālūm hai ki baṛe śahar kī zindagī kaisī hotī hai…maĩ ek choṭe gā̃v mẽ rahnā cāhtā hū̃!

Unit 8

Four children

१ जी हाँ, ओम शंकर से बड़ा है ।
jī hā̃, Om Śankar se baṛā hai.

२ दो बच्चे रीता से छोटे हैं ।
do bacce Rītā se choṭe haĩ.

३ सबसे बड़ा लड़का शिव है ।
sabse baṛā laṛkā Śiv hai.

४ सबसे छोटा लड़का शंकर है ।
sabse choṭā laṛkā Śankar hai.

५ ओम सिर्फ़ एक बच्चे से बड़ा है ।
Om sirf ek bacce se baṛā hai.

६ जी नहीं, रीता शिव से छोटी है ।
jī nahī̃, Rītā Śiv se choṭī hai.

७ जी हाँ, रीता ओम से छोटी नहीं है ।
jī nahī̃, Rītā Om se choṭī nahī̃ hai.

८ जी नहीं, रीता शंकर से बड़ी है ।
jī nahī̃, Rītā Śankar se baṛī hai.

९ मुझे तो सभी तस्वीरें बहुत पसंद हैं !
mujhe to sabhī tasvīrẽ bahut pasand haĩ!

Practise what you've learnt

१ जावेद पत्र लिख रहा है ।
Jāved patr likh rahā hai.

२ दो लड़कियाँ ताश खेल रही हैं ।
do laṛkiyā̃ tāś khel rahī haĩ.

३ कोई आदमी खाना तैयार कर रहा है ।
koī ādmī khānā taiyār kar rahā hai.

४ कुत्ता सो रहा है ।
kuttā so rahā hai.

५ सीता फ़ोन पर बात कर रही है ।
Sītā fon par bāt kar rahī hai.

६ गीता और राजू शराब पी रहे हैं ।
Gītā aur Rājū śarāb pī rahe haĩ.

७ राम बरतन माँज रहा है ।
Rām bartan mā̃j rahā hai.

८ उषा दौड़ रही है ।
Uṣā dauṛ rahī hai.

8a

१ आप उनसे ज़्यादा होशियार नहीं हैं ।
āp unse zyādā hośiyār nahī̃ haĩ.

२ मैं अपने भाई से बड़ी हूँ लेकिन आपसे छोटी हूँ ।
maĩ apne bhāī se baṛī hū̃ lekin āpse choṭī hū̃.

३ मेरी दूसरी बहिन सबसे होशियार है ।
merī dūsrī bahin sabse hośiyār hai.

४ कुछ लोग कहते हैं कि हिन्दी अँग्रेज़ी से ज़्यादा आसान है ।
kuch log kahte haĩ ki hindī ā̃grezī se zyādā āsān hai.

५ माँ सोचती हैं कि मेरी बहिन मुझसे ज़्यादा सुंदर है ।
mā̃ soctī haĩ ki merī bahin mujhse zyāda sundar hai.

६ पिताजी माताजी से ज़्यादा जानते हैं लेकिन वे कुछ नहीं कह सकते हैं ।
pitājī mātājī se zyādā jānte haĩ lekin ve kuch nahī̃ kah sakte haĩ.

७ उनका मकान हमारे मकान से ज़्यादा बड़ा और सुंदर है ।
unkā makān hamāre makān se zyādā baṛā aur sundar hai.

८ मैं आपसे ज़्यादा होशियार हूँ ।
maĩ āpse zyādā hośiyār hū̃.

९ आपकी भाषा मेरी भाषा से ज़्यादा मुश्किल है ।
āpkī bhāṣā merī bhāṣā se zyādā muśkil hai.

8b

१० हम लोग अपने दोस्तों को खाना खाने बुला रहे हैं ।
ham log apne dostõ ko khānā khāne bulā rahe haĩ. We're inviting our friends for a meal.

११ मैं खाना तैयार कर रहा हूँ ।
maĩ khānā taiyār kar rahā hū̃. I am preparing the food.

१२ वे लोग शाम को आ रहे हैं ।
ve log śām ko ā rahe haĩ. They are coming in the evening.

१३ वे अपने बच्चों और दोस्तों को भी ला रहे हैं ।
ve apne baccõ aur dostõ ko bhī lā rahe haĩ. They're bringing their children and friends too.

१४ मेरी पत्नी कह रही है कि उनके बच्चे मोती को मार रहे हैं ।
merī patnī kah rahī hai ki unke bacce Motī ko mār rahe haĩ. My wife is saying that their children are hitting Moti.

१५ दादी जी हमारी मदद नहीं कर रही हैं, सिर्फ़ रेडियो सुन रही हैं ।

dādī jī hamārī madad nahī̃ kar rahī haĩ, sirf reḍiyo sun rahī haĩ. Grandma isn't helping us, she's only listening to the radio.

१६ हमारा कुकर ठीक से काम नहीं कर रहा है ।
hamārā kukar ṭhīk se kām nahī̃ kar rahā hai.
Our cooker isn't working properly.

१७ हमारे दोस्त कह रहे हैं कि बाथरूम में पानी नहीं आ रहा है ।

hamāre dost kah rahe haĩ ki bāthrūm mẽ pānī nahī̃ ā rahā hai. Our friends are saying that there isn't any water ['coming'] in the bathroom.

8c **(sample answers)**

१८ अपने ख़ाली समय में मैं अपने दोस्तों से मिलता हूँ ।
apne khālī samay mẽ maĩ apne dostõ se miltā hū̃.

१९ मुझे दोनों पसंद हैं – घर पर रहना भी और बाहर जाना भी !
mujhe donõ pasand haĩ — ghar par rahnā bhī aur bāhar jānā bhī. (Note भी...भी *bhī…bhī* 'both…and'.)

२० क्योंकि मेरे बहुत-से हिन्दुस्तानी दोस्त हैं ।
kyõki mere bahut-se hindustānī dost haĩ.

२१ जी नहीं, मेरे ख़याल में दोनों भाषाएँ काफ़ी मुश्किल हैं !
jī nahī̃, mere khyāl se donõ bhāṣāẽ kāfī muśkil haĩ!

२२ जी हाँ, मेरे हिन्दुस्तानी दोस्त हिन्दी बोलते हैं ।
jī hā̃, mere hindustānī dost hindī bolte haĩ.

२३ आज मैं यह किताब लिख रहा हूँ !
āj maĩ yah kitāb likh rahā hū̃!

२४ अपनी छुट्टियों में मैं भारत या ग्रीस [Greece] जाता हूँ ।
apnī chuṭṭiyõ mẽ maĩ bhārat yā grīs jātā hū̃.

२५ मैं अभी सोच रहा हूँ कि यह पाठ [lesson] बहुत लंबा है !
maĩ abhī soc rahā hū̃ ki yah pāṭh bahut lambā hai!

Unit 9

Practise what you've learnt (sample answers)

१ आज रात को मैं हिन्दुस्तानी खाना खाऊँगा ।
āj rāt ko maĩ hindustānī khānā khāū̃gā.

२ मैं शायद बीयर पिऊँगा ।
maĩ śāyad bīyar piū̃gā.

३ आज मैं काम करूँगा और अपने बड़े बेटे से मिलने जाऊँगा ।
āj maĩ kām karū̃gā aur apne baṛe beṭe se milne jāū̃gā.

४ कल सुबह् मैं ब्रिटिश लाइब्रेरी [British Library] जाऊँगा ।
kal subah maĩ briṭiś lāibrerī jāū̃gā.

५ अगर आप परसों लंदन आएँगे/आएँगी, तो आपसे ही मिलूँगा !
agar āp parsõ landan āẽge/āẽgī, to āpse hī milū̃gā!

Geeta's diary

सोमवार घर पर रहना *somvār ghar par rahnā*

मंगलवार दिल्ली जाना *mangalvār dillī jānā*

बुधवार कुछ चीज़ें ख़रीदना *budhvār kuch cīzẽ kharīdnā*

गुरुवार घर वापस आना *guruvār ghar vāpas ānā*

शुक्रवार आराम करना *śukravār ārām karnā*

शनिवार सीता के यहाँ जाना *śanivār Sītā ke yahā̃ jānā*

रविवार अगले हफ़्ते की तैयारियाँ करना *ravivār agle hafte kī taiyāriyā̃ karnā*

9a

1E If the vegetable market is closed, get ['take'] the vegetables tomorrow morning.

2D If you don't know the way, buy a map.

3C If you don't know the meaning of some/any word, look in a dictionary.

4B If you don't find a policeman at the roundabout, go to the police station.

5A If you don't get a room at the hotel, stay at my place.

6F If you turn into that narrow lane you'll see the café on your left ['the café will appear…'].

9b

७ दो लोगों के लिए कमरा चाहिए । हम दो दिन रहेंगे ।
do logõ ke lie kamrā cāhie. ham do din rahẽge.

८ आज शाम को हमारे कुछ दोस्त हमसे मिलने आएँगे ।
āj śam ko hamāre kuch dost hamse milne āẽge.

९ नाश्ते में क्या मिलेगा ? *nāśte mẽ kyā milegā?*

१० क्या रात का खाना भी मिलेगा ? *kyā rāt kā khānā bhī milegā?*

११ यहाँ से सिनेमा जाने में कितना समय लगेगा ? हम पैदल जाना चाहते हैं । *yahā̃ se sinemā jāne mẽ kitnā samay lagegā? ham paidal jānā cāhte haĩ.*

१२ मैं लंदन फ़ोन करना चाहता हूँ । क्या मैं अपने कमरे से ही फ़ोन कर सकता हूँ ?
maĩ landan fon karnā cāhtā hū̃. kyā maĩ apne kamre se hī fon kar saktā hū̃?

१३ अगले हफ़्ते हम लोग आगरे और दिल्ली जाएँगे ।
agle hafte ham log āgre aur dillī jāẽge.

१४ क्या आज रात को हमारे दोस्त हमारे साथ खाना खा सकते हैं ?
kyā āj rāt ko hamāre dost hamāre sāth khānā khā sakte haĩ?

9c

१५ कल शनिवार है, इसलिए हम बाहर जाएँगे ।
kal śanivār hai, islie ham bāhar jāẽge.

१६ हम सोच रहे थे कि हम सिनेमा जाएँगे ।
ham soc rahe the ki ham sinemā jāẽge.

१७ मेरा भाई कह रहा था कि वह घर पर रहेगा ।
merā bhāī kah rahā thā ki vah ghar par rahegā.

१८ अगर आप चाहें तो आप भी हमारे साथ आइए ।
agar āp cāhẽ to āp bhī hamāre sāth āie.

१९ हम जल्दी जाएँगे ताकि अच्छी सीटें मिलें ।
ham jaldī jāẽge tāki acchī sīṭẽ milẽ.

२० अगर बारिश हो रही है तो हम गाड़ी से जाएँगे ।
agar bāriś ho rahī hai to ham gāṛī se jāẽge.

Unit 10

Practise what you've learnt

१ मनोज घर गया । *Manoj ghar gayā.*

२ राजू और राम बाहर गए । *Rājū aur Rām bāhar gae.*

३ सीता दिल्ली गई । *Sītā dillī gaī.*

४ कुछ नहीं हुआ । *kuch nahī̃ huā.*

५ मीना कल पहुँची । *Mīnā kal pahũcī.*

६ दादीजी परसों आईं । *Dādījī parsõ āī̃.*

७ मनोज मंगलवार को आया । *Manoj mangalvār ko āyā.*

How many did you see?

१ मैंने दो किताबें देखीं । *maĩne do kitābẽ dekhī̃.*

२ मैंने एक सिग्रेट देखा । *maĩne ek sigreṭ dekhā.*

३ मैंने एक अख़बार देखा । *maĩne ek a<u>kh</u>bār dekhā.*

४ मैंने दो गाड़ियाँ देखीं । *maĩne do gāṛiyā̃ dekhī̃.*

५ मैंने एक गिलास देखा । *maĩne ek gilās dekhā.*

६ मैंने एक ट्रेन देखी । *maĩne ek ṭren dekhī.*

७ मैंने दो जूते देखे । *maĩne do jūte dekhe.*

८ मैंने तीन चाबियाँ देखीं । *maĩne tīn cābiyā̃ dekhī̃.*

९ मैंने दो हाथी देखे । *maĩne do hāthī dekhe.*

१० मैंने एक मकान देखा । *maĩne ek makān dekhā.*

११ मैंने दो कुत्ते देखे । *maĩne do kutte dekhe.*

१२ मैंने एक बंदर देखा । *maĩne ek bandar dekhā*

१३ मैंने एक बिल्ली देखी । *maĩne ek billī dekhī.*

१४ मैंने एक क़मीज़ देखी । *maĩne ek qamīz dekhī.*

१५ मैंने एक दरवाज़ा देखा । *maĩne ek darvāzā dekhā.*

१६ मैंने तीन बोतलें देखीं । *maĩne tīn botalẽ dekhī̃.*

What did Geeta see?

१ गीता ने एक नई फ़िल्म देखी । *Gītā ne ek naī film dekhī.*

२ राजू ने दो अख़बार ख़रीदे । *Rājū ne do akhbār kharīde.*

३ मोती ने दस चपातियाँ खाईं । *Motī ne das capātiyā̃ khāī̃.*

४ मीना ने दो कहानियाँ पढ़ीं । *Mīnā ne do kahāniyā̃ paṛhī̃.*

५ हमने चार कुरते ख़रीदे । *hamne cār kurte kharīde.*

६ उन्होंने मेज़ पर कुछ किताबें रखीं । *unhõne mez par kuch kitābẽ rakhī̃.*

७ मैंने दीवार पर अपना नाम लिखा । *maĩne dīvār par apnā nām likhā.*

८ मैंने कई बातें सुनीं । *maĩne kaī batẽ sunī̃.*

९ मैंने एक ही भाषा सीखी । *maĩne ek hī bhāṣā sīkhī.*

Geeta's version of the morning

१ राजू पहले उठा ।
Rājū pahle uṭhā.

२ राजू ने गीता के लिए नाश्ता तैयार किया ।
Rājū ne Gītā ke lie nāśtā taiyār kiyā.

३ गीता को जगाने से पहले राजू आँगन में बैठा और चाय पी ।
Gītā ko jagāne se pahle Rājū ā̃gan mẽ baiṭhā aur cāy pī.

४ गीता की शिकायत यह थी कि राजू ने चाय में बहुत ज़्यादा चीनी डाली थी ।
Gītā kī śikāyat yah thī ki Rājū ne cāy mẽ bahut zyādā cīnī ḍālī thī.

५ गीता ने नाश्ता रसोई में किया ।
Gītā ne nāśtā rasoī mẽ kiyā.

६ गीता ने गोलियाँ खाईं । उसके सिर में दर्द था ।
Gītā ne goliyā̃ khāī̃. uske sir mẽ dard thā.

७ नहीं, सिर्फ़ राजू को जल्दी उठना पसंद है, गीता को नहीं ।
nahī̃, sirf Rājū ko jaldī uṭhnā pasand hai, Gītā ko nahī̃.

८ उसने सोचा कि शाहरुख़ आया था ।
usne socā ki Śāhrukh āyā thā.

९ शायद गीता के सपने में ही !
śāyad Gītā ke sapne mẽ hī!

10a

१ जावेद ने मुझे फ़ोन करके बताया कि तबियत ख़राब है ।
Jāved ne mujhe fon karke batāyā ki tabiyat <u>kh</u>arāb hai.

२ मैं जावेद के घर जाकर उसके कमरे में गया ।
maĩ Jāved ke ghar jākar uske kamre mẽ gayā.

३ जावेद का हाल देखकर मैंने डाक्टर को बुलाया ।
Jāved kā hāl dekhkar maĩne ḍākṭar ko bulāyā.

४ थोड़ी देर में आकर डाक्टर ने कहा कि जावेद बहुत ही कमज़ोर है।
thoṛī der mẽ ākar ḍākṭar ne kahā ki Jāved bahut hī kamzor hai.

५ जावेद को कुछ गोलियाँ देकर डाक्टर ने कहा कि रोज़ दो गोलियाँ लेना ।
Jāved ko kuch goliyā̃ dekar ḍākṭar ne kahā ki roz do goliyā̃ lenā.

६ जावेद ने मुस्कराकर डाक्टर से धन्यवाद कहा ।
Jāved ne muskarākar ḍākṭar se dhanyavād kahā.

७ डाक्टर ने मेरी तरफ़ देखकर कहा कि “अच्छा, तो मैं चलता हूँ ।”
ḍākṭar ne merī taraf dekhkar kahā ki ‘acchā, to maĩ caltā hū̃’.

८ मैंने कहा कि चाय पीकर जाइए ।
maĩne kahā ki cāy pīkar jāie.

९ डाक्टर ने हँसकर कहा कि मैं चाय नहीं लूँगा, अपनी फ़ीस लूँगा !
ḍākṭar ne hãskar kahā ki maĩ cāy nahī̃ lū̃gā, apnī fīs lū̃gā!

10b

कल सुबह मैं छह बजे उठा । नाश्ता करके मैंने अपने भाई को फ़ोन किया । वह सो रहा था । मेरी आवाज़ सुनकर उसने कहा, "तुमने मुझे इतनी जल्दी क्यों जगाया ?" । मैंने कहा, "तुमको याद नहीं ? आज हम जयपुर जा रहे हैं !" उसने पूछा, "हम कितने बजे जा रहे हैं ?" । मैंने जवाब दिया, "हम दस बजे की गाड़ी पकड़ेंगे । तुम जल्दी तैयार हो जाओ !" उसने जँभाई लेकर कहा कि रात में उसने सपना देखा था । सपने में एक बूढ़ी औरत ने उससे कहा था कि आज तुम कहीं मत जाना ! घर पर ही रहना ! मैंने हँसकर कहा, "यह तो सपना ही था । उठो न ! तैयार हो जाओ ।"

गाड़ी ठीक दस बजे स्टेशन से चलने लगी । पर बीस-पच्चीस मिनट बाद वह रुकी । इंजन ख़राब हो गई थी । सुनसान जगह थी; पास में कोई गाँव या मकान नहीं था । जुलाई की गरमी में सारे यात्रियों ने गाड़ी से उतरकर कई घंटों तक कुछ छोटे पेड़ों के साये में इंतज़ार किया । भयंकर गरमी थी । तीन बजे एक दूसरी गाड़ी आकर रुकी । यह दूसरी गाड़ी यात्रियों को वापस दिल्ली ले आने आई थी ।

गाड़ी की कहानी हमने रेडियो पर ही सुनी । हमने उस बूढ़ी औरत की सलाह ली थी ! हम जयपुर कल जाएँगे...

kal subah maĩ chah baje uṭhā. nāśtā karke maĩne apne bhāī ko fon kiyā. vah so rahā thā. merī āvāz sunkar usne kahā, 'tumne mujhe itnī jaldī kyõ jagāyā?' maĩne kahā, 'tumko yād nahī̃? āj ham jaypur jā rahe haĩ!' usne pūchā, 'ham kitne baje jā rahe haĩ?'. maĩne javāb diyā, 'ham das baje kī gāṛī pakaṛẽge. tum jaldī taiyār ho jāo!' usne jā̃bhāī lekar kahā ki rāt mẽ usne sapnā dekhā thā. sapne mẽ ek būṛhī aurat ne usse kahā thā ki āj tum kahī̃ mat jānā! ghar par hī rahnā! maĩne hā̃skar kahā, 'yah to sapnā hī thā. uṭho na! taiyār ho jāo.'

gāṛī ṭhīk das baje sṭeśan se calne lagī. par bīs-paccīs minaṭ bād vah rukī. injan <u>kh</u>arāb ho gaī thī. sunsān jagah thī; pās mẽ koī gā̃v yā makān nahī̃ thā. julāī kī garmī mẽ sare yātriyõ *ne gāṛī se utarkar kaī ghaṇṭõ tak kuch choṭe peṛõ ke sāye mẽ intazār kiyā. bhayankar garmī thī. tīn baje ek dūsrī gāṛī ākar rukī. yah dūsrī gāṛī yātriyõ ko vāpas dillī le āne āī thī.*

gāṛī kī kahānī hamne reḍiyo par hī sunī. hamne us būṛhī aurat kī salāh lī thī! ham jaypur kal jāẽge…

Unit 11

India: states and languages

१ तमिल तमिलनाडु में बोली जाती है ।
tamil tamilnāḍu mẽ bolī jātī hai.

२ मराठी महाराष्ट्र में बोली जाती है ।
marāṭhī mahārāṣṭra mẽ bolī jātī hai.

३ केरल में मलयालम बोली जाती है ।
keral mẽ malayālam bolī jātī hai.

४ हिन्दी दस प्रदेशों में बोली जाती है ।
hindī das pradeśõ mẽ bolī jātī hai.

५ दिल्ली और बिहार के बीच उत्तर प्रदेश पाया जाता है ।
dillī aur bihār ke bīc uttar pradeś pāyā jātā hai.

Sharma ji in his shop

१ गोपाल को शर्मा जी से बुलाया गया ।
Gopāl ko Śarmā jī se bulāyā gayā.

२ सामान छोटे कमरे में रखा जाएगा ।
sāmān choṭe kamre mẽ rakhā jāegā.

३ कमरे की सफ़ाई गोपाल से की जाएगी ।
kamre kī safāī Gopāl se kī jāegī.

४ दुकान को आठ बजे बंद किया जाएगा ।
dukān ko āṭh baje band kiyā jāegā.

५ शर्मा जी के साफ़ कपड़े धोबी के यहाँ से लाए जाएँगे ।
Śarmā jī ke sāf kapṛe dhobī ke yahā̃ se lāe jāẽge.

६ क्योंकि गोपाल रेडियो सुन रहा था !
kyõki Gopāl reḍiyo sun rahā thā!

Your help is needed

१ गीता को आराम करना चाहिए ।
Gītā ko ārām karnā cāhie.

२ मनोज को गोली लेनी चाहिए और पानी पीना चाहिए ।
Manoj ko golī lenī cāhie aur pānī pīnā cāhie.

३ राजू को फ़र्श को साफ़ करना चाहिए ।
Rājū ko farś ko sāf karnā cāhie.

४ मीना को कुछ खाना चाहिए ।
Mīnā ko kuch khānā cahie.

५ उन लोगों को नया घर लेना (या ख़रीदना) चाहिए ।
un logõ ko nayā ghar lenā (yā kharīdnā) cāhie.

11a

१ कोई तीस लोग बुलाए जाएँगे ।
koī tīs log bulāe jāẽge.

२ शुक्रवार को घर को साफ़ किया जाएगा ।
śukravār ko ghar ko sāf kiyā jāegā.

३ रविवार की सुबह को खाना बनाया जाएगा ।
ravivār kī subah ko khānā banāyā jāegā.

४ दोपहर को कुछ रिश्तेदारों को स्टेशन से लाए जाएँगे ।
dopahar ko kuch riśtedārõ ko sṭeśan se lāe jāẽge.

५ बच्चों को तोहफ़े दिए जाएँगे ।
baccõ ko tohfe die jāẽge.

६ रात को बग़ीचे में बत्तियाँ जलाई जाएँगी ।
rāt ko bagīce mẽ battiyā̃ jalāī jāẽgī.

७ संगीत भी बजाया जाएगा ।
sangīt bhī bajāyā jāegā.

८ पड़ोसियों को भी बुलाया जाएगा ।
paṛosiyõ ko bhī bulāyā jāegā.

11b

९ आज का खाना ताज़ा नहीं था । लगता है वह कल ही बनाया गया था ।

āj kā khānā tāzā nahī̃ thā. lagtā hai vah kal hī banāyā gayā thā.

१० कल रात को हमारे दोस्त हमसे मिलने आए थे लेकिन हमें नहीं बताया गया कि वे आए हैं ।

kal rāt ko hamāre dost hamse milne āe the lekin hamẽ nahī̃ batāyā gayā ki ve āe haĩ.

११ किसी के गंदे कपड़े मेरे कमरे रखे गए थे ।

kisī ke gande kapṛe mere kamre mẽ rakhe gae the.

१२ आज शाम को मैंने देखा कि हमारे कमरे के दरवाज़े को ठीक से बंद नहीं किया गया था ।

āj śām ko maĩne dekhā ki hamāre kamre ke darvāze ko ṭhīk se band nahī̃ kiyā gayā thā.

१३ एक बात और — हमारे सामान को खोला गया था !

ek bat aur — hamare sāmān ko kholā gayā thā!

१४ हमको नहाने के लिए गरम पानी नहीं दिया गया ।

hamko nahāne ke lie garam pānī nahī̃ diyā gayā.

१५ मैंने परसों कुछ कपड़े दिए थे धोने के लिए, लेकिन अभी तक वे वापस नहीं दिए गए ।

maĩne parsõ kuch kapṛe die the dhone ke lie, lekin abhī tak ve vāpas nahī̃ die gae.

१६ मेरे ड्राइवर को बताया गया कि उसे गाड़ी में ही सोना होगा ।

mere ḍrāivar ko batāyā gayā ki use gāṛī mẽ hī sonā hogā.

11c

Why do these people hassle me? Everyday they complain about something. It seems they're very fond of complaining. I don't know which country they're from ['they've come from']. In my opinion when people come to our country they shouldn't complain about everything. They should respect this country. It's true that their luggage shouldn't have been opened, but all the other matters were quite minor. I should tell the manager about this but I don't want to tell him. I won't tell him. These people can go to hell!

Unit 12

1 ब	2 हा	3 दु	र				4 दु
5 द	ल	श		6 अ	7 ध्या	पि	का
सू		8 म	धु	ब	न		न
र		न				9 स	दा
10 त	ब		11 मं	ग	ल	वा	र
			दि			ल	
12 अ	13 ख़	बा	र	14 वा	15 ला		16 या
17 म	त			18 रा	ख	19 दा	नी
री	20 रा	21 मा	य	ण		ल	
क		र		22 सी	23 घा		24 ए
25 न	हा	ना			26 गा	य	क

Practise what you've learnt

१ हम शर्मा जी से बच्चों को हिन्दी सिखवाएँगे ।
ham Śarmā jī se baccõ ko hindī sikhvāẽge.

२ मैंने नौकरों से कुछ खाना बनवाया ।
maĩne naukarõ se kuch khānā banvāyā.

३ हमें गाड़ी को ठीक करवाना है ।
hamẽ gāṛī ko ṭhīk karvānā hai.

४ मैं मास्टरजी से कुछ करते सिलवाना चाहता हूँ ।
maĩ māsṭarjī se kuch kurte silvānā cāhtā hū̃.

५ मैंने इन पत्रों को किसी से लिखवाया ।
maĩne in patrõ ko kisī se likhvāyā.

The doctor asks *you* some questions

१ मेरी तबियत दो दिन से ख़राब है ।
merī tabiyat do din se <u>kh</u>arāb hai.

२ जी नहीं, बुख़ार नहीं है ।
jī nahī̃, bu<u>kh</u>ār nahī̃ hai.

३ जी हाँ, सिर में दर्द है ।
jī hā̃, sir mẽ dard hai.

४ जी नहीं, मैं बाहर का खाना कभी नहीं खाता हूँ ।
jī nahī̃, maĩ bāhar kā khānā kabhī nahī̃ khātā hū̃.

५ जी नहीं, मैं बोतल का पानी ही पीता हूँ ।
jī nahī̃, maĩ botal kā pānī hī pītā hū̃.

६ जी हाँ, उलटी हो रही है ।
jī hā̃, ulṭī ho rahī hai.

७ हाँ, दस्त भी है ।
hā̃, dast bhī hai.

८ मैं शराब पीता तो हूँ लेकिन बहुत ज़्यादा नहीं ।
maĩ śarāb pītā to hū̃ lekin bahut zyādā nahī̃.

९ आम तौर पर नींद ठीक से आती है ।
ām taur par nī̃d ṭhīk se ātī hai.

१० मैं ग्यारह-बारह बजे सोता हूँ ।
maĩ gyārah-bārah baje sotā hū̃.

११ मैं कम से कम [at least] सात घंटे सोता हूँ ।
maĩ kam se kam [at least] *sāt ghanṭe sotā hū̃.*

१२ जी नहीं, और कोई तकलीफ़ नहीं है ।
jī nahī̃, aur koī taklīf nahī̃ hai.

12a

१ किसी बड़े आर्टिस्ट ने उसको बनाया होगा ।
kisī baṛe ārṭisṭ ne usko banāya hogā.

२ जहाँ हीरालाल रहता है वहाँ कई दूसरे रिक्शेवाले भी रहते हैं ।
jahā̃ Hīrālāl rahtā hai vahā̃ kaī dūsre rikśevāle bhī rahte haĩ.

३ उस शहर का नाम आगरा है ।
us śahar kā nām āgrā hai.

४ जी नहीं, बारिश में भी हीरालाल को काम करना पड़ता है ।
jī nahī̃, bāriś mẽ bhī Hīrālāl ko kām karnā paṛtā hai.

५ रिक्शे का वज़न तब बहुत ज़्यादा हो जाता है जब मोटे लोग अपने भारी सामान को लेकर रिक्शे में चढ़ते हैं ।
rikśe kā vazan tab bahut zyādā ho jātā hai jab moṭe log apne bhārī sāmān ko lekar rikśe mẽ caṛhte haĩ.

६ हीरालाल की जेब तब ख़ाली रहती है जब कोई सवारी नहीं आती ।
Hīrālāl kī jeb tab <u>kh</u>ālī rahtī hai jab koī savārī nahī̃ ātī.

७ जो लोग रिक्शे चलाते हैं उनकी ज़िन्दगी मुश्किल होती है ।
jo log rikśe calāte haĩ unkī zindagī muśkil hotī hai.

12b (sample answers)

८ जो लोग भारत के बारे में कुछ सीखना चाहते हैं उनको हिन्दी सीखनी चाहिए ।
jo log bhārat ke bāre mẽ kuch sīkhnā cāhte haĩ unko hindī sīkhnī cāhie.

९ जब मैंने पहली बार ताज महल को देखा तो मैंने सोचा कि मैं भी एक ऐसी इमारत बनाऊँगा !
jab maĩne pahlī bār tāj mahal ko dekhā to maĩne socā ki maĩ bhī ek aisī imārat banāū̃gā!

१० जहाँ मेरे रिश्तेदार रहते हैं, वहाँ पहुँचने में कई घंटे लगते हैं ।
jahā̃ mere riśtedār rahte haĩ, vahā̃ pahũcne mẽ kaī ghaṇṭe lagte haĩ.

११ जो आदमी मेरे साथ काम करता है उसकी पत्नी मेरी पत्नी की सहेली है ।
jo ādmī mere sāth kām kartā hai uskī patnī merī patnī kī sahelī hai.

१२ जो आदमी मेरे घर के सामने रहता है वह कोई बड़ा नेता है ।
jo ādmī mere ghar ke sāmne rahtā hai vah koī baṛā netā hai.

१३ जिन लोगों के पास बहुत पैसा है वे ही लंदन में बड़ा मकान ख़रीद सकते हैं ।
jin logõ ke pās bahut paisā hai ve hī landan mẽ baṛā makān <u>kh</u>arīd sakte haĩ.

१४ जो कपड़े मैंने कल ख़रीदे उनको तुमने कहाँ रखा ?
jo kapṛe maĩne kal <u>kh</u>arīde unko tumne kahā̃ rakhā?

12c

१५ जब मैं आगरे जाता हूँ तो अक्सर राजू के यहाँ रहता हूँ ।
jab maĩ āgre jātā hū̃ to aksar Rājū ke yahā̃ rahtā hū̃.

१६ जो आदमी हमको हिन्दी पढ़ाता है वह राजू का भाई है ।
jo ādmī hamko hindī paṛhātā hai vah Rājū kā bhāī hai.

१७ जो तोहफ़ा मैंने आज राजू को दिया वह काफ़ी सस्ता था ।

jo tohfā maĩne āj Rājū ko diyā vah kāfī sastā thā.

१८ जब मैंने उसे उसको दिया तो उसने उसे अपनी माँ को दिखाया ।
jab maĩne use usko diyā to usne use apnī mā̃ ko dikhāyā.

१९ जब राजू की माँ ने मेरा तोहफ़ा देखा तो वे हँसने लगीं ।
jab Rājū kī mā̃ ne merā tohfā dekhā to ve hãsne lagī̃.

२० जो सवाल उन्होंने राजू से मेरे बारे में पूछा मैं उसको कभी नहीं भूलूँगा ।
jo savāl unhõne Rājū se mere bāre mẽ pūchā usko maĩ kabhī nahī̃ bhūlū̃gā.

२१ जो जवाब राजू ने दिया वह हमेशा याद रहेगा ।
jo javāb Rājū ne diyā vah hameśā yād rahegā.

12d

Dear Manoj,

I got your letter, thanks. I hadn't had a letter for a year so I'd begun wondering what had happened to my friend Manoj.

Everything's fine here. My brother has married. He's rented a small house in Delhi.

My father says I should get married too now. But I've told him clearly that I won't get married yet. I'm still young. When I turn thirty then maybe I'll start thinking about these things. But Father doesn't want to listen to what I say. Just a little while ago he again began talking about marriage. I got a bit angry. I said, 'Yes Papa, I heard!'

Tell me your email address.

Yours, Motu

Hindi–English vocabulary

KEY

m.	masculine
f.	feminine
pl.	plural
m., f.	used for both sexes
m./f.	used in either gender

DICTIONARY ORDER

The order of the characters in the Devanagari script follows the chart given in the introduction. Vowels precede consonants; nasalized vowels precede unnasalized vowels; plain consonants precede conjunct consonants.

अँगूठा *ãgūṭhā* m. thumb

अँग्रेज़ *ãgrez* m., f. English person

अँग्रेज़ी *ãgrezī* f. English (language); and adj.

अंदर *andar* inside

अख़बार *a<u>kh</u>bār* m. newspaper

अख़बारवाला *a<u>kh</u>bārvālā* m. newspaper seller

अकेला *akelā* alone

अकेलापन *akelāpan* m. loneliness

अगर *agar* if

अगला *aglā* next

अच्छा *acchā* good, nice

अध्यापक *adhyāpak* m. teacher

अध्यापिका *adhyāpikā* f. teacher

अपना *apnā* one's own (my, etc.)

अभी *abhī* right now; still

अमरीकन *amrīkan* American

अरे *are* hey! Oh!

अलमारी *almārī* f. cupboard

अस्पताल *aspatāl* m. hospital

आँख *ãkh* f. eye

आँगन *ãgan* m. courtyard

आकाश *ākāś* m. sky

आगे *āge* ahead

आज *āj* today; आजकल *ājkal* nowadays, these days; आज रात को *āj rāt ko* tonight; आज शाम को *āj śām ko* this evening

आठ *āṭh* eight

आदमी *ādmī* m. man

आदर *ādar* m. respect

आदरणीय *ādaraṇīy* respected (used for 'Dear...' in formal corresponence)

आधा *ādhā* m. half

आना *ānā* to come

आप *āp* you

आपका *āpkā* your, yours

आम *ām* [1] m. mango

आम *ām* [2] ordinary; आम तौर पर *ām taur par* usually

आराम *ārām* m. rest; आराम करना *ārām karnā* to rest; आराम से *ārām se* comfortably, easily

आवाज़ *āvāz* f. voice; sound

आशा *āśā* f. hope

आसान *āsān* easy

इंजन *injan* m. engine (train)

इंतज़ार *intazār* m. waiting, *expecting*; का इंतज़ार करना *kā intazār karnā* to wait for

इतना *itnā* so much, so

इतिहास *itihās* m. history

इधर *idhar* here, over here

इमारत *imārat* f. building

इलाज *ilāj* m. cure, treatment

इसका *iskā* his, her/hers, its

इसलिए *islie* so, because of this

उँगली *ũglī* f. finger

उगना *ugnā* to grow (of plants)

उठना *uṭhnā* to get up, rise

उठाना *uṭhānā* to pick up, raise

उतरना, उतर जाना *utarnā, utar jānā* to get down, alight

उत्तर *uttar* north

उधर *udhar* there, over there

उम्र *umra, umar* f. age

उर्दू *urdū* f. Urdu

उलटी *ulṭī* f. vomiting, sickness

उसका *uskā* his, her/hers, its

ऊपर *ūpar* up, upstairs

ऋण *ṛṇ* m. debt

एक *ek* one; a

ऐसा *aisā* such, of this kind

ओ *o* oh!

ओर *or* f. side, direction

और *aur* and; more

औरत *aurat* f. woman

कंधा *kandhā* m. shoulder

कई *kaī* several

कटना *kaṭnā* to be cut

कपड़ा *kapṛā* m. cloth; garment

कब *kab* when?

कभी *kabhī* ever; कभी कभी *kabhī kabhī* sometimes; कभी नहीं *kabhī nahī̃* never

कम *kam* little, less

कमज़ोर *kamzor* weak

कमर *kamar* f. waist

कमरा *kamrā* m. room

कमी *kamī* f. lack, shortage

क़मीज़ *qamīz* f. shirt

कम्प्यूटर *kampyūṭar* m. computer

करना *karnā* to do

करवाना *karvānā* to get done (by someone else)

कराची *karācī* f. Karachi

कल *kal* yesterday; tomorrow

क़लम *qalam* m./f. pen

कलाई *kalāī* f. wrist

कहना *kahnā* to say

कहाँ *kahā̃* where?

कहानी *kahānī* f. story

कहीं *kahī̃* anywhere, somewhere

का–की–के *kā–kī–ke* [shows possession, like English apostrophe 's]

काठमांडु *kāṭhmāṇḍu* m. Kathmandu

कान *kān* m. ear

काफ़ी *kāfī* [1] f. coffee

काफ़ी *kāfī* [2] quite, very; enough

काम *kām* m. work; job, task; काम करना *kām karnā* to work; to function

काला *kālā* black

कालेज *kālej* m. college

कि *ki* that (conjunction); कि *ki* when, when suddenly; or

कितना kitnā how much/many?

किताब *kitāb* f. book

किनारा *kinārā* m. bank, edge

किलो *kilo* m. kilo, kilogram

किराया *kirāyā* m. rent; fare

किसी *kisī* oblique of कोई *koī*

की ओर *kī or* towards

की तरफ़ *kī taraf* towards

की तरह *kī tarah* like

कुछ *kuch* some; something; कुछ और *kuch aur* some more; कुछ नहीं *kuch nahī̃* nothing

कुरता *kurtā* m. kurta, loose shirt

कुहनी *kuhnī* f. elbow

कुत्ता *kuttā* m. dog

कुरता *kurtā* m. kurta

कुरसी *kursī* f. chair

कुल मिलाकर *kul milākar* all together, in total

कृपया *kṛpayā* please (formal)

के अंदर *ke andar* inside

के अलावा *ke alāvā* as well as

के ऊपर *ke ūpar* above, on top of

के चारों तरफ़ *ke cārõ taraf* all around

के द्वारा *ke dvārā* by (in formal passive sentences)

के नज़दीक *ke nazdīk* near

के नीचे *ke nīce* below, under

के पास *ke pās* near; in the possession of

के बाहर *ke bāhar* outside

के यहाँ *ke yahā̃* at the place of

के लिए *ke lie* for

के साथ *ke sāth* with, in the company of

के सामने *ke sāmne* opposite

केला *kelā* m. banana

कैसा *kaisā* how?

को *ko* to; [also marks an individualized direct object: पानी को पियो *pānī ko piyo* 'Drink the water']

कोई *koī* some, any, a; (with number) about; कोई दूसरा *koī dūsrā* some other, another; कोई नहीं *koī nahī̃* nobody
कौन *kaun* who?
कौनसा *kaunsā* which?
क्या *kyā* what?; and question marker
क्यों *kyõ* why?
क्योंकि *kyõki* because
क्रिकेट *kriket̤* m. cricket
खड़ा *khaṛā* standing
ख़त *khat* m. letter (correspondence)
ख़त्म *khatm* finished; ख़त्म करना *khatm karnā* to finish
ख़याल *khyāl*, m. opinion, thought, idea
ख़राब *kharāb* bad; ख़राब हो जाना *kharāb ho jānā* to break down
ख़रीदना *kharīdnā* to buy
ख़र्च *kharc m.* expenditure; ख़र्च करना *kharc karnā* to spend
ख़ाली *khālī* empty, free, vacant
खाना *khānā* [1] m. food
खाना *khānā* [2] to eat
खिड़की *khiṛkī* f. window
खिलौना *khilaunā* m. toy
ख़ुद *khud* oneself (myself, etc.)
ख़ुश *khuś* pleased, happy
ख़ूब *khūb* a lot, freely
खेल *khel* m. game
खेलना *khelnā* to play (a game)
खोलना *kholnā* to open
गंगा *gangā* f. Ganges
गंदा *gandā* dirty
गरम *garam* hot, warm
गरमी *garmī* f. heat; गरमियाँ *garmiyā̃* f.pl. summer
ग़रीब *garīb* poor
गर्दन *gardan* f. neck
गली *galī* f. lane, narrow street
गाँव *gā̃v* m. village
गाड़ी *gāṛī* f. car; train, vehicle
गाना *gānā* m. song, singing
गाना *gānā* to sing
गाल *gāl* f. cheek
गिलास *gilās* m. tumbler
गुजराती f. Gujarati
गुरुवार *guruvār* m. Thursday
गोलचक्कर *golcakkar* m. roundabout
गोली *golī* f. tablet, pill; bullet
गोश्त *gośt* m. meat
घंटा *ghaṇṭā* m. hour
घर *ghar* m. house, home
घास *ghās* f. grass
घुटना *ghuṭnā* m. knee
घुसना *ghusnā* to enter, sneak in
घूमना *ghūmnā* to turn, revolve
घोड़ा *ghoṛā* m. horse; घोड़े बेचकर सोना *ghoṛe beckar sonā* to sleep like a log
चढ़ना *caṛhnā* to climb, get into vehicle
चढ़ाव *caṛhāv* m. rise, incline
चपाती *capātī* f. chapati
चमकना *camaknā* to shine
चम्मच *cammac* m. spoon

चलना *calnā* to move, blow, flow; चलते जाना *calte jānā* to keep going
चलाना *calānā* to drive
चश्मा *caśmā* m. glasses, spectacles
चाक़ू *cāqū* m. knife, penknife
चाचा *cācā* m. uncle (father's younger brother)
चाबी *cābī* f. key
चाय *cāy* f. tea
चार *cār* four; चारों ओर *cārõ or* all around
चालू करना *cālū karnā* to turn on
चावल *cāval* m. rice
चाहना *cāhnā* to want, wish
चाहिए *cāhie* (is) wanted, needed
चिंता *cintā* f. anxiety
चिट्ठी *ciṭṭhī* f. letter, note
चीज़ *cīz* f. thing
चीनी *cīnī* f. sugar
चुकना *cuknā* to have already done (with verb stem: वह जा चुका है *vah jā cukā hai* 'He's already gone')
चूहा *cūhā* m. mouse, rat
चेहरा *cehrā* m. face
चौड़ा *cauṛā* wide, broad
चौथा *cauthā* fourth
छठा *chaṭhā* sixth
छत *chat* f. roof
छह *chah* six
छाती *chātī* f. chest
छुट्टी *chuṭṭī* f. holiday; free time
छोटा *choṭā* small
जँभाई *jãbhāī* f. yawn
जगह *jagah* f. place
जगाना *jagānā* to awaken
जब *jab* when
ज़माना *zamānā* m. period, time
जरूर *zarūr* of course
ज़रूरत *zarūrat* f. need; मुझको X की ज़रूरत है *mujhko X kī* zarūrat *hai* I need X
जलना *jalnā* to burn
जलवाना *jalvānā* to cause to burn
जलाना *jalānā* to light, burn
जल्दी *jaldī* quickly, early; f. hurry
जवान *javān* young
जवाब *javāb* m. answer, reply; जवाब देना *javāb denā* to reply
जहाँ *jahā̃* where
जाँघ *jā̃gh* f. thigh
जान *jān* f. life, soul
जानना *jānnā* to know
जाना *jānā* to go
ज़िंदगी *zindagī* f. life
ज़िंदा *zindā* (invariable *-ā* ending) alive
जी *jī* word of respect used after names etc.and as a short form of जी हाँ *jī hā̃* 'yes'
जी नहीं *jī nahī̃* no
जी हाँ *jī hā̃* yes
जीतना *jītnā* to win, conquer
जीवन *jīvan* m. life
जुकाम *zukām* m. head cold
ज़ोर से *zor se* with force, loudly

जूता *jūtā* m. shoe
जेब *jeb* f. pocket
जैसा ... वैसा *jaisā... vaisā* as [one thing], so [another]
जो *jo* who, which
ज़्यादा *zyādā* more, much
झूठ *jhūṭh m.* a lie
टाँग *ṭā̃g* f. leg
टार्च *ṭārc* m. torch, flashlight
टिकट *ṭikaṭ* f./m. ticket; stamp
टिकिया *ṭikiyā* f. cake (e.g. of soap)
टूटना *ṭūṭnā* to break
टैक्सी *ṭaiksī* f. taxi
टोस्ट *ṭosṭ* m. toast, piece of toast
ट्रेन *ṭren* f. train
ठंड *ṭhaṇḍ* f. cold; ठंड लगना *ṭhaṇḍ lagnā* to feel cold
ठंडा *ṭhaṇḍā* cold
ठीक *ṭhīk* OK, all right; exactly
ठुड्डी *ṭhuḍḍī* f. chin
डाक *ḍāk* f. post; डाक घर *ḍāk ghar* m. post office; डाक की टिकट *ḍāk kī ṭikaṭ* f. stamp
डाक्टर *ḍākṭar* m. doctor
डालना *ḍālnā* to put, pour
डिब्बा *ḍibbā* m. box
ड्राइवर *ḍrāivar* m. driver
ढाबा *ḍhābā* m. roadside cafe
तंग *tang* narrow, confined; तंग करना *tang karnā* to harass
तक *tak* up to, until, as far as
तकलीफ़ *taklīf* f. suffering, pain, discomfort, inconvenience, trouble
तनख़्वाह *tan<u>kh</u>vāh,* तनख़ाह *tankhāh* f. pay, wages
तब *tab* then
तबला *tablā* m. tabla (drum)
तबियत *tabiyat* f. health, disposition
तमिल f. Tamil
तस्वीर *tasvīr* f. picture
ताकि *tāki* so that, in order that
ताज महल *tāj mahal* m. Taj Mahal
ताज़ा *tāzā* (-*ā* ending sometimes treated as invariable) fresh
ताश *tāś* m. playing cards
तीन *tīn* three
तीसरा *tīsrā* third
तुम *tum* you (familiar)
तुम्हारा *tumhārā* your, yours
तू *tū* you (intimate)
तैयार *taiyār* ready, prepared; तैयार करना *taiyār karnā* to prepare; तैयार हो जाना *taiyār ho jānā* to get ready
तैयारी *taiyārī* f. preparation
तो *to* so, then; as for...
तोड़ना *toṛnā* to break, smash
तोता *totā* m. parrot
तोहफ़ा *tohfā* m. gift, present
थकना *thakna* to get tired
थाना *thānā* m. police station
थोड़ा *thoṛā* (a) little; थोड़ी देर *thoṛī der* f. a little while
दक्षिण *dakṣiṇ* south
दफ़्तर *daftar* m. office
दयालु *dayālu* kind, merciful

दरवाज़ा *darvāzā* m. door
दर्ज़ी *darzī* m. tailor
दर्द *dard* m. pain
दवा *davā* f. medicine
दवाख़ाना *davākhānā* m. pharmacy, chemist's shop
दस *das* ten
दस्त *dast* m. diarrhoea; दस्त आना *dast ānā* to have diarrhoea
दाँत *dā̃t* m. tooth
दादा *dādā* m. grandfather (father's father)
दादी *dādī* f. grandmother (father's mother)
दाल *dāl* f. daal, lentil
दाहिना *dāhinā* right (direction)
दिखाना *dikhānā* to show
दिन *din* m. day
दिया *diyā* m. lamp
दिल *dil* m. heart
दिल्ली *dillī* f. Delhi
दीवार, दीवाल *dīvār, dīvāl* f. wall
दुकान *dukān* f. shop
दुकानदार *dukāndār* m. shopkeeper
दुखी *dukhī* sad
दुर्घटना *durghaṭnā* f. accident
दूध *dūdh* m. milk
दूधवाला *dūdhvālā* m. milkman
दूर *dūr* far, distant
दूसरा *dūsrā* second; other
देखना *dekhnā* to look, to see
देना *denā* to give; to allow to, let (with oblique infinitive: हमको जाने दो *hamko jāne do* 'Let us go')
देर *der* f. a while, length of time; delay; देर से *der se* late
देरी *derī* f. delay
देश *deś* m. country
दो *do* two
दोनों *donõ* both, the two
दोस्त *dost* m., f. friend
दौड़ना *dauṛnā* to run
धन्यवाद *dhanyavād* thank you
धीरे धीरे *dhīre dhīre* slowly
धुलना *dhulnā* to be washed
धुलवाना *dhulvānā* to get washed
धोना *dhonā* to wash
धोबी *dhobī* m. washerman
ध्यान *dhyān* m. attention; ध्यान से *dhyān se* attentively; ध्यान रखना *dhyān rakhnā* to pay attention to, look after
न *na* don't; isn't that so?
नक़्शा *naqśā* m. map, plan
नदी *nadī* f. river
नमस्कार *namaskār* hello, goodbye
नमस्ते *namaste* hello, goodbye
नया *nayā* (f. नई *naī*; m. pl. नए *nae*) new
नर्स *nars* m., f. nurse
नल *nal* m. tap, pipe
नहाना *nahānā* to bathe
नहीं *nahī̃* not, no
नाक *nāk* f. nose
नाम *nām* m. name
नाराज़ *nārāz* angry, displeased

नाव *nāv* f. boat

नाश्ता *nāśtā* m. breakfast, snack; नाश्ता करना *nāśtā karnā* to have breakfast

निकलना *nikalnā* to emerge, come/go out नीचे *nīce* down, downstairs

नींद *nīd̃* f. sleep; नींद आना *nīd̃ ānā* (sleep to come) to get to sleep

नीला *nīlā* blue

नेता *netā* m. leader, politician

नेपाल *nepāl* m. Nepal

नौ *nau* nine

नौकर *naukar* m. servant

नौकरी *naukarī* f. job, employment

पंखा *pankhā* m. fan

पकड़ना *pakaṛnā* to catch

पचास *pacās* fifty

पड़ना *paṛnā* to fall; to have to (with preceding infinitive: मुझे जाना पड़ेगा *mujhe jānā paṛegā* 'I'll have to go')

पड़ा *paṛā* lying

पड़ोसी *paṛosī* m., पड़ोसिन *paṛosin* f. neighbour

पढ़ना *paṛhnā* to read, to study

पढ़ाई *paṛhāī* f. studies, studying

पढ़ाना *paṛhānā* to teach

पतला *patlā* thin

पता *patā* m. address; whereabouts

पति *pati* m. husband

पत्नी *patnī* f. wife

पत्र *patr* m. letter (correspondence)

पर *par*[1] but

पर *par*[2] on; at ('at home' etc.)

परसों *parsõ* two days away (the day after tomorrow; the day before yesterday)

परिवार *parivār* m. family

पश्चिम *paścim* west

पसंद *pasand* pleasing *(*यह मुझको पसंद है *yah mujhko pasand hai* I like this*);* पसंद आना *pasand ānā* to appeal to, to be liked

पहला *pahlā* first

पहाड़ *pahāṛ* m. hill

पहुँचना *pahũcnā* to reach, arrive

पाँच *pā̃c* five; पाँचवाँ *pā̃cvā̃* fifth

पाँव *pā̃v* m. foot, leg

पाकिस्तान *pākistān* m. Pakistan

पागल *pāgal* mad, crazy

पाना *pānā* to find, obtain; to be able, to manage to (with verb stem: मैं नहीं जा पाया *maĩ nahī̃ jā pāyā* 'I didn't manage to go')

पानी *pānī* m. water

पापा *pāpā* m. papa, father

पार *pār* across; पार करना *pār karnā* to cross; उस पार *us pār* on the other side (of, के *ke)*

पार्टी *pārṭī* f. party

पास में *pās mẽ* nearby

पिछला *pichlā* previous, last

पिता *pitā* m. father

पीटना *pīṭnā* to beat, thrash

पीना *pīnā* to drink; to smoke
पीला *pīlā* yellow
पुकारना *pukārnā* to call out
पुराना *purānā* old (for inanimates, not for people)
पुल *pul* m. bridge
पुलिस *pulis* f. police; पुलिसवाला *pulisvālā* m. policeman
पुस्तकालय *pustakālay* m. library
पूछना *pūchnā* to ask
पूरा *pūrā* full, complete
पूर्व *pūrv* east
पेट *peṭ* m. stomach
पेड़ *peṛ* m. tree
पैदल *paidal* on foot
पैर *pair* m. foot; पैर की उँगली *pair kī ũglī* f. toe
पैसा *paisā* m. money
प्यारा *pyārā* dear, sweet, cute
प्यास *pyās* f. thirst; प्यास लगना *pyās lagnā* (thirst to strike) to feel thirsty
प्रदेश *pradeś* m. state, region
प्रधान मंत्री *pradhān mantrī* m./f. prime minister
प्रिय *priy* dear; 'Dear...' (in informal letter writing)
प्रेस करना *pres karnā* to iron
प्लेट *pleṭ* f. plate
फल *phal* m. fruit
फलवाला *phalvālā* m. fruitseller
फ़र्श *farś* m. floor
फिर, फिर से *phir, phir se* again
फ़िल्म *film* f. film
फ़ीस *fīs* f. fee, fees
फूल *phūl* m. flower
फ़ोन *fon* m. phone; फ़ोन करन *fon karnā* to phone
बंद *band* closed, shut
बकवास *bakvās* f. nonsense, idle chatter
बग़ीचा *bagīcā* m. garden
बचपन *bacpan* m. childhood
बच्चा *baccā* m. child
बजना *bajnā* to play, resound, chime
बजाना *bajānā* to play (music)
बजे *baje* o'clock
बड़ा *baṛā* big
बढ़िया *baṛhiyā* (invariable *-ā* ending) excellent, really good, fine
बटुआ *baṭuā* m. purse, wallet
बताना *batānā* to tell
बत्ती *battī* f. light, lamp
बनवाना *banvānā* to cause to be made
बनाना *banānā* to make
बरतन *bartan* m. dish, utensil
बस *bas* f. bus
बहिन *bahin* f. sister
बहुत *bahut* very; बहुत ज़्यादा *bahut zyādā* very great, too much
बाँह *bā̃h* f. arm, upper arm
बाज़ार *bāzār* m. market, bazaar
बात *bāt* f. thing said, idea; बात करना *bāt karnā* to talk
बाप *bāp* m. dad; बाप रे बाप ! *bāp re bāp!* Oh God!

बायाँ *bāyā̃* left (direction)

बार *bār* f. time, occasion; इस बार *is bār* this time; कितनी बार *kitnī bār* how many times?; कई बार *kaī bār* several times

बारिश *bāriś* f. rain; बारिश होना *bāriś honā* to rain

बाल *bāl* m. hair

बाहर *bāhar* outside

बिजली *bijlī* f. electricity

बिलकुल *bilkul* quite, completely

बिल्ली *billī* f. cat

बिस्कुट *biskuṭ* m. biscuit

बीमार *bīmār* ill, sick

बीयर *bīyar* f. beer

बुख़ार *bukhār* m. fever

बुधवार *budhvar* m. Wednesday

बुरा *burā* bad

बुलवाना *bulvānā* to cause to be called

बुलाना *bulānā* to call, invite, summon

बूढ़ा *būṛhā* elderly

बेचना *becnā* to sell

बेटा *beṭā* m. son

बेटी *beṭī* f. daughter

बेहतर *behtar* better

बैठणा *baiṭhnā* to sit

बैठा *baiṭhā* seated, sitting

बोतल *botal* f. bottle

बोलना *bolnā* to speak

भयंकर *bhayankar* terrible

भरना *bharnā* to be filled

भरोसा *bharosā* m. trust, reliance

भाई *bhāī* m. brother

भाड़ में जाए *bhāṛ mẽ jāe* '(he/she) can go to hell' (भाड़ *bhāṛ* m. grain-parching oven)

भारत *bhārat* m. India

भारी *bhārī* heavy

भाषा *bhāṣā* f. language

भिजवाना *bhijvānā* to have sent, to cause to be sent

भी *bhī* also; even

भूख *bhūkh* f. hunger; भूख लगना *bhūkh lagnā* (hunger to strike) to feel hungry

भेजना *bhejnā* to send

मंगलवार *maṅgalvār* f. Tuesday

मंदिर *mandir* m. temple

मकान *makān* m. house

मज़ा *mazā* m. enjoyment, fun; मज़े करना *maze karnā* to enjoy oneself, have fun

मत *mat* don't

मतलब *matlab* m. meaning

मदद *madad* f. help; किसी की मदद करना *kisī kī madad karnā* to help someone

मराठी *marāṭhī* f. Marathi

मरीज़ *marīz* m. patient

महँगा *mahãgā* expensive

महसूस करना *mahsūs karnā* to feel; महसूस होना *mahsūs honā* to be felt, experienced

महिला *mahilā* f. lady

महीना *mahīnā* m. month

माँ *mā̃* f. mother; माँ-बाप *mā̃-bāp* m. pl. parents

माँगना *mā̃gnā* to ask for,

demand

माँजना *mā̃jnā* to scour, clean, cleanse

माता *mātā* f. mother

माता-पिता *mātā-pitā* m.pl. parents

माथा *māthā* m. forehead

माफ़ी *māfī* f. forgiveness; माफ़ी माँगना *māfī mā̃gnā* to apologize

मामूली *māmūlī* ordinary

मारना *mārnā* to hit, beat, strike

माल *māl* m. goods, stuff

मालूम *mālūm* (is) known; मालूम नहीं *mālūm nahī̃* [I] don't know

मार्ग *mārg* m. road, street (used in street names)

मिठाई *miṭhāī* f. sweet, sweetmeat

मिठास *miṭhās* f. sweetness

मिलना *milnā* to meet, to be available

मीठा *mīṭhā* sweet

मुंबई *mumbaī* f. Mumbai, Bombay

मुँह *mũh* m. mouth; face

मुड़ना *muṛnā* to turn

मुफ़्त (का) *muft (kā)* free; मुफ़्त में *muft mẽ* for nothing, free

मुश्किल *muśkil* difficult; मुश्किल से *muśkil se* with difficulty, hardly

मुस्कराना *muskarānā* to smile

में *mẽ* in

मेज़ *mez* f. table

मेमसाहब *memsāhab* f. memsahib

मेरा *merā* my, mine

मेहनत *mehnat* f. hard work; मेहनती *mehntī* hard-working

मैं *maĩ* I

मैला *mailā* dirty

मोटा *moṭā* fat

मौसम *mausam* m. weather

यह *yah* he, she, it, this

यहाँ *yahā̃* here

यहीं *yahī̃* right here

या *yā* or

यात्री *yātrī* m. traveller, passenger

याद *yād* f. memory

यानी *yānī* in other words, that is to say

ये *ye* they, these

रखना *rakhnā* to put, place, keep

रविवार *ravivār* m. Sunday

रसोई *rasoī* f. kitchen

रहना *rahnā* to live, to stay

राजा *rājā* m. king, raja

रात *rāt* f. night; रात का खाना *rāt kā khānā* m. dinner

रास्ता *rāstā* m. road

रिक्शा *rikśā* m. rickshaw

रिक्शेवाला *rikśevālā* m. rickshaw driver

रिश्तेदार *riśtedār* m. relation, relative

रुपया *rupayā* m. rupee

रेडियो *reḍiyo* m. radio

रोज़ *roz* every day

रोना *ronā* to cry, weep
लंबा *lambā* tall
लगना *lagnā* time to be taken; घर जाने में १० मिनट लगते हैं / एक घंटा लगता है *ghar jāne mẽ 10 minaṭ lagte haĩ / ek ghaṇṭā lagtā hai* It takes 10 minutes / one hour to get home; लगना *lagnā* to seem; to be felt (of hunger, thirst etc.); to have an effect; to begin (following an oblique infinitive)
लन्दन *landan* m. London
लड़का *laṛkā* m. boy
लड़की *laṛkī* f. girl
लाइट *lāiṭ* f. light, electric power
लाना *lānā* to bring
लाल *lāl* red
लिखना *likhnā* to write
लेकिन *lekin* but
लेखक *lekhak* m. writer
लेटना *leṭnā* to lie down
लेटा *leṭā* lying, lying down
लेना *lenā* to take
लोग *log* m. pl. people
लौटना *lauṭnā* to return
व *va* and
वग़ैरह *vagairah* etc., and so on
वज़न *vazan* m. weight
वह *vah* he, she, it, that
वहाँ *vahā̃* there
वापस *vāpas* 'back' in वापस आना/जाना/देना *vāpas ānā/jānā/denā* to come/go/give back
वाराणसी *vārāṇasī* f. Varanasi, Banaras
विदेश *videś* abroad
विदेशी *videśī* m. foreigner; adj. foreign
विद्यार्थी *vidyārthī* m. student
वे *ve* they, those
शक्ति *śakti* f. power
शनिवार *śanivār* m. Saturday
शब्द *śabd* m. word
शब्दकोश *śabdkoś* m. dictionary
शराब *śarāb* f. alcoholic drink, liquor
शरीर *śarīr* m. body
शहर *śahar* m. town, city
शांति *śānti* f. peace
शादी *śādī* f. wedding, marriage; शादी करना *śādī karnā* to marry
शादी-शुदा *śādī-śudā* (*-ā* ending invariable) married
शानदार *śāndār* splendid, magnificent
शाबाश *śābāś* bravo
शाम *śām* f. evening
शायद *śāyad* maybe, perhaps
शिकायत *śikāyat* f. complaint; शिकायत करना *śikāyat karnā* to complain
शुक्रवार *śukravār* m. Friday
शुक्रिया *śukriyā* thank you
शुद्ध *śuddh* pure
शुभ *śubh* good, auspicious
शुभकामना *śubhkāmnā* f. good wish

शोला *śolā* m. flame

शौक़ *śauq* m. liking, hobby, interest

श्री *śrī* Mr; श्रीमती *śrīmatī* Mrs

संगीत *saṅgīt* m. music

संगीतकार *saṅgītkār* m. musician

संतरा *santarā* m. orange

सकना *saknā* to be able (with verb stem: तुम जा सकते हो *tum jā sakte ho* 'You can go')

सच *sac* m. truth; adj. true

सड़क *saṛak* f. road, street

सपना *sapnā* m. dream; सपना देखना *sapnā dekhnā* to dream, to have a dream

सब *sab* all; सब कुछ *sab kuch* everything; सबसे *sabse* of all (in superlatives, e.g. सबसे अच्छा *sabse acchā* best, best of all)

सब्ज़ी *sabzī* f. vegetable(s); सब्ज़ी मंडी *sabzī maṇḍī* f. vegetable market; सब्ज़ीवाला *sabzīvālā* m. vegetable seller

समझना *samajjnā* to understand

समय *samay* m. time

समोसा *samosā* m. samosa

सरकार *sarkār* f. government

सलाह *salāh* f. advice

सवारी *savārī* f. passenger, rider

सस्ता *sastā* cheap

सहायता *sahāytā* f. assistance

सहित *sahit* with (formal)

सही *sahī* correct, true, exact

सहेली *sahelī* f. female's female friend

-सा *-sā* '-ish' (suffix that qualifies an adjective, as in बड़ा-सा *baṛā-sā* 'biggish')

साइकिल *sāikil* f. bicycle

साड़ी *sāṛī* f. sari

सात *sāt* seven

सादर *sādar* respectful

साफ़ *sāf* clean, clear; साफ़ करना *sāf karnā* to clean

साबुन *sābun* m. soap

सामने *sāmne* opposite

सामान *sāmān* m. goods, furniture, luggage

साया *sāyā* m. shade, shadow

साल *sāl* m. year

साहब *sāhab* m. sahib

सिखवाना *sikhvānā* to cause to be taught

सिखाना *sikhānā* to teach

सिग्रेट *sigreṭ* m. cigarette

सितार *sitār* m. sitar

सिनेमा *sinemā* m. cinema

सिर *sir* m. head

सिर्फ़ *sirf* only

सिलवाना *silvānā* to have sewn

सीना *sīnā* to sew

सुखी *sukhī* happy

सीखना *sīkhnā* to learn

सुंदर *sundar* beautiful, handsome

सुनना *sunnā* to hear, to listen

सुनसान *sunsān* desolate, empty

सुबह *subah* f. morning

से *se* from

सैर *sair* f. trip

सोचना *socnā* to think
सोना *sonā* to sleep
सोमवार *somvār* m. Monday
सौ *sau* m. hundred
स्कूल *skūl* m. school
हँसना *hãsnā* to laugh
हफ़्ता *haftā* m. week
हम *ham* we, us
हमारा *hamārā* our, ours
हमेशा *hameśā* always
हर *har* every, each
हवा *havā* f. air, breeze
हाँ *hā̃* yes
हाथ *hāth* m. hand
हाथी *hāthī* m. elephant
हाल *hāl* m. condition, state (in क्या हाल है ? *kyā hāl hai?* 'How's things? How are you?'
हिन्दी *hindī* f. Hindi
हिन्दुस्तानी *hindustānī* Indian
हिलाना *hilānā* to move, shake
ही *hī only* (emphatic)
हीरा *hīrā* m. diamond
हुआ *huā* [past tense of होना *honā*] 'happened'
हूँ *hū̃* am
हैं *haĩ* are
है *hai* is
हो *ho* are (with तुम *tum*)
होटल *hoṭal* m. hotel, restaurant, cafe
होना *honā* to be; *ho jānā* to become
होशियार hośiyār clever

English–Hindi vocabulary

KEY

adj. adjective (only stated to resolve ambiguities)

f. feminine

m. masculine

m., f. used for both sexes

m./f. used in either gender

N regularly uses the ने *ne* construction in perfective tenses

n sometimes uses the ने *ne* construction in perfective tenses

p. plural

a एक *ek*, कोई *koī*

able, to be सकना *saknā* (after verb stem — मैं जा सकता हूँ *maĩ jā saktā hū̃* I can go)

about (approx.) क़रीब *qarīb*, लगभग *lagbhag*; (with number) कोई *koī* (कोई दस लोग *koī das log* some ten people); (concerning) के बारे में *ke bāre mẽ*

above ऊपर *ūpar*

abroad विदेश *videś*

accept, to स्वीकार करना *svīkār karnā* N; मानना *mānnā* N

accident हादसा *hādsā* m., दुर्घटना *durghaṭnā* f.

actually वैसे *vaise*

add, to जोड़ना *joṛnā* N

address पता *patā* m.

advice सलाह *salāh* f.

aeroplane हवाई जहाज़ *havāī jahāz* m.

affection प्यार *pyār* m.

after के बाद *ke bād*

again फिर *phir*, फिर से *phir se*

age (of person) उम्र f. *umra, umar*

Agra आगरा *āgrā* m.

ahead (of) (के) आगे *(ke) āge*

air हवा *havā* f.

airmail हवाई डाक *havāī ḍāk* f.

alcoholic drink शराब *śarāb* f.

all सब *sab*, सभी *sabhī*; whole सारा *sārā*

allow to, to oblique inf. + देना *denā* N (मुझे जाने दो *mujhe jāne do* 'let me go')

alone अकेला *akelā*; (adv.) अकेले *akele*

also भी *bhī*

although हालाँकि *hālā̃ki*

always हमेशा *hameśā*

America अमरीका *amrīkā* m.; American अमरीकन *amrīkan*

among के बीच *ke bīc*; among themselves आपस में *āpas mẽ*

and और *aur*

anger ग़ुस्सा *gussā* m.

angry नाराज़ *nārāz*

answer जवाब *javāb* m.; to answer जवाब देना *javāb denā* N

anxiety परेशानी *pareśānī* f.; चिंता *cintā* f.

anyone (at all) कोई (भी) *koī (bhī)*

anywhere (at all) कहीं (भी) *kahī̃ (bhī)*

apart from के सिवा/ सिवाय *ke sivā/sivāy*; को छोड़कर *ko choṛkar*

apologize (to), to (से) माफ़ी माँगना *(se) māfī mā̃gnā* N

appear, to दिखना *dikhnā*, दिखाई देना *dikhāī denā*; to seem लगना *lagnā*

area, district इलाक़ा *ilāqā* m.

arm बाँह *bā̃h* f.

around, in vicinity of के आस-पास *ke ās-pās*

arrange, to का इंतज़ाम करना *kā intazām karnā* N

arrangement इंतज़ाम *intazām* m.

arrive, to पहुँचना *pahũcnā*

as if, as though जैसे *jaise*, मानों *mānõ*

as soon as जैसे ही *jaise hī*

ask, to पूछना *pūchnā* N; ask Ram राम से पूछो *Rām se pūcho*

at को *ko*; पर *par*

at least कम से कम *kam se kam*

attention ध्यान *dhyān* m.; to pay attention (to) (पर) ध्यान देना *(par) dhyān denā* N

attentively ध्यान से *dhyān se*

August अगस्त *agast* m.

available, to be मिलना *milnā*

back (in sense 'return') वापस *vāpas*

back (part of body) पीठ *pīṭh* f.

bad ख़राब *kharāb*, बुरा *burā*

bag, cloth bag थैला *thailā* m.

Banaras बनारस *banāras* m., वाराणसी *vārāṇasī* f.

bathe, to नहाना *nahānā*

be, to होना *honā*; बनना *bannā*

beat, to मारना *mārnā* N

beautiful सुन्दर *sundar*

because क्योंकि *kyõki*

because of की वजह से *kī vajah se,* के कारण *ke kāraṇ*

become, to बनना *bannā*

before (के/से) पहले *(ke/se) pahle*

begin to, to oblique inf. + लगना *lagnā* (पानी पड़ने लगा *pānī paṛne lagā* it began to rain); शुरू करना *śurū karnā* ᴺ (हम काम शुरू करें *ham kām śurū karẽ* let's begin work)

beginning शुरू *surū* m.

behind (के) पीछे *(ke) pīche*

bell घंटी *ghaṇṭī* f.

below, beneath (के) नीचे *(ke) nīce*

between के बीच *ke bīc*; between themselves आपस में *āpas mẽ*

bicycle साइकिल *sāikil* f.

big बड़ा *baṛā*

bird चिड़िया *ciṛiyā* f.

birth जन्म *janm* m.

birthday जन्मदिन *janmdin* m.

blanket कंबल *kambal* m.

boil, to उबलना *ubalnā*; उबालना *ubālnā* ᴺ

book किताब *kitāb* f.; पुस्तक *pustak* f.

bored, to be ऊबना *ūbnā*

born, to be पैदा होना *paidā honā* (पैदा *paidā* inv.); का जन्म होना *kā janm honā*

both दोनों *donõ*

bottle बोतल *botal* f.

boy लड़का *laṛkā* m.

bread रोटी *roṭī* f.; (loaf) डबल रोटी *ḍabal roṭī* f.

break, be broken, to टूटना *ṭūṭnā*

break, to तोड़ना *toṛnā* ᴺ

breakfast नाश्ता *nāśtā* m.

bridge पुल *pul* m.

bring, to लाना *lānā*, ले आना *le ānā*

brother भाई *bhāī* m.

brother-in-law (husband's younger bro.) देवर *devar* m.; (wife's bro.) साला *sālā* m.

building इमारत *imārat* f.

bullet गोली *golī* f.

burn, to जलना *jalnā*; जलाना *jalānā* ᴺ

bus बस *bas* f.

but लेकिन *lekin*, पर *par*, मगर *magar*

butter मक्खन *makkhan* m.

buy, to ख़रीदना *kharīdnā* ᴺ

by से *se*; by means of (के) द्वारा *(ke) dvārā*

call (invite), to बुलाना bulānā ᴺ

camera कैमरा *kaimrā* m.

can see 'able, to be'

capital city राजधानी *rājdhānī* f.

car गाड़ी *gāṛī* f., कार *kār* f.

care (about), to (की) परवाह करना *(kī) parvāh karnā* ᴺ

cat बिल्ली *billī* f.

catch, to पकड़ना *pakaṛnā* N; (of fire or illness) लगना *lagnā*

cause कारण *kāraṇ* m.

certainly ज़रूर *zarūr*

chair कुरसी *kursī* f.

chance, opportunity मौक़ा *mauqā* m.

change, to बदलना *badalnā* n

chapatti चपाती *capātī* f.

cheap सस्ता *sastā*

child बच्चा *baccā* m.

childhood बचपन *bacpan* m.

choose, to चुनना *cunnā* N

cigarette सिग्रेट *sigreṭ* f.

cinema सिनेमा *sinemā* m.

city शहर *śahar* m.

class क्लास *klās* m./f.

clean साफ़ *sāf*; to clean साफ़ करना *sāf karnā* N

cleaning सफ़ाई *safāī* f.

clear साफ़ *sāf*; evident ज़ाहिर *zahir*

clever (intelligent) होशियार *hośiyār*, (cunning) चतुर *catur*

closed बंद *band*

close, to बंद करना *band karnā* N

cloth कपड़ा *kapṛā* m.

clothing, garment कपड़ा *kapṛā* m.

cloud बादल *bādal* m.

coffee काफी *kāfī* f.

cold ठंड *ṭhanḍ* f.; (adj.) ठंडा *ṭhanḍā*; (nose cold) ज़ुकाम *zukām* m.

come, to आना *ānā*

come out, to निकलना *nikalnā*

comfort आराम *ārām* m.; comfortably आराम से *ārām se*

companion साथी *sāthī* m.

complain, to शिकायत करना *śikāyat karnā* N; to complain to Sita about Ram, सीता से राम की शिकायत करना *Sītā se Rām kī śikāyat karnā* N

complaint शिकायत *śikāyat* f.

computer कम्प्यूटर kampyūṭar m.

concern चिंता *cintā* f.

condition, state हाल *hāl* m., हालत *hālat* f.

congratulation बधाई *badhāī* f.

conversation बातचीत *bātcīt* f.

copy (of book etc.) प्रति *prati* f.

corner कोना *konā* m.

correct सही *sahī*

cough, to खाँसी आना *khā̃sī ānā*

country देश *deś* m.

cow गाय *gāy* f.

cross (road etc.), to पार करना *pār karnā* N

crowd भीड़ *bhīṛ* f.

cup प्याला *pyālā* m.

cupboard अलमारी *almārī* f.

cure इलाज *ilāj* m.

curtain परदा *pardā* m.

cut, to be कटना *kaṭnā*

cut, to काटना *kāṭnā* N

daal, lentils दाल *dāl* f.

daily (adverb) रोज़ *roz*

dance नृत्य *nṛtya* m., नाच *nāc* m.; to dance नाचना *nācnā*

dark अँधेरा *ãdherā*; (of colour) गहरा *gahrā*; darkness अँधेरा *ãdherā* m.

date तारीख़ *tārīkh* f.

daughter बेटी *beṭī* f.

daughter-in-law बहू *bahū* f.

day दिन *din* m.; all day दिन भर *din bhar*; **day before yesterday / after tomorrow** परसों *parsõ*

dear प्रिय *priy*

death मौत *maut* f., मृत्यु *mṛtyu* f.

degree (academic) डिगरी *ḍigrī* f.

delay देर f.

Delhi दिल्ली *dillī* f.

deliberately जान-बूझकर *jān-būjhkar*

description वर्णन *varṇan* m.; to describe का वर्णन करना *kā varṇan karnā* N

despair निराशा *nirāśā* f.

Devanagari (the Hindi script) देवनागरी *devnāgarī* f.

dhobi, washerman धोबी *dhobī* m.

dialect बोली *bolī* f.

dictionary शब्दकोश *śabdkoś* m.

die, to मरना *marnā*

difference फ़र्क *farq* m. it makes no difference कोई फ़र्क नहीं पड़ता *koī farq nahī̃ paṛtā*

different भिन्न *bhinn*; (separate) अलग *alag*

difficult मुश्किल *muśkil*

difficulty मुश्किल *muśkil* f.

direction तरफ़ *taraf* f., ओर *or* f.

dirty गंदा *gandā*, मैला *mailā*

disappointment निराशा *nirāśā* f.; disappointed निराश *nirāś*

distant दूर *dūr*

do, to करना *karnā* N

doctor डाक्टर *ḍākṭar* m.

dog कुत्ता *kuttā* m.

don't (in commands) न *na*, मत *mat*

door दरवाज़ा *darvāzā* m.

doubt शंका *śankā* f.

down, downstairs नीचे *nīce*

draw, to खींचना *khī̃cnā* N

drawer दराज़ *darāz* f.

dream सपना *sapnā* m.; to dream सपना देखना *sapnā dekhnā* N

drink, to पीना *pīnā* N

drive, to चलाना *calānā* N

driver ड्राइवर *ḍrāivar* m.

each हर *har*, हरेक *harek*

ear कान *kān* m.

early जल्दी *jaldī*

earn, to कमाना *kamānā* N

easily आसानी से *āsānī se*, आराम से *ārām se*

easy आसान *āsān*; simple सरल *saral*

eat, to खाना *khānā* N

edge किनारा *kinārā* m.

either... or या तो... या *yā to... yā*

electricity बिजली *bijlī* f.
e-mail ई-मेल *ī-mel* f.
emerge, to निकलना *nikalnā*
employment नौकरी *naukrī* f.
end अंत *ant* m.; in the end, after all आख़िर (में) *ā<u>kh</u>ir (mẽ)*
English person अँग्रेज़ *ãgrez* m., f.
enough! that's all! बस *bas*
envelope लिफ़ाफ़ा *lifāfā* m.
escape, to बचना *bacnā*
etc. वग़ैरह *vagairah*, इत्यादि *ityādi*
evening शाम *śām* f.
everything सब *sab*, सब कुछ *sab kuch*
exactly, precisely ठीक *ṭhīk*
examination परीक्षा *parīkṣā* f.; to take (sit) an exam परीक्षा देना *parīkṣā denā* ᴺ; to examine की परीक्षा लेना *kī parīkṣā lenā* ᴺ
except for (को) छोड़कर *ko choṛkar*, के सिवाय *ke sivāy*
expensive महँगा *mahãgā*
experience अनुभव *anubhav* m.
explain, to समझाना *samjhānā* ᴺ
extremely बहुत ही *bahut hī*
face मुँह *mũh* m.; चेहरा *cehrā* m.
facing, opposite (के) सामने *(ke) sāmne*
fall, to गिरना *girnā*
family परिवार *parivār* m.
famous मशहूर *maśhūr*, प्रसिद्ध *prasiddh*
fan पंखा *pankhā* m.
far away दूर *dūr*
fare (taxi etc.) किराया *kirāyā* m.
fat मोटा *moṭā*
father पिता *pitā* m. (inv.), बाप *bāp* m.
fault, guilt कसूर *kasūr* m.
fear डर *ḍar* m.; to fear (से) डरना *(se ḍarnā)*
feel, to महसूस करना *mahsūs karnā* ᴺ; to be felt महसूस होना *mahsūs honā*
fetch, to लाना *lānā*, ले आना *le ānā*
fever बुख़ार *bu<u>kh</u>ār* m.
fight, to (से) लड़ना *(se) laṛnā* ᴺ
film फ़िल्म *film* f.
find, to पाना *pānā* ᴺ
finger उँगली *ũglī* f.
finish, to ख़त्म करना *<u>kh</u>atm karnā* ᴺ
finished ख़त्म *<u>kh</u>atm*
fire आग *āg* f.
first पहला *pahlā*; (adverb) पहले *pahle*
fix, to ठीक करना *ṭhīk karnā* ᴺ
floor फ़र्श *farś* m./f.
flower फूल *phūl* m.
fly (insect) मक्खी *makkhī* f.
fly, to उड़ना *uṛnā*
follow, to का पीछा करना *kā pīchā karnā* ᴺ
food खाना *khānā* m.
for के लिए *ke lie*

forbidden मना *manā* (inv.)
force, strength ज़ोर *zor* m.
foreign country विदेश *videś* m.
foreigner विदेशी *videśī* m.
forget, to भूलना *bhūlnā*, भूल जाना *bhūl jānā*
forgive, to माफ़ करना *māf karnā* N
forgiveness माफ़ी *māfī* f.
fork (utensil) काँटा *kā̃ṭā* m.
free (vacant) ख़ाली *khālī*; (of cost) मुफ़्त *muft*; free time फ़ुरसत *fursat* f.
fresh ताज़ा *tāzā*
friend दोस्त *dost* m., f., मित्र *mitr* m., f.; girl's girlfriend सहेली *sahelī* f.
from से *se*
fruit फल *phal* m.
full पूरा *pūrā*, भरा *bharā*
fun मज़ा *mazā* m.
furniture सामान *sāmān* m.
future भविष्य *bhaviṣya* m.
Ganges गंगा *gangā* f.
garden बग़ीचा *bagīcā* m.
get up, to उठना *uṭhnā*
ghost भूत *bhūt* m.
gift तोहफ़ा *tohfā* m., भेंट *bhẽṭ* f.
girl लड़की *laṛkī* f.
give, to देना *denā* N; to give up छोड़ना *choṛnā* N
glasses, specs चश्मा *caśmā* m.
go, to जाना *jānā*
gold सोना *sonā* m.
good अच्छा *acchā*; decent भला *bhalā*
goodbye नमस्ते *namaste*, नमस्कार *namaskār*
government सरकार *sarkār* f.; governmental सरकारी *sarkārī*
grandfather (father's father) दादा *dādā* m. (invariable -*ā* ending.) ; (mother's father) नाना *nānā* m. (invariable -*ā* ending)
grandmother (father's mother) दादी *dādī* f.; (mother's mother) नानी *nānī* m.
grass घास *ghās* f.
guest मेहमान *mehmān* m.
guru गुरु *guru* m.
half आधा *ādhā* adj. & m.
hand हाथ *hāth* m.
happiness ख़ुशी *khuśī* f.
happy ख़ुश *khuś*
harass, to तंग करना *tang karnā* N
hard, difficult मुश्किल *muśkil*
hard-working मेहनती *mehntī*
harm नुक़सान *nuqsān* m.
hate नफ़रत *nafrat* f.; to hate (से) नफ़रत करना *(se) nafrat karnā* N
he वह *vah*
head सिर *sir* m.
health तबियत *tabiyat* f.
hear, to सुनना *sunnā* N

heart दिल *dil* m.
heat गरमी *garmī* f.
heaven स्वर्ग *svarg* m.
heavy भारी *bhārī*
height लंबाई *lambāī* f.
hello नमस्ते *namaste*, नमस्कार *namaskār*; (on phone) हलो *halo*
help मदद *madad* f.; to help him उसकी मदद करना *uskī madad karnā* N
here यहाँ *yahā̃*, इधर *idhar*
high ऊँचा *ū̃cā*
hill पहाड़ *pahāṛ* m.
Hindi हिन्दी *hindī* f.
Hindu हिन्दू *hindū*
history इतिहास *itihās* m.
hit, to मारना *mārnā* N
holiday छुट्टी *chuṭṭī* f.
home घर *ghar* m.; at home घर पर *ghar par*
hope आशा *āśā* f., उम्मीद *ummīd* f.
hospital अस्पताल *aspatāl* m.
hot गरम *garam*
hotel होटल *hoṭal* m.
hour घंटा *ghanṭā* m.
house मकान *makān* m.
how much/many कितना *kitnā*; how much does that come to? कितना हुआ? *kitnā huā?*
hunger भूख *bhūkh* f.; to feel hungry भूख लगना *bhūkh lagnā*
hungry भूखा *bhūkhā*
husband पति *pati* m.
I मैं *maĩ*
ice बर्फ़ *barf* f.
idea विचार *vicār* m., ख़याल *khyāl* m.
if अगर *agar*
ill बीमार *bīmār*
immediately तुरंत *turant*
important ज़रूरी *zarūrī*
impossible असंभव *asambhav*, नामुमकिन *nāmumkin*
in में *meṃ*
in front (of) (के) आगे *(ke) āge*
increase, to बढ़ना *baṛhnā*, बढ़ाना *baṛhānā* N
India हिन्दुस्तान *hindustān* m., भारत *bhārat* m.; Indian हिन्दुस्तानी *hindustānī*, भारतीय *bhāratīy*
individual, person व्यक्ति *vyakti* m.
inside (के) अंदर *(ke) andar*
instead of के बजाय *ke bajāy*
intelligent होशियार *hośiyār*, तेज़ *tez*
intention इरादा *irādā* m.
interesting दिलचस्प *dilcasp*
invite, to बुलाना *bulānā* N
-ish -सा *-sā*
it वह *vah*
job, employment नौकरी *naukrī* f.
joke मज़ाक़ *mazāk* m.; joking, fun हँसी-मज़ाक *hãsī-mazāk* m.

journey यात्रा *yātrā* f., सफ़र *safar* m.

jungle जंगल *jangal* m.

keep, to रखना *rakhnā* ^{N}

key चाबी *cābī* f.

kill, to मारना *mārnā* ^{N}, मार डालना *mār ḍālnā* ^{N}

kind, type तरह *tarah* f., प्रकार *prakār* m.

king राजा *rājā* m. (inv.)

kitchen रसोईघर *rasoīghar* m.

knife छुरी *churī* f.

know, to जानना *jānnā* ^{N}; मालूम होना *mālūm honā*

kurta कुरता *kurtā* m.

lack, want कमी *kamī* f.

lady महिला *mahilā* f.

lamp, light बत्ती *battī* f.

land ज़मीन *zamīn* f.

lane गली *galī* f.

language भाषा *bhāṣā* f., ज़बान *zabān* f.

last, previous पिछला *pichlā*

late, delayed देर से *der se*

later बाद (में) *bād (mẽ)*, आगे चलकर *āge calkar*

laugh, to हँसना *hãsnā* ^{N}; to make laugh हँसाना *hãsānā* ^{N}

lazy आलसी *ālsī*; (workshy) कामचोर *kāmcor*

leader, politician नेता *netā* m.

learn, to सीखना *sīkhnā* ^{N}; to study पढ़ना *paṛhnā*

leave, to छोड़ना *choṛnā* ^{N}

left (opp. of right) बायाँ *bāyā̃*; to the left (hand) बायें/ उलटे (हाथ) *bāyẽ/ulṭe (hāth)*

left (remaining) बाक़ी *bāqī*

length लंबाई *lambāī* f.

lentil(s) दाल *dāl* f.

less कम *kam*

letter ख़त *khat* m., पत्र *patr* m., चिट्ठी *ciṭṭhī* f.

lie झूठ *jhūṭh* m.; to lie झूठ बोलना *jhūṭh bolna* ^{N}

lie, recline, to लेटना *leṭnā*

life ज़िंदगी *zindagī* f., जीवन *jīvan* m.

lift, to उठाना *uṭhānā* ^{N}

light (brightness) रोशनी *rośnī* f.; (lamp, electric light) बत्ती *battī* f.

light (in weight) हल्का *halkā*

like की तरह *kī tarah*; (equal to) (के) समान *ke samān*; (such as) जैसा *jaisā*

like, to पसंद करना *pasand karnā* ^{N}, पसंद होना *pasand honā*

listen, to सुनना *sunnā* ^{N}

little, a थोड़ा-सा *thoṛā-sā*

live, to (reside) रहना *rahnā*; (be alive) जीना *jīnā* ^{n}

lock ताला *tālā* m.

London लंदन *landan* m.

loneliness अकेलापन *akelāpan* m.

look for, to ढूँढ़ना *ḍhū̃ṛhnā* ^{N}, की तलाश करना *kī talāś karnā* ^{N}

look, to देखना *dekhnā* N

lose, to खोना *khonā* N

love प्रेम *prem* m., प्यार *pyār* m.; to love us हमसे प्रेम/प्यार करना *hamse prem/pyār karnā* N

luggage सामान *sāmān* m.

lunch दोपहर का खाना *dopahar kā khānā* m.

luxury ऐश *aiś* m.

lying (for inanimate things) पड़ा *paṛā*; (for people, 'lying down') लेटा *leṭā*

Ma माँ *mā̃* f.

mad पागल *pāgal*

mail, post डाक f.

make, to बनाना *banānā* N

man, person आदमी *ādmī* m.

mango आम *ām* m.

market बाज़ार *bāzār* m.

married शादी-शुदा *śādī-śudā* (invariable *-ā* ending.)

marry, to शादी करना *śādī karnā* N; to marry Ram, राम से शादी करना *Rām se śādī karnā* N; to marry Ram to Sita, राम की शादी सीता से करना *Rām kī śādī Sītā se karnā* N

matter बात *bāt* f.; it doesn't matter कोई बात नहीं *koī bāt nahī̃*

mean, miserly कंजूस *kanjūs*

meaning मतलब *matlab* m., अर्थ *arth* m.

meat गोश्त *gośt* m., माँस *mā̃s* m.

medicine दवा *davā* f.

meet, to (से) मिलना *(se) milnā*

meeting मुलाक़ात *mulāqāt* f., भेंट *bhẽṭ* f.

memory याद *yād* f.

midnight आधीरात *ādhīrāt* f.

milk दूध *dūdh* m.

mine मेरा *merā*

minute मिनट *minaṭ* m.

mistake ग़लती *galtī* f., भूल *bhūl* f.; to make a mistake ग़लती/भूल करना *galtī/bhūl karnā* N

Monday सोमवार *somvār* m.

money पैसा *paisā* m.

monkey बंदर *bandar* m.

month महीना *mahīnā* m.

moon चाँद *cā̃d* m.

more और *aur*, ज़्यादा *zyādā*, अधिक *adhik*

morning सुबह *subah* f.

mosquito मच्छर *macchar* m.

most ज़्यादा *zyādā*, अधिक *adhik*; at the most अधिक से अधिक *adhik se adhik*, ज़्यादा से ज़्यादा *zyādā se zyādā*

mostly ज़्यादातर *zyādātar*

mother माता *mātā* f., माँ *mā̃* f.

mountain पहाड़ *pahāṛ* m.

mouth मुँह *mũh* m.

move , to चलना *calnā*; हिलना *hilnā*; to move house शिफ़्ट करना *śifṭ karnā* N, घर बदलना *ghar badalnā* N

much ज़्यादा *zyādā*, अधिक *adhik*
Muslim मुसलमान *musalmān* adj. and m.
my मेरा *merā*
narrow तंग *tang*
near (के) नज़दीक *(ke) nazdīk*, (के) पास *(ke) pās*
necessary ज़रूरी *zarūrī*
neck गर्दन *gardan* f.
need ज़रूरत *zarūrat* f.
needed चाहिए *cāhie*
neighbour पड़ोसी *paṛosī* m.
neither... nor न ... न *na... na*
new नया (नए, नई) *nayā (nae, naī)*
news ख़बर *<u>kh</u>abar* f., समाचार samācār m.
newspaper अख़बार *a<u>kh</u>bār* m.
next अगला *aglā*
next to, close by की बग़ल में *kī bagal mẽ*
night रात *rāt* f.
no नहीं *nahī̃*; जी नहीं *jī nahī̃*
no one कोई नहीं *koī nahī̃*
nobody कोई नहीं *koī nahī̃*
noise, tumult शोर *śor* m.
noon, afternoon दोपहर *dopahar* f.
nose नाक *nāk* f.
not नहीं *nahī̃*, न *na*
nothing कुछ नहीं *kuch nahī̃*
now अब *ab*
nowadays आजकल *ājkal*
nowhere कहीं नहीं *kahī̃ nahī̃*
o' clock बजे *baje*
of का *kā*
of course ज़रूर *zarūr*, अवश्य *avaśya*
office दफ़्तर *daftar* m.
often अक्सर *aksar*
old (of people) बूढ़ा *būṛhā*; (of things) पुराना *purānā*
old man बूढ़ा *būṛhā* m.
old woman बुढ़िया *buṛhiyā* f.
on पर *par*
on top (of) के ऊपर *ke ūpar*
one एक *ek*; one and a half डेढ़ *ḍeṛh*; one and a quarter सवा *savā*
oneself ख़ुद *<u>kh</u>ud*, स्वयं *svayam*
only सिर्फ़ *sirf*, केवल *keval*; ही *hī*
open खुला *khulā*; to open खुलना *khulnā*; खोलना *kholnā*[N]
opinion राय *rāy* f.; ख़याल *<u>kh</u>yāl* m.; in my opinion मेरे ख़याल में/से *mere <u>kh</u>yāl mẽ/se*
opportunity मौक़ा *mauqā* m.
or या *yā*
order (send for), to मँगवाना *mā̃gvānā* [N]
ordinary आम *ām*, साधारण *sādhāraṇ*
other, second दूसरा *dūsrā*
otherwise नहीं तो *nahī̃ to*
our, ours हमारा *hamārā*
out बाहर *bāhar*
out of, from among में से *mẽ se*

outside (के) बाहर *(ke) bāhar*

own, one's own अपना *apnā*

pain दर्द *dard* m.; (mental) दुःख *duḥkh* m.

paper काग़ज़ *kāgaz* m.

park (car), to खड़ा करना *kharā karnā* [N]

particular ख़ास *khās*, विशेष *viśeṣ*

party (political) दल *dal* m.

party (social event) पार्टी *pārṭī* f.

passenger यात्री *yātrī* m., मुसाफ़िर *musāfir* m., सवारी *savārī* f.

pearl मोती *motī* m.

pen क़लम *qalam* m./f.

pencil पेंसिल *pensil* f.

people लोग *log* m. pl.; the people, public जनता *jantā* f. (used in singular)

perhaps शायद *śāyad*

period, age ज़माना *zamānā* m.

person, individual व्यक्ति *vyakti* m.

phone, to फ़ोन करना *fon karnā* [N]

photograph फ़ोटो *foṭo* m.; to take photo फोटो खींचना *foṭo khĩcnā* [N]

pick up, to उठाना *uṭhānā* [N]

picture तस्वीर *tasvīr* f., चित्र *citr* m.

piece, bit टुकड़ा *ṭukṛā* m.

pill गोली *golī* f.

place जगह *jagah* f.

play (game), to खेलना *khelnā* [N]

play (music), to बजाना *bajānā* [N]

please कृपया *kṛpayā*, मेहरबानी करके *meharbānī karke*

pocket जेब *jeb* f.

poem; poetry कविता *kavitā* f.

police पुलिस *pulis* f. (used in singular)

politician नेता *netā* m.

poor ग़रीब *garīb*

possible मुमकिन *mumkin*, संभव *sambhav*

post, mail डाक *ḍāk* f.

post office डाकघर *ḍākghar* m.

pour, to डालना *ḍālnā* [N]

power शक्ति *śakti* f.

practice अभ्यास *abhyās* m.

praise तारीफ़ *tārīf* f.; to praise की तारीफ़ करना *kī tārīf karnā* [N]

prepare, to तैयार करना *taiyār karnā* [N]

present, gift तोहफ़ा *tohfā* m., उपहार *uphar* m., (presentation) भेंट *bhẽṭ* f.

previous पिछला *pichlā*; previously पहले *pahle*

price दाम *dām* m., क़ीमत *qīmat* f.

pride गर्व *garv* m.

problem समस्या *samasyā* f.

profession पेशा *peśā* m.

properly ठीक से *ṭhīk se*

public, the people जनता *jantā* f. (used in singular)

pure, unmixed शुद्ध *śuddh*

put on, to पहनना *pahannā* N
put, to रखना *rakhnā* N
quarrel झगड़ा *jhagṛā* m.
question सवाल *savāl* m., प्रश्न *praśn* m.
quick तेज़ *tez*
quickly जल्दी *jaldī*
quite (fairly) काफ़ी *kāfī*; (completely) बिलकुल *bilkul*
radio रेडियो *reḍiyo* m.
rain बारिश *bāriś* f.; to rain बारिश होना *bāriś honā*, पानी पड़ना *pānī paṛnā*
reach, to पहुँचना *pahũcnā*
read, to पढ़ना *paṛhnā* N
ready तैयार *taiyār*
real असली *aslī*
reason कारण *kāraṇ* m., वजह *vajah* f.
recognize, to पहचानना *pahcānnā* N
red लाल *lāl*
refuse (to), to (से) इनकार करना *(se) inkār karnā* N
relative रिश्तेदार *riśtedār* m., f.
remain, to रहना *rahnā*
remaining बाक़ी *bāqī*
remember, to याद करना *yād karnā* N ; याद होना *yād honā*
remind, to याद दिलाना *yād dilānā* N
rent किराया *kirāyā* m.; to rent किराये पर लेना/देना *kirāye par lenā/denā* N
reply जवाब *javāb* m.; to reply जवाब देना *javāb denā* N
rest, ease आराम *ārām* m.; to rest आराम करना *ārām karnā* N
return, to लौटना *lauṭnā*
rice चावल *cāval* m.
rich, wealthy अमीर *amīr*
rickshaw रिक्शा *rikśā* m.
right (correct) ठीक *ṭhīk*, सही *sahī*
right (opp. of left) दाहिना *dāhinā*; to the right (hand) दाहिने (हाथ) *dāhine (hāth)*
river नदी *nadī* f.
robbery चोरी *corī* f.
room कमरा *kamrā* m.
run, to दौड़ना *dauṛnā*; to run away भागना *bhāgnā*
rupee रुपया *rupayā* m.
salt नमक *namak* m.
samosa समोसा *samosā* m.
sandal चप्पल *cappal* f.
Sanskrit संस्कृत *sanskṛt* f.
sari साड़ी *sāṛī* f.
Saturday शनिवार *śanivār* m.
save, to बचाना *bacānā* N
say, to (से) कहना *(se) kahnā* N
scold, to डाँटना *ḍā̃ṭnā* N
script (alphabet) लिपि *lipi* f.
sea समुद्र *samudra* m.
search तलाश *talāś* f.; to search for की तलाश करना *kī talāś karnā* N

seated, sitting बैठा *baiṭhā*
see, to देखना *dekhnā* N
seem, to लगना *lagnā*; मालूम होना *mālūm honā*
sell, to बेचना *becnā* N
send, to भेजना *bhejnā* N
sentence वाक्य *vākya* m.
separate, separately अलग *alag*
servant नौकर *naukar* m.
several कई *kaī*
she वह *vah*
shoe; pair of shoes जूता *jūtā* m.
shop दुकान *dukān* f.; shop-keeper दुकानदार *dukāndār* m.
should चाहिए *cāhie* (after infinitive: 'I should go' मुझको जाना चाहिए *mujhko jānā cāhie*)
shout, to चिल्लाना *cillānā* N
shut बंद *band*; to shut बंद करना *band karnā* N
side, direction तरफ़ *taraf* f., ओर *or* f.
silent चुप *cup*, ख़ामोश *khāmoś*
simple, easy सरल *saral*
since the time when... since then जब से ... तब से *jab se... tab se*
sing, to गाना *gānā* N
sister बहिन *bahin* f.
sit, to बैठना *baiṭhnā*
sitar सितार *sitār* m.
sky आकाश *ākāś* m., आसमान *āsmān* m.
sleep नींद *nīd̃* f.
sleep, to सोना *sonā*
small छोटा *choṭā*
smile, to मुस्कराना *muskarānā* N
smoke, to (सिग्रेट) पीना *(sigreṭ) pīnā* N
so (then) तो *to*, सो *so*; so much इतना *itnā*
soap साबुन *sābun* m.
sold, to be बिकना *biknā*
some (with single countable noun) कोई *koī*; (with uncountable) कुछ *kuch*; something else कुछ और *kuch aur*; something or other कुछ न कुछ *kuch na kuch*
somehow कहीं *kahī̃*
someone कोई *koī*; someone else और कोई *aur koī*, कोई और *koī aur*; someone or other कोई न कोई *koī na koī*
sometime कभी *kabhī*; sometimes कभी कभी *kabhī kabhī*
somewhere कहीं *kahī̃*; somewhere else कहीं और *kahī̃ aur*; somewhere or other कहीं न कहीं *kahī̃ na kahī̃*
son बेटा *beṭā* m.
song गाना *gānā* m., गीत *gīt* m.
soon जल्दी *jaldī*
sound आवाज़ *āvāz* f.
south दक्षिण *dakṣiṇ* m.

speak, to बोलना *bolnā* [n]
spoon चम्मच *cammac* m.
stair, staircase सीढ़ी *sīṛhī* f.
stamp टिकट *ṭikaṭ* m./ f.
standing खड़ा *khaṛā*
state, province प्रदेश *prades´* m.
station स्टेशन *sṭeśan* m.
stay, to रहना *rahnā*
steal, to चोरी करना *corī karnā* [N]
still (up to now) अभी *abhī*
stomach पेट *peṭ* m.
stone पत्थर *patthar* m.
stop, to रुकना *ruknā*; रोकना *roknā* [N]
story कहानी *kahānī* f.
straight, straightforward सीधा *sīdhā*
strange अजीब *ajīb*
stranger अजनबी *ajnabī* m.
street सड़क *saṛak* f.
string रस्सी *rassī* f.
stroll, to टहलना *ṭahalnā*
strong मज़बूत *mazbūt*, तेज़ *tez*
student विद्यार्थी *vidyārthī* m., f.
studies, studying पढ़ाई *paṛhāī* f.
study, to पढ़ना *paṛhnā*
stupid बेवक़ूफ़ *bevaqūf*; stupid person उल्लू *ullū* m. (lit. 'owl')
subject, topic विषय *viṣay* m.
success सफलता *saphaltā* f.; successful सफल *saphal*, कामयाब *kāmyāb*
suddenly, unexpectedly अचानक *acānak*, एकाएक *ekāek*
suggestion सुझाव *sujhāv* m.; to suggest सुझाव देना *sujhāv denā* [N]
summer गरमियाँ *garmiyā̃* f. pl; summer holidays गरमी की छुट्टियाँ *garmī kī chuṭṭiyā̃* f. pl
sun सूरज *sūraj* m.; sunlight, sunshine धूप *dhūp* f.
Sunday रविवार *ravivār* m.
surprise आश्चर्य *āścarya* m.; I'm surprised मुझे आश्चर्य है *mujhe āścarya hai*
sweet मीठा *mīṭhā*; sweet dish मिठाई *miṭhāī* f.
swim, to तैरना *tairnā* [N]
tabla तबला *tablā* m.
table मेज़ *mez* f.
tablet, pill गोली *golī* f.
tailor दर्ज़ी *darzī* m.
take, to (receive) लेना *lenā* [N]; (deliver) ले जाना *le jānā*
take away, to ले जाना *le jānā*
take care of, to का ख़याल/ध्यान रखना *kā khyāl/dhyān rakhnā* [N]
talk, converse, to (से) बात/बातें करना *(se) bāt/bātẽ karnā* [N]
tall लंबा *lambā*; (high) ऊँचा *ū̃cā*
tap (faucet) नल *nal* m.
taxi टैक्सी *ṭaiksī* f.
tea चाय *cāy* f.
teach, to (a subject) पढ़ाना *paṛhānā* [N], (a skill) सिखाना *sikhānā* [N]
teacher अध्यापक *adhyāpak* m.

tell, to बताना *batānā* [N]

temple मंदिर *mandir* m.

thank you शुक्रिया *śukriyā*, धन्यवाद *dhanyavād*

that (conjunction) कि *ki*

that (pronoun) वह *vah*

that is to say यानी *yānī*

theft चोरी *corī* f.

then फिर *phir*, तब *tab*

there वहाँ *vahā̃*; right there वहीं *vahī̃*; over there उधर *udhar*

these ये *ye*

they ये *ye*, वे *ve*

thick, coarse मोटा *moṭā*

thief चोर *cor* m.

thin पतला *patlā*; (lean) दुबला-पतला *dublā-patlā*

thing चीज़ *cīz* f.; (abstract, 'matter') बात *bāt* f.

think, to सोचना *socnā* [N]

thirst प्यास *pyās* f.; to feel thirsty, thirst to strike प्यास लगना *pyās lagnā*

this यह *yah*

those वे *ve*

thought विचार *vicār* m., ख़याल *khyāl* m.

throat गला *galā* m.

throw, to डालना *ḍālnā* [N], फेंकना *phẽknā* [N]

ticket टिकट *ṭikaṭ* m./ f.

time समय *samay* m., वक़्त *vaqt* m.; occasion बार *bār* f., दफ़ा *dafā* f.

tired थका *thakā*; to be tired थकना *thaknā*

to को *ko*

today आज *āj*

together (in company with) एक साथ *ek sāth*, के साथ *ke sāth*

tomorrow कल *kal*

too (also) भी *bhī*; (excessive) बहुत ज़्यादा *bahut zyādā*

touch, to छूना *chūnā* [N]

towards की तरफ़/ ओर *kī taraf/ or*

town शहर *śahar* m.

toy खिलौना *khilaunā* m.

train ट्रेन *ṭren* f., गाड़ी *gāṛī* f., रेलगाड़ी *relgāṛī* f.

translation अनुवाद *anuvād* m.; to translate (का) अनुवाद करना *(ka) anuvād karnā* [N]

travel यात्रा *yātrā* f., सफ़र *safar* m.; to travel यात्रा/सफ़र करना *yātrā/ safar karnā* [N]

traveller यात्री *yātrī* m., मुसाफ़िर *musāfir* m.

tree पेड़ *peṛ* m.

true सच *sac*

trust भरोसा *bharosā* m., विश्वास *viśvās* m.

truth सच्चाई *sacāī* f.

try, to की कोशिश करना *kī kośiś karnā* [N]

turn, bend मोड़ *moṛ* m.

turn, to मुड़ना *muṛnā*, मोड़ना *moṛnā* [N]

two दो *do*; two and a half ढाई *ḍhāī*

uncle (father's younger brother) चाचा *cācā* m. (inv.)

understand, to समझना *samajhnā* [n]

understanding समझ *samajh* f.

until तक *tak*

up, upstairs ऊपर *ūpar*

up to तक *tak*

upset परेशान *pareśān*

Urdu उर्दू *urdū* f.

urgent ज़रूरी *zarūrī*

us हम *ham*

useless बेकार *bekār*

usually आम तौर पर *ām taur par*

vacant ख़ाली *khālī*

vacate, to ख़ाली करना *khālī karnā* [N]

valuable क़ीमती *qīmtī*

Varanasi वाराणसी *vārāṇasī* f.

vegetable(s) सब्ज़ी *sabzī* f.

very बहुत *bahut*

via से होकर *se hokar*

village गाँव *gā̃v* m.

visible, to be दिखाई देना *dikhāī denā*

voice आवाज़ *āvāz* f.

wait, waiting इंतज़ार *itnazār* m.; to wait (for) (का) इंतज़ार करना *(kā) intazār karnā* [N]

walk, to पैदल चलना/जाना *paidal calnā/jana*

wall दीवार *dīvār* f.

want, to चाहना *cāhnā* [N] (in past, use imperfective – मैं चाहता था *maĩ cāhtā thā* – rather than perfective)

warm गरम *garam*

wash, to धोना *dhonā* [N]; (bathe) नहाना *nahānā;* to wash dishes बरतन *mā̃jnā* [N]

washed, to be धुलना *dhulnā*

watch, wristwatch घड़ी *ghaṛī* f.

water पानी *pānī* m.

way, manner ढंग *ḍhang* m., तरह *tarah* f., प्रकार *prakār* m.

we हम *ham*

weak कमज़ोर *kamzor*

wear, to पहनना *pahannā* [N]

weather मौसम *mausam* m.

wedding शादी *śādī* f.

week हफ़्ता *haftā* m., सप्ताह *saptāh* m.

weep, to रोना *ronā* [n]

well, anyway ख़ैर *khair*

well, in a good way अच्छा *acchā*, अच्छी तरह (से) *acchī tarah (se)*

wet (soaked) भीगा *bhīgā*; (damp) गीला *gīlā*

what like, what kind of? कैसा *kaisā*

what? क्या *kyā*

when... then जब... तब *jab... tab*

when? कब *kab*

where... there जहाँ ... वहाँ *jahā̃...vahā̃*

where? कहाँ *kahā̃*, किधर *kidhar*

which, the one which जो *jo*; which/what ever जो भी *jo bhī*

which? कौनसा *kaunsā*

while (on the other hand) जब कि *jab ki*

white सफ़ेद *safed*; white person गोरा *gorā* m., f.

who, the one who जो *jo*; whoever जो भी *jo bhī*

who? कौन *kaun*

why? क्यों *kyõ*

wife पत्नी *patnī* f.

wind हवा *havā* f.

window खिड़की *khiṛkī* f.

with से *se*; (in company of) के साथ *ke sāth*

without के बिना *ke binā*; without doing/saying/thinking बिना किए/बोले/सोचे *binā kie/bole/soce*

woman औरत *aurat* f.

wood लकड़ी *lakṛī* f.

word शब्द *śabd* m.

work काम *kām* m.; (occupation) धंधा *dhandhā* m.; (employment) नौकरी *naukrī* f.

world दुनिया *duniyā* f.

write, to लिखना *likhnā* ᴺ

writer लेखक *lekhak* m.

wrong, incorrect ग़लत *galat*

year साल *sāl* m., वर्ष *varṣ* m.; (of calendar, era) सन् *san* m.

yes हाँ *hā̃*, जी हाँ *jī hā̃*

yesterday कल *kal*

you (intimate) तू *tū*; (familiar) तुम *tum*; (formal) आप *āp*

young छोटा *choṭā*, जवान *javān*

your, yours (intimate) तेरा *terā*; (familiar) तुम्हारा *tumhārā*; (formal) आपका *āpkā*

glossary of grammatical terms

adjective A word that describes: 'green, small, nice'.

adverb A word or phrase that describes the way in which something happens: 'quickly, carefully, immediately, next week'.

agreement Having the same number, gender and case: in 'we go', the verb 'go' agrees with 'we'; in 'he goes', 'goes' agrees with 'he'.

case A way of showing the relationship of a word to other words in a sentence: 'she hit her' distinguishes agressor and victim by having 'she' and 'her' in different cases. In Hindi, the main distinction is between 'direct case' and 'oblique case'.

conjunction A link-word between parts of a sentence, such as 'that' and 'but' in 'I heard that my brother was ill but I did nothing'.

continuous The tense that describes things going on at a particular time, conveyed in English by an '-ing' verb and in Hindi by a रहा *rahā* construction: वह बोल रहा है *vah bol rahā hai* 'he is speaking'.

direct The case used by default for nouns (and pronouns and adjectives); it is replaced by the 'oblique' when a noun (etc.) is followed by a postposition, and in some adverbial phrases.

gender The status of a noun as being either masculine or feminine. For animates, grammatical gender follows sexual gender (आदमी *ādmī* 'man' is masculine, औरत *aurat* 'woman' is feminine), but for inanimates the allocation of gender is not easily predictable (कान *kān* 'ear' is masculine, नाक *nāk* 'nose' is feminine).

imperfective A verb tense whose action is not a completed, one-off event: मैं हिन्दी बोलता हूँ *maĩ hindī boltā hū̃* 'I speak Hindi'; see **perfective**.

intransitive verb One that cannot take a direct object. Verbs of motion are typical examples: आना *ānā* to come, जाना *jānā* to go.

noun A word that names something: 'mouse, love, brother, Ram'.

number The status of a word as being either singular or plural.

infinitive The form of the verb listed in dictionaries: in Hindi it ends -ना *-nā,* as in करना *karnā*; in English it features the word 'to', as in 'to do'. An infinitive is used in many constructions such as मुझको जाना चाहिए *mujhko jānā cāhie* 'I ought to go'.

object The part of the sentence that is affected by the verb, or to which the action is done. In वह राम को पैसा देगा *vah Rām ko paisā degā* 'He'll give money to Ram', वह *vah* 'he' is the subject, पैसा *paisā* 'money' is the direct object, राम *Rām* 'Ram' the indirect object.

oblique The case that is used before a postposition. In मेरे कमरे में *mere kamre mẽ* 'in my room', मेरे कमरे *mere kamre* is made oblique by में *mẽ.* An oblique also appears (without postposition) in some adverbs such as इन दिनों *in dinõ* 'these days'.

participle A form of the verb used as the basis for various tenses: जाता *jātā* is the imperfective participle from जाना *jānā* 'to go' and is used to form वह जाता है/था *vah jātā hai/thā* 'he goes/ used to go'.

passive A verb whose focus is on the action being done rather than the person doing it: 'the food is being cooked' is passive, 'I am cooking the food' is active.

perfective A verb tense that describes a completed, one-off action, as in हमने गाड़ी ख़रीदी *hamne gāṛī kharīdī* 'we bought a car'.

possessive Having a meaning that indicates ownership: 'my' and 'our' are possessive pronouns.

postposition Words like में *mẽ* 'in', पर *par* 'on' and के लिए *ke lie* 'for', which express a relationship to the word or phrase preceding it, as in मेज़ पर *mez par* 'on the table', आप के लिए *āp ke lie* 'for you'; postpositions are the Hindi equivalents of English *pre*positions.

pronoun A word that stands for a noun: 'Manoj read a book' uses nouns, 'he read it' uses pronouns.

relative A relative pronoun such as 'who, which' gives further information about something already mentioned, as in 'Find the boy who took my jacket': such a word introduces a relative clause.

stem The base form of a verb, to which endings are added: कर *kar* in करना *karnā* 'to do'.

subject That person or thing who acts or is: हम *ham* 'we' in हम खाना तैयार करेंगे *ham khānā taiyār karẽge* 'we will prepare food'.

subjunctive A form of the verb that typically expresses possibility or suggestion rather than definitive actions.

transitive A transitive verb is one that can take a direct object: 'to eat, to write, to ask' ('to eat *food*, to write *letters*, to ask *questions*').

verb A word or phrase that denotes an action or a state of being: 'ate' in 'I ate the banana', 'am' in 'I am unwell'. It usually has a subject ('I') and may also take an object ('the banana').

index

References are to Unit and section number.